DATE DUE

DE 16 '97		
NV 8 '98		
NO 2 '98		
DE 9 '98		
MY 25 '99		
Sep 14		

DEMCO 38-296

SERIOUS VIOLENCE

Second Edition

SERIOUS VIOLENCE

Patterns of Homicide and Assault in America

By

KEITH D. HARRIES, Ph.D.

University of Maryland
Baltimore County

CHARLES C THOMAS • PUBLISHER, LTD.
Springfield • Illinois • U.S.A.

Distributed Throughout the World by

CHARLES C THOMAS • PUBLISHER, LTD.
2600 South First Street
Springfield, Illinois 62794-9265

© *1997 by* CHARLES C THOMAS • PUBLISHER, LTD.
ISBN 0-398-06718-X (cloth)
ISBN 0-398-06719-8 (paper)

Library of Congress Catalog Card Number: 96-31513

First Edition, 1990
Second Edition, 1997

With THOMAS BOOKS *careful attention is given to all details of manufacturing
and design. It is the Publisher's desire to present books that are satisfactory as to their
physical qualities and artistic possibilities and appropriate for their particular use.*
THOMAS BOOKS *will be true to those laws of quality that assure a good name
and good will.*

*Printed in the United States of America
SC-R-3*

Library of Congress Cataloging-in-Publication Data

Harries, Keith D.
    Serious violence : patterns of homicide and assault in America /
by Keith D. Harries. — 2nd ed.
        p.   cm.
    Includes bibliographical references and index.
    ISBN 0-398-06718-X (cloth). — ISBN 0-398-06719-8 (pbk.)
    1. Violent crimes—United States.   2. Violent crimes—United
States—Prevention.   3. Homicide—United States.   4. Assault and
battery—United States.   I. Title.
HV6789.H27   1996   96-31513
364.1'5'0973—dc20   CIP

ACKNOWLEDGMENTS

The author is indebted to several authors and publishers who have given permission for the quotation or adaptation of their copyrighted material. These are *Newsweek, The Washington Post,* Pergamon Press for the journal *Geoforum,* Routledge, Chapman, and Hall, Inc., *U.S. News and World Report, Geografiska Annaler,* the Association of American Geographers, the American Society of Criminology and Dr. Bryan Vila, the National Council for Crime Prevention (Stockholm), and Dr. Hugh Whitt and his coauthors, Jay Corzine and Lin Huff-Corzine.

My former colleague, Dr. Stephen Stadler, generously permitted my adaptation of part of our coauthored chapter published in 1989 as "Assault and heat stress: Dallas as a case study," in: D.J. Evans and D.T. Herbert (Eds.), *The Geography of Crime* (London: Routledge, Chapman, and Hall).

Graphics were prepared or adapted by the Cartographic Services Laboratory at the University of Maryland Baltimore County, directed by Joseph School. Student interns Paul Erdman and Melanie Orwig Parker were responsible for the work in the first edition; Beth Richardson assisted with the preparation of additional graphics for the second edition.

PREFACE

The first edition of this book was written at the end of the 1980s when drug-related violence associated with the then-recent cocaine epidemic had overwhelmed America's inner cities. The book was written originally in order to add more emphasis to the violence issue but also to make explicit the connection between *place* and violence.

The second edition is written in the mid-1990s. What has changed? Levels of violence are still high, though generally somewhat lower than a few years ago for reasons both drug-related (territorial conflict over drug turf· is thought to have abated) and demographic. But an extremely disturbing new trend has emerged—the vastly increased involvement of juveniles in violent crime. Not only are younger children performing violent acts, but like their older counterparts, they are doing so with ever more lethal weapons. While there is no hard evidence, it also seems that the juvenile violence is increasingly gratuitous—done for "kicks." We can only look to this piece of the future with trepidation in the realization that yet another generation of deprived inner city youth is being lost, the by-product of lack of parental control, abysmal schools, and a litany of other social stresses.

Does American society at large see the situation as a crisis? Is the public response any different than it was in the 1980s? The political shift to the right with the 1992 general election reinforced the trend toward curtailment of social programs and a general turning away from inner city issues. Policy emphasis was to be on a tide of unfettered economic development that would lift all boats. To appease public fears, more resources would be put into policing. Also, welfare would be "reformed," albeit in different ways in different places. Ultimately, however, there would be no coherent effort to look to root causes of violence, perhaps because there is no reward for such focus at the ballot box, or perhaps because those root causes are poorly understood, or both. For suburban-ites the carnage of the inner city is out of sight if not out of mind, something to be watched on the evening news; take it or leave it. The

vii

public response is ambivalent—general agreement that there is a major problem, but utter confusion when it comes to "what to do about it."

An extraordinary feature of violence continues to be its localized nature, with fantastically high levels in one neighborhood and next to nothing within a very short distance. Herein lies the essential fascination of a geographic approach; why so much *spatial* variation? What are the qualitative aspects of that variation? In the last decade, interest in this geographic variation has blossomed as police departments have nearly universally adopted geographic information systems (GIS) technology to facilitate the monitoring of crime hot spots in order to mobilize their own resources but also as a basis for informing the community about emerging problems. Geography in this context has gone from being seemingly irrelevant to the status of "tool" and "perspective," providing new insights on community interactions.

Over the last decade I have benefitted greatly from association with several individuals whose knowledge of crime and its patterns and processes is remarkable: Derral Cheatwood (formerly of the University of Baltimore, currently at the University of Texas, San Antonio), Philip Canter of the Baltimore County Police Department, Jacqueline Campbell (Johns Hopkins University), James Lebeau (Southern Illinois University), George Rengert (Temple University), and Roland Reboussin (FBI Academy). Participation in the Homicide Research Working Group based in Chicago has also led to helpful insights. I am also grateful to the University of Maryland Baltimore County for granting a sabbatical leave during part of which this second edition was prepared.

K.D.H.

CONTENTS

SERIOUS VIOLENCE

Chapter 1

INTRODUCTION: BACKGROUND, RATIONALE, PLAN OF ATTACK

This book is about violence, with particular emphasis on where it happens and why. However, it is limited in its scope to the related crimes of homicide and assault. Other crimes of violence (including rape and robbery) are interwoven with homicide and assault in that the latter may occur in concert with rapes or robberies, but rape and robbery are sufficiently unique that they have attracted their own specialized research literatures. While rape and robbery will be referred to here insofar as they are incorporated in the fabric of homicide and assault, they will not be treated as separate topics. For specialized treatments, the reader is referred to, for example, Reiss and Roth (1993) on rape and robbery, Gabor (1987), Cook (1983), and Perez (1992) on robbery, and Amir (1971), Brownmiller (1976), Ellis (1989), Macdonald (1971), Parrot and Bechofer (1991), and Allison (1993), on rape. Comprehensive overviews of violence phenomena are found in Reiss and Roth (1993) and Rosenberg and Fenley (1991).

Why another book on violence? The short answer is that until there is in place a national, effective policy to reduce violence at its roots—in poverty and discrimination wherever they are found—it is impossible to bring too much attention to the problem. The nation has been distracted since the War on Poverty, which officially ended with the closing of the Office of Economic Opportunity in 1974, first with Viet Nam, then with inflation and more recently with budget balancing efforts. In addition to the "normal" political distractions, however, there has been no political will, no mandate from powerful interest groups, to alleviate poverty and its associated violence. Presumably, the point has not been lost on Congress that, for the most part, it is the poor who kill and injure each other in the poverty zones of the cities (and of rural areas, too). These are people without substantial political clout, which is bought for cash by political action committees in the halls of Congress, and is not, in all too many situations, an expression of public will at the ballot box.

After dipping in the mid-1980s, the homicide rate has worked back towards its historic high achieved around 1980. The rate as it stands (Figure 1.2) is extraordinary compared to other more developed countries. A focused national violence policy has yet to be put in place; the emphasis is still on control of violence via the police and courts rather than on elimination of causes. After all, reinstating and extending the federal death penalty, for example, costs little or nothing; murderers have no support in Congress. Whether such an act would be effective or not is irrelevant; it is politically "good," and better yet, cheap, since few capital incidents actually fall under federal jurisdiction.

This chapter provides a comprehensive background to the violence issue. Initially, the inability of the U.S. to prevent violence or to develop coherent policy responses is dramatized via discussion of the emergence of the national capital as the intermittently most violent city, as represented by conventional measures. Then, international comparisons demonstrate that the U.S. is remarkably unlike its more developed siblings with respect to levels of violence. Finally, several recurring themes relating to violence are outlined, and fundamental demographic and other relationships are discussed.

WASHINGTON, D.C. AS A SYMBOL OF VIOLENCE

As Ronald Reagan stepped down from the Presidency in January, 1989, Washington, D.C. had recently been named "homicide capital of the United States." This dubious distinction was achieved on the basis of 372 homicides in 1988 for a population of 626,000 yielding a rate of 59.4 per 100,000. The District has been among the cities with a higher homicide rate for decades; in 1970, for example, it ranked fifth, but with a rate of 26.4, less than half the current rate (Klebba, 1975). In 1988, Detroit ran a close second with 58/100,000. Dallas, another city with a reputation for violence, ran third with a mere 36.57/100,000 (Mann, 1989). Just across the border in Canada, however, Toronto, a metropolitan area of some 3.3 million, had 53 murders in 1988, or a rate of 1.6/100,000, about one thirty-seventh the D.C. rate (Denton, 1989). As a basis for comparison, the U.S. rate for homicide was about 8.5/100,000 in the same year.

It seems incredible that, virtually within sight of Capitol Hill and the

White House, citizens were afraid to go out into their own neighborhoods. Many were afraid to venture out of their apartments and go to the laundry rooms in their buildings for fear of being mugged, or worse. A *Washington Post* poll in May, 1988, asked residents "Is there any area in your neighborhood—that is, within five or six blocks—where you would be afraid to walk at night?" Some 55 percent of those aged 65 and older answered affirmatively, while younger respondents, while also often fearful, were not as apprehensive as the elderly (Sinclair, 1988). On some occasions, citizens were shot by stray bullets as they minded their own business *inside* their own homes. One woman was killed as she stood by her kitchen sink. A man was shot when he got up out of bed to get a drink of water. Citizens reported hearing gunfire nightly in some neighborhoods, sometimes as a result of gun battles, often as drug dealers put new weapons through their paces, avoiding the inconvenience of going to a firing range by letting loose clips in the street. People have been killed and injured (apparently mainly in Southern states) as a result of bullets falling after guns have been fired in the air in celebrations on New Year's Eve. Milloy (1988) reported that in the four years 1985 through 1988, 860 homicides occurred in Washington, combined with over 100,000 arrests, statistics "more than tripling the number of deaths and arrests in all race riots since 1917." What we have instead of the riots of the 1960s, however, is what are being referred to as "Quiet Riots", a phrase coined by Harris and Wilkins (1988) to describe the process of poor African Americans turning anger and frustration inward to themselves and their communities in a kind of slow burn, or, in the word of Rev. Jesse Jackson, "implosion."

Perhaps it is ironically fitting that the capital city of the United States (one of the most violent of societies and certainly the most violent among more developed countries) should be its most violent municipality. The legendary inefficiency and corruption of District of Columbia government notwithstanding, it appeared throughout 1988 that no police department, no city government, could have thwarted the social forces at work in the area, particularly the turf battle for what has by now become a hackneyed as well as euphemistic phrase: "the lucrative drug trade." Tragically, homicide was to get worse before it would get better. The year 1988 was a low point—murders would not go below 400 again until 1994, when 399 were recorded (Bowles, 1995).

POLICY FAILURE

That public policy in the realm of violence prevention has failed is obvious. Indeed, it has never been clear how to address the violence issue, in part because there has never been agreement among scholars on the causes of crime. However, while "crime" is an extraordinarily complex problem, encompassing as it does everything from stock fraud to pocket picking, it will be argued here that serious violence tends to be spatially focused in particular neighborhoods and those neighborhoods tend to be poor and African American. The evidence that will be represented here will suggest that to eliminate the causes of poverty, particularly African American poverty, would be to take a significant step in the reduction of violence in America (Chapter 9).

In perhaps the only major policy initiative to make explicit the link between crime and poverty, Lyndon Johnson's "War on Poverty" in the 1960s actually had its roots as a war on juvenile delinquency, inspired as it was by Cloward and Ohlin's *Delinquency and Opportunity,* published in 1960 (Lemann, 1988; 1989). In recent years, however, no coherent policy has existed, and social problems have been all but ignored. Reagan economic policy assumed that reduced taxes and economic growth would automatically lift all boats, a scenario that has been tragically wrong. Official poverty measures, which had shown marked improvement between the 1960s and 1970s, leveled off or worsened somewhat between the late seventies and 1985. In 1979, 9.0 percent of whites were below the poverty line, a proportion that had risen to 11.4 percent by 1985. Among blacks, comparable numbers were 31.0 and 31.3 (Harris & Wilkins, 1988: 50). There was no War on Poverty in the 1980s. Furthermore, racism seemed to resume manifestations of openness and ugliness with the Howard Beach incident in New York in 1988, riots in Miami in early 1989, the election of former Ku Klux Klan Grand Wizard David Duke to a seat in the Louisiana legislature from the Metairie district, also in 1989, the infamous Rodney King beating in 1991 (replayed ad nauseam on television), and the Los Angeles Detective Mark Furman revelations in the O.J. Simpson trial (also in Los Angeles), in 1995. The Miami disturbances seemed to epitomize the apparent detachment of American society at large (in contrast to those affected on a day-to-day basis) from the pattern of inner city violence. Miami officials, according to media accounts, seemed to be more concerned about the economic impact of the disturbances on attendance at the scheduled Super Bowl game and related spending by fans, than about substantive issues concerning causes of the unrest. The Commissioner of the National Football League, Pete Rozelle, was quoted to the effect that it was lucky that the riots were early in the week so that they did not interfere with the game.

Concern for violence did not appear to be a high priority for the incoming Bush administration in early 1989, or for the Clinton administration in 1993. A search of campaign promises and goals drawn from the Bush campaign indicated no explicit undertaking to reduce violence, although some initiatives did relate to drug abuse. A search of references to violence policy on the White House World Wide Web site in 1996 came up empty, as did a query directed to the Democratic National Committee. However, the overall tenor of the goals in the realm of crime and drug abuse remains punitive rather than ameliorative, such as restoring the federal death penalty and developing neighborhood watch programs in public housing areas (see also Hoffman, 1989).

It is, then, against a background of polarization in American society and policy failure that this book is written. Those who can leave areas of violence and deprivation do so, leaving behind an increasingly helpless minority likely to constitute the great majority of both victims and offenders in violent incidents. Perhaps never before in America has the difference between city and suburb been so pronounced. In order to better understand the current context, it is useful to take an historical and comparative perspective.

INTERNATIONAL COMPARISONS

Comparisons of homicide across nations suggest that the U.S. has relatively high rates, but is not among the highest, which tend to be Latin American, Caribbean, North African, or Middle Eastern (Wolfgang, 1986). However, U.S. rates are much higher than those of northwest European nations, or Canada (Fig. 1.1).

In a ranking of 61 "literate societies" based on data from around 1960, the U.S. was 15th, Japan 29th, Sweden 50th, and the Irish Republic 61st. Top ranking nations in this list were Colombia, Mexico, and Nicaragua. Data drawn from more recent sources tended to confirm the approximate rankings. In the quinquennium 1982 through 1986, the U.S. rate averaged 8.4/100,000, or on the order of four to eight times higher than Northern European countries (FBI, 1983–87). This finding is corrobo-

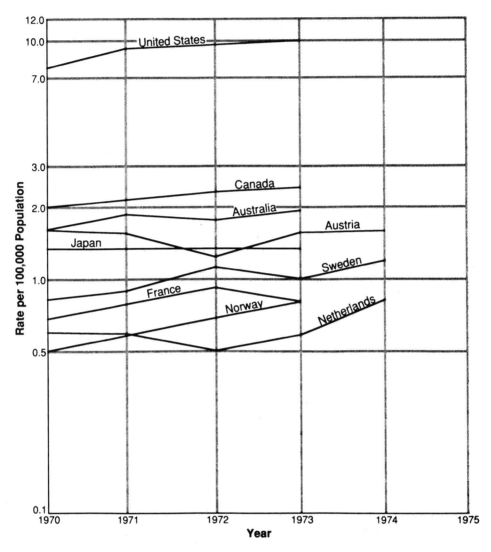

Figure 1.1. International homicide rates per 100,000 population, 1970–74. In 1990, rates were similar. *Source:* Adapted from Wolfgang, 1986.

rated by Kalish (1988), drawing on data for 1980–84 from the United Nations, the International Police Organization, and the World Health Organization. She observed that the U.S. homicide rate ranged between 7.9 and 10.5/100,000 while the comparable European composite rate was below 2/100,000. The rate for Japan was 0.8 for 1980–84. Similar analysis by Fingerhut (1994) for 1989–90 showed a U.S. rate of approximately 10/100,000, and rates for Canada, Japan, and England and Wales of 2 or less per 100,000.

Wolfgang concluded that the observed patterns suggested two hypotheses; first, that if high homicide rate countries such as those in Latin America, "westernize without turmoil," their rates will decline. If, on the other hand, westernization is accompanied by conflict, rates will probably increase further (Wolfgang, 1986). Relevant to this observation is the finding that the existence of heterogeneous cultural groupings in societies tend to be linked to higher rates of homicide (Hansmann and Quigley, 1982). Straus (1988) noted that in any given nation, a certain minimum amount of violence, ascribed to intrafamily conflict, is inevitable; thus in nations with relatively low rates of homicide, a higher proportion will be family violence. Based on data for 1966–84, Straus found that in the U.S., with its high overall homicide rate, intrafamily events made up about half the total, in Canada about half, and in Denmark, some 67 percent.

Within nations, according to analysis by Archer and Gartner (1986), it appears homicide rates in the principal, or primary, cities tend to be higher than national average rates; this relationship holds in the U.S., also, where city size correlates with homicide rates. Data for 1926 through 1970 showed that homicide rates for primary cities are consistently high compared to their national rates. However, it could not be demonstrated that city growth correlated with homicide rate increase; half the city rates analyzed increased, half decreased. For a small sample (7) of primary cities with data available for the period 1926–70, no trend of increasing rates over time was observed. Archer and Gartner concluded that a city's homicide rate is determined not by its absolute size, but rather by its relative size in the context of its society. "Any jurisdiction more urban than its national environment," they suggested, "will have a homicide rate higher than the national average" (Archer and Gartner, 1986:116).[1]

---

[1] Archer and Gartner also found, in an analysis of both combatant and non-combatant nations, that homicide rates were consistently higher after wars, a condition explained by the *legitimation of violence* model, arguing that "legal" war killing affects the peacetime society. (See also: Archer and Gartner, 1976.) Another finding of indirect interest in the present context was that the abolition of capital punishment "was followed more often than not by absolute *decreases* in homicide rates, not by the increases predicted by deterrence theory" (Archer and Gartner, 1986:136).

VIOLENCE TRENDS

Violence trends in the U.S. may be seen in the context of broader patterns of variation. In a comprehensive review, Gurr (1981) suggested that the evidence shows "a distended U-shaped curve" of serious crime in Western Europe and the U.S., based on a review of data commencing with the thirteenth century. Included in the evidence is a study of homicide arrest trends between 1860 and 1920 in 23 cities, showing that the rate peaked in the Civil War, fell in the 1880s, then increased again by 1920. The Civil War-related crime waves—actually two, in the late 1860s and mid-1870s—have been explained in terms of the degradation of war (cf. Archer and Gartner, 1976), recession, social disruption caused by the mobility engendered by the war, anomie caused by destruction of the social structure, and the notion that crime waves somehow have a role in "redefining the acceptable boundaries of behavior" (Monkkonen, 1981; 78–79).

Overall, the nineteenth century trend was "stable or declining" (Gurr), with an increase in the 1860s and 1870s. Gurr also drew attention to the differential between African American and white homicide rates. While white rates have remained relatively constant, rates for African Americans have tended to increase. Also, Gurr concluded that two upturns in homicide in twentieth century America "may be attributable mainly to increases in killings among blacks" (Gurr; 324). Significantly, Gurr found that the evidence shows that black and white violence rates react quite differently to changing economic conditions and, therefore, "quantitative studies of determinants of crime trends in the United States ought to be disaggregated along racial lines" (Gurr, 1981;332–333).

The last 130 years in the U.S. have seen three waves of violence in cycles with about 50 years between each, beginning about 1860, 1900, and 1960 (Gurr, 1981). However, sharp racial differences make problematical the question of whether these upsurges were universal or actually disproportionately due to particular age or race cohorts. Gurr's interpretation was that rates among whites had tended to decline while those among African Americans had tended to be higher and to increase (Gurr, 1981).

Other historical studies of homicide patterns provide some insights applicable to the understanding of twentieth century trends. Based on research on nineteenth century Philadelphia, Lane (1980) suggested that the homicide rate was going down—"raggedly", as he put it, throughout the period. British studies, too, indicated declining rates of serious violence. Nineteenth century rates were greatly understated, owing to the weakness of police work and general data-gathering deficiencies. Infanticide, for example, was virtually unaccounted for, owing to the inadequacy of forensic science. The "best available" rate for Philadelphia for 1839–1901 was about 3.0/100,000, but an accounting making allowance for gaps in the data indicated a "real" rate on the order of 15.0–20.0.

When technologically improved handguns first became available in the 1850s, the homicide rate immediately jumped. Lane argued that handguns have facilitated violence and would have made for higher rates in the nineteenth century had they been readily available. From around 1870 to 1900, the homicide rate declined in spite of handgun availability, a trend interpreted by Lane in terms of public school enrollments and increases in employment in factories and bureaucracies. The public schools inculcated behavior patterns stressing conformity and suppression of emotions or discomfort, thus suppressing violent behavior, but (arguably) at the price of increasing the probability of suicide.

A continuing source of concern has been the tendency for rates of serious violence among blacks to exceed those among whites. Lane saw the roots of this discrepancy in the subservient, marginal status of African Americans, which made the environment in which they lived a hostile one, encouraging the possession of knives, and later handguns, for protection. Thus African American neighborhoods, even in the nineteenth century, were dangerous places. Black rates of violence were high as initially measured, and rose further through the nineteenth century, while white rates fell. The regimented lifestyle of school, factory, and office were not available to African Americans; in effect, there was no broadly based paradigm for behavior. With intermittent breaks in periods of war, this condition has persisted to the present day. (Poor) African American neighborhoods are still dangerous—more dangerous than ever—and behavioral paradigms are still missing, weak, or hopelessly inappropriate for the majority (such as the "professional athlete" and "professional entertainer" models). Indeed, black-white differences in homicide patterns are so pronounced that they account for differences in life expectancy. In 1975, for example, a white male had about six more years of life expectancy compared to a black, and about 20 percent of that difference was traceable to homicide rate differences. Furthermore, homicide is the leading cause of death among younger African American males (Farley, 1980).

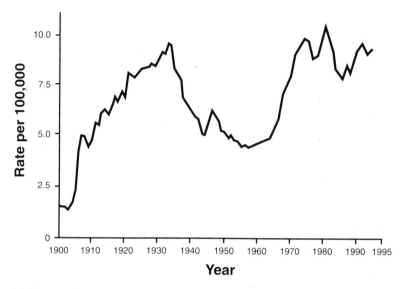

Figure 1.2. Twentieth century homicide trend chart. Rates per 100,000, U.S. population. *Source:*
U.S. Department of Justice, 1988, 1995.

In the twentieth century, the homicide rate in the U.S. reached a peak
in 1980 and has been declining somewhat since (Figure 1.2). As the
chart shows, rates were low at the beginning of the century, rose rapidly
to about 1910, then continued to increase irregularly until 1933, when
the rate stood at 9.7/100,000. Rates dropped until the end of World War
II, increased briefly in the mid forties, and declined again until about
1958 (4.5). Between 1961 and 1980, the rate increased to 11.0 (U.S.
Department of Justice, 1988a; Klebba, 1975).

The increase in rates between 1900 and 1920 is attributable in part to
the in-migration of large numbers of people from more violent cultures,
overcoming, in a statistical sense, the tendency toward declining violence in the established population (Lane, 1980). Prohibition is thought
to have contributed to the increase between 1919 and 1933; the abolition
of prohibition contributed to declining rates through World War II. The
nadir of modern homicide rates in the mid- to late-fifties also coincided
with full employment in the industrial city. But the opening of factory
jobs to African Americans came too late; by the time they gained access,
such jobs were obsolete. The upturn of rates in the sixties marked the
post-industrial era and relatively few employment opportunities for the
unskilled, including African Americans (Lane, 1980). Some interpretations of mortality in general, including deaths resulting from violence,

argue that economic instability is associated with trends in homicide, suicide, accidents, and perhaps (after a lag) chronic disease (Holinger and Klemen, 1982).

However, no one social or economic phenomenon can explain all the variation in homicide rates; another important dimension of variation is found in the interpretation of the influence of population age cohorts, defined as groups of persons born in a particular 5-year period. Klebba (1975), for example, noted that the precipitous decline in the homicide rate during World War II was due in part to the absence of some 5.5 million men, of whom some 3.5 million were in the prime homicide victimization cohorts, 20–24 and 25–29. Furthermore, employment was high, and overtime was common, thus reducing opportunities for hostile interpersonal interaction.

The Klebba study examined homicide trends through 1972 and found that the post-1958 increase had three components:

1. A large increase in the 15–29 age group which has figured prominently in both the offender and victim categories,

2. A large increase in death rates in this age group, beginning about 1960, and

3. Higher homicide rates in the period 1960–72 for the 35 and over age group, compared to the 25–34 group, which is usually more heavily involved.

Most of the increase in homicide rates between 1962–72 was ascribed to the 20–24 cohort, born in 1948–52. Almost a quarter of all arrests for homicide came from this cohort in 1972. The 15–19 cohort (born 1953–57) accounted for nearly 19.1 of homicide arrests in 1973. Overall, the 15–29 age group included 40 percent of victims and 59 percent of arrestees in 1973 (Klebba, 1975). Another element contributing to an understanding of the dynamics of homicide in the 1960–73 period is the increase in firearm involvement from 55 percent to 67 percent of the incidents.

Smith (1986) examined the issue of whether violence is seen most clearly as an *age* effect (i.e., one affecting certain age groups), a *period* effect (one impacting all age groups across a particular time period), or a *cohort* effect, in which one or more 5-year age groups consistently have high rates through their life cycles. Using data for the quarter century 1952–76, he found that cohort was the strongest effect. Combined with the age effect (the greater involvement in homicide of younger cohorts), the cohort effect accounts for much of the increase in the homicide rate during the period 1952–56. However, each cohort is unique, and an additional avenue of explanation suggests that we must look at the characteristics of each cohort in order to better understand the processes at work. The mere fact that a younger cohort is large does not in itself influence the overall crime rate; for a cohort to elevate rates, its *rate* must be higher than that of preceding cohorts.[2] It is in this context that we consider the influence of the notorious "baby boomers", born between about 1945 and 1960. Their relatively large numbers diminished their value in an economic sense and made the affluence of the fifties and sixties harder to sustain. Sub-groups within the cohort have fared very badly, suffering extraordinarily high rates of unemployment. As recently as 1986, for example, young blacks (16–19) were more than twice as likely to be unemployed (39% versus 15%) as their white counterparts (U.S. Bureau of the Census, 1988: Table 611).

In order to test the hypothesis that the structural characteristics of cohorts affect their economic well-being, which in turn influences the rate of violence, Smith measured the structural and economic characteristics of each cohort, using the variables *cohort size, age-specific unemployment rates,* and *proportion African American,* and examined their relationship to the homicide rate. All three variables were significant; the strongest correlation was between age-specific homicide rate and the unemployment rate. This finding suggests that such structural characteristics help explain the behavior of particular cohorts, although social-psychological effects, such as thwarted aspirations, should also be taken into account (Smith, 1986).

In the mid-1990s, a welcome downward trend in homicide was noted, with frequencies having declined from 1992–94, including a 7 percent drop from 25,470 in 1993 to 23,730 in 1994 (AP, 1995a), followed by a 12 percent drop in the first half of 1995 compared to the same period in 1994 (AP, 1995b). Significant declines were noted in several major cities, including New York, Chicago, Los Angeles, Philadelphia, Houston, Washington D.C., and Miami, and Kansas City, Missouri. Suggested explanations included a decline in the size of the youthful male population, the maturing and stabilization of drug markets, improved policing, community involvement, and displacement to the suburbs. The latter

---

[2] If a cohort is relatively large, it will, other things being equal, generate more crime. However, the larger amount of crime will be spread among more persons, so that the *population-based rate* (e.g., rate per 100,000) is not affected. On the other hand, a cohort generating more than its "share" of crime will contribute to the inflation of overall rates.

phenomenon is exemplified by Washington D.C. where homicide fell 10 percent in 1995, but increased in neighboring Prince George's County by 10 percent (Thomas, 1995a,b), in a "less than par" increment, given that 10 percent in Washington D.C. meant more incidents than 10 percent in Prince George's County. Indeed, displacement cannot explain declining *national* rates; fundamental changes are occurring to some degree.

Data Accuracy

The accuracy of homicide series, particularly in the earlier years, is questionable. Zahn (1980) has noted that complete national statistics were not available until the 1930s. Furthermore, police data and coroner's data are both inconsistent to some degree. For example, police data, ultimately incorporated in the *Uniform Crime Reports* (UCR) of the FBI, are probably quite accurate in terms of counts of incidents. But the accuracy of data on the victim-offender relationship or other aspects of the case may merely reflect the sophistication of the agency or be a function of the social status of the victim or offender, with lower status persons having less effort devoted to their cases. Also, coroners and medical examiners generate homicide data for national *Vital Statistics* (VS). These data, too, have been quite inconsistent over time, depending on whether they came through a coroner or medical examiner system, the adequacy of their staffs, and, again, the social status of the victim or offender.

Complicating the picture further, all states were not included in the national reporting of VS until the 1930s, when the UCR also began. On balance, however, both the UCR and VS have been congruent over time, with the VS usually higher than the UCR, the difference being attributable to definitional variation (Zahn, 1980).[3]

EMERGENT THEMES

Several themes emerge from interpretation of variations in twentieth century homicide rates. First, homicide has been predominantly an event occurring between males, on an intraracial basis. Rates among

---

[3] VS defines homicide in medical terms, as taking the life of another intentionally, while the UCR uses a legal definition—"willful killing." Thus a police killing would appear in the VS but not in the UCR (Zahn, 1980:115).

African Americans have tended to be relatively high. There would appear to be an analogy between increased violence in the period of alcohol prohibition (1919–33), and increased violence in the era of prohibited drug use, particularly cocaine in the late 1980s and early 1990s. Under both types of prohibition, violence has been employed as a rapid solution to problems in the marketplace, including, for example, the conflict between dealers over control of territory (see Chapter 9 for further discussion on this point).

Second, the issue of regional variation in violence has generated a stream of research that continues today. The South has consistently exhibited higher rates. (For extended discussion on this issue, see Chapter 4.)

Third, there has been a tendency for homicide rates to increase while other causes of mortality have diminished. Since 1980, this trend may have reversed, but the impact of greatly increased rates of drug-related violence in some areas in the late 1980s and early 1990s has not yet been assessed. In seeking explanation for the increasing rates of the sixties and seventies, Farley (1980) reviewed the adequacy of the *deterrence* and *social structural* models. The former argues that the virtual *de facto* elimination of capital punishment in the 1960s removed its deterrent effect and therefore contributed to increased violent crime. The social-structural model suggests that conditions such as poverty, unemployment, and high population density are associated with high rates of violence. However, Farley offered an alternative explanation to the effect that much of the increased rate of violence was associated with increased firearm availability rather than to failure of deterrence, social structure, or changes in the propensity of the population to use violence. The role of guns came to the fore following the urban violence of the sixties, during which handgun sales escalated; in 1969, over three million handguns were produced domestically or imported (Farley, 1980). By decomposing vital statistics homicide data for 1960–75, Farley concluded that "within the nonwhite community, the increase in homicide results almost exclusively from more murders by guns" (p. 184). Guns also contributed substantially to increased mortality in the white community. In 1975, the age-standardized homicide rate for non-white men was 622 deaths per million higher than for white men. Of that difference, 74 percent was due to firearms (Farley, Table 3).

By and large, historical trends in violence are not well understood, in spite of a substantial amount of related research. Much of the work done has been fragmented, and earlier studies, in particular, had to make do with data of dubious quality. Just as temporal patterns need more explanation, spatial patterns and their explanation are also fuzzy. Clearly, substantial trend differences between age and race cohorts in terms of their violence experience are also translatable into spatial differences. The high rate groups have not been randomly distributed with respect to space or time; thus some areas have been greatly impacted while others have been relatively free of serious violence.

THE SCOPE AND STRUCTURE OF HOMICIDE AND ASSAULT RATES

For the purpose of this discussion, it is assumed that homicide and aggravated assault rates are closely correlated in terms of their patterns of occurrence and demographic relationships. (This point will be elaborated in Chapter 3.) As noted elsewhere, an assault can be regarded as a failed homicide and it is very unlikely that a given area would have high rates of one type of serious violence without the other. For example, FBI data for 1986 showed that the homicide rate in the Burlington, Vermont, Metropolitan Statistical Area (MSA) was 1.9/100,000. The comparable aggravated assault rate was 75.3. In contrast, the homicide rate in the Dallas MSA was 19.9, the assault rate 493.8, illustrative of the crude correlation between rates (FBI, 1987). Various attributes of both homicide and assault will be examined in greater depth in later chapters, and the present discussion will sketch only the broadest characteristics of age, gender, race and other conditions.

Age

In 1986, the 20–29 age group accounted for 6,542 (34%) of the nation's 19,257 homicide victims, a proportion that has remained roughly constant into the 1990s. If the age range is expanded to 15–34, the percentage accounted for increased to 56. Homicide, then is a crime that disproportionately affects young adults (Figure 1.3). Rates increase rapidly through the teens and the highest rate tends to be in the 25- to 29-year-old cohort. Rates then decline after age 29 (FBI, 1987; Centers for Disease Control, 1983). The age structure of those arrested is comparable. The average age of homicide offenders in 1985 was 30 at the time of their arrest; the comparable age for aggravated assault was 29. In

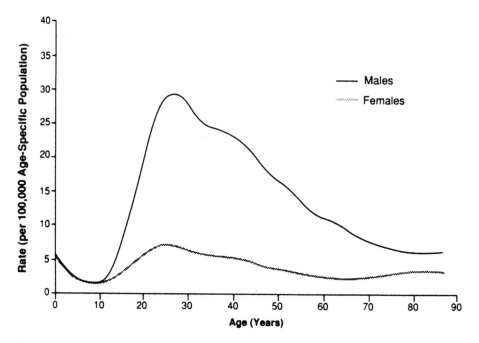

Figure 1.3. Homicide rates by age and gender of victim, U.S., 1978. *Source:* Centers for Disease Control, 1983.

general, the probability of arrest for violent crimes was greatest between the ages of 18 and 34 (U.S. Department of Justice, 1988a).

Gender

Serious violence overwhelmingly involves males as both victims and offenders. In 1986, 75 percent of the 19,257 homicide victims were male, as were some 88 percent of those arrested for homicide and 87 percent arrested for aggravated assault (U.S. Department of Justice, 1988a). The concentration of homicide among young adults applies to both males and females. The proportions of males remain quite constant; in 1992, 77 percent of victims were male, while 91 percent of persons arrested were male (Maguire and Pastore, 1995).

Race

The public health literature uses the concept of *years of potential (or productive) life lost before age 65* (YPLL) to express the impact of various

TABLE 1.1. HOMICIDE AS A CAUSE OF DEATH, BY RACE AND AGE

	WHITE				*BLACK*			
				AGE				
RANK	1–14	15–24	25–34	35–44	1–14	15–24	25–34	35–44
1	Acc	Acc	Acc	MN	Acc	HOM	HOM	Heart
2	MN	Suic	Suic	Heart	MN	Acc	Acc	MN
3	Con	HOM	MN	Acc	HOM	Suic	Heart	Acc
4	Heart	MN	HOM	Suic	Con	Heart	MN	Con
5	HOM	Heart	Heart	Liver	Heart	MN	Suic	Liver

KEY: Acc: Accidents. Con: Congenital anomalies. Heart: Heart diseases. HOM: Homicide. Liver: Liver diseases and cirrhosis. MN: Malignant neoplasms. Suic: Suicide.

Source: Centers for Disease Control, 1986, Tables 2a and 2b, pp. 14 and 15.

forms of premature mortality. In 1985, for example, homicides were responsible for a total of 612,556 YPLL. Homicide was the third ranked cause of YPLL for blacks, while for whites and others it was the sixth ranked source. In a study of homicide among African Americans and Hispanics conducted by the Centers for Disease Control using data for the period 1970 to 1983, it was shown that the homicide rate for African Americans was 37.4/100,000, some 6.7 times that for whites. Homicide was found to be the leading cause of death among African Americans in the 15–34 age category (Table 1.1). Rates of homicide were near 100/100,000 for black males in the 25–34 age group. This compares to national homicide rates, whether taken from mortality data or from the FBI, in the range 8 to 10/100,000 for the same period (Centers for Disease Control, 1986). In 1993, 51 percent of homicide victims were African American (Maguire & Pastore, 1995).

The lifetime risk of being murdered has been put as high as 1 in 20 for black males (Hilts, 1988), and about 1 in 178 for white males (U.S. Department of Justice, 1988b). Recent data have shown that African American life expectancy has dropped, for the first time in the twentieth century, and the principal components of that drop are homicide and accidents. Between 1985 and 1986, black homicides increased 15 percent, compared to a 5 percent increase among whites (Hilts, 1988). Rate differences by race, age and gender are summarized graphically in Figure 1.4.

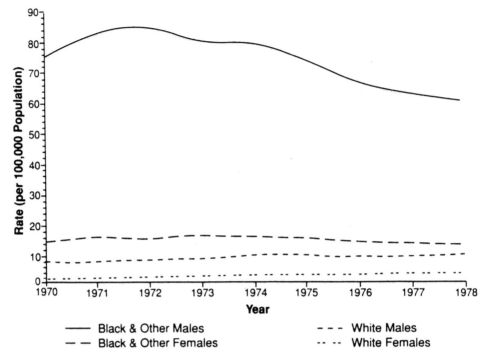

Figure 1.4. Age-adjusted homicide rates by race and gender of victim, U.S., 1970–78. *Source:* Centers for Disease Control, 1983.

Other Related Conditions

Historically, the majority of victims died as a result of altercations in which the offender was known personally by the victim.[4] Generally, about half of aggravated assault victims, too, are acquaintances, relatives, or otherwise known to the victims. However, in the mid-1990s there began to be new indications that stranger-to-stranger homicides and assaults were in the majority (see Chapter 3). Of all family violence, it is estimated that some 57 percent is committed by spouses or ex-spouses (Klaus and Rand, 1984). Single, unemployed, and lower income persons

---

[4]Incidents in which victim and offender are known to each other are sometimes referred to as "primary". These are also usually of the so-called "non-felony" type, meaning that another crime was not being perpetrated at the time that the violence occurred. Other incidents (stranger-to-stranger) are referred to as "secondary" and are more likely to be of the "felony" type. For example, a burglar (stranger) enters a home and shoots and kills the occupant. This would be a felony-type, secondary event.

are more likely to be the victims of violent crimes (U.S. Department of Justice, 1988a).

About 20 percent of homicide victims are killed by offenders in the course of another crime, e.g., armed robbery. Of the felony homicides, about 64 percent in 1986 involved situations in which the victim was classified as a "stranger" or of "unknown relationship" to the offender; 26 percent involved "acquaintances."

Most homicides are performed with firearms, and most of the firearms are handguns. In 1986, for example, of the 19,257 homicides, 59 percent were firearm incidents. Of that number, 8,460 (74%) involved handguns (FBI, 1987). By 1993, 70 percent of the 24,526 homicides were firearm related, an all-time high. Fifty-seven percent (of 24,526) were with handguns (Maguire and Pastore, 1995). Blacks are more likely to use handguns in the course of a homicide (51% for 1976–83), compared to whites (42%). Firearms are more likely to be used in the killing of men than of women.

Temporal patterns suggest a pronounced seasonality for assault. The Centers for Disease Control (1983) reported that "there appears to be a seasonal trend in the occurrence of homicide," on the basis of analysis of data for 1970–78. Other analyses, however, have been unable to confirm this finding (e.g., Cheatwood, 1988; Harries, 1989; see Chapter 7 for more detailed discussion).

Research on violence at various levels of urbanization has shown that urban rates exceed suburban which in turn exceed rural, regardless of personal characteristics of victims (Gibbs, 1979). At the local level, suburban residents are more likely to be victimized while in the central city of their metropolitan area compared to central city residents in adjoining suburbs. At the neighborhood level, the home is the single most likely location of a fatal assault. In a study of Dade county, Florida, for example, Wilbanks (1984) found that some 26 percent of homicides occurred in the home, 15 percent in public buildings, and another 15 percent on streets or sidewalks. However, about 11 percent occurred in homes other than the victim's, giving a total of 37 percent of incidents taking place in home settings.

COSTS OF VIOLENCE

The costs of violence have several dimensions: immediate medical expenses, lost earnings, and impacts on the dependents of the victims and offenders. Data for such costs are not collected in any systematic fashion and aggregate dollar amounts can only be estimated. In a study of all gunshot patients admitted to San Francisco General Hospital, the principal trauma center for the city, in 1984, it was found that the total cost for 131 victims was $905,809. On the basis of this data, it was estimated that the total national cost of gunshot treatments only in 1984 was $429 million. The best recent comparable estimate is about one billion dollars (Martin, Hunt, & Hulley, 1988). The impact of drug related violence has been traumatic in some locations; the Washington (D.C.) Hospital Center's Medstar Trauma Center treated 180 gunshot admissions in 1987, a number that increased over 300 percent to 551 by 1988 (McCarthy, 1989).

A 1994 cost analysis of shootings in Washington, D.C. showed a cost of $7,000 if a murder victim died before medical attention, but about $22,000 if the victim survived through surgery. To this should be added the cost of searching for, and prosecuting, an offender, followed by incarceration at about $25,000 per year (Thomas, 1994). Analysis based on a pilot survey of patients admitted to the R. Adams Cowley Shock Trauma Center at the University of Maryland Hospital in Baltimore led to the conclusion that the overall average cost for each patient was $32,000, with an average of $47,000 for the gunshot victims, the majority of whom were uninsured (Read, 1993).

Lost Earnings

A crude estimate of lost earnings can be provided by multiplying years of productive life lost (YPLL) by some factor to represent income. If a value of $20,000 is used as the income constant, the loss in 1985, based on the previously quoted YPLL value of 612,556, would be estimated at more than $12 billion. Higher income estimates, of course, yield correspondingly higher loss estimates. If lost earnings could be mapped, the distribution would certainly be nonrandom, and would peak in inner cities, illustrating an important, yet often overlooked, component of the impact of violence.

Impacts on Dependents

The effects of violence on households are virtually incalculable in monetary terms—the losses of shared joys and sorrows, love and affection—all the myriad nuances of human relationships. Such losses are profound, and, like estimates of monetary losses, are distributed nonrandomly in geographic space. Residents of neighborhoods disproportionately affected by violence are likely to experience above-average levels of mental illness, particularly depression, as a consequence of such stresses. (For further discussion of this point, see Aneshensel, 1992; Jargowsky and Bane, 1990; Mulroy and Lane, 1992; Pappas et al., 1993; Pearlin, 1989, and Ratner, 1992.)

THE REST OF THE BOOK

In Chapter 2, perspectives and theories underlying the explanation of serious violence are discussed. As the title of the book indicates, the approach is basically an ecological one, demonstrating how various elements of the urban and regional system are interrelated, and how some of those interrelationships tend to be associated with violence. Attention will focus particularly on the reasons for the concentration of violence in relatively few areas in cities. The approach may be character-ized as one of uncovering spatial relationships, but with the addition of a longitudinal perspective wherever possible. For example, it is virtually impossible to explain patterns of violence in the contemporary Ameri-can city without an understanding of the recent qualitative and quantita-tive history of drug use.

Chapter 3 deals with the issue of classification, an unusually impor-tant topic in the context proposed here since an underlying argument is that misclassification of homicide and assault incidents has historically limited our ability to undertake comprehensive, meaningful, analyses. It will be suggested that we should develop a new way of classifying homicide and assault in order to combine incidents which are generi-cally comparable. The justification for this will be illustrated by drawing on recent research on patterns in Dallas.

Chapter 4 examines regional variations in homicide. One of the most persistent cultural traits of the United States, setting it apart from other developed nations, is its extraordinarily high homicide rate. The high rate is substantially attributable to very high rates in the South. This issue will be examined in order to illustrate how the situation has come about and the various interpretations offered to account for it.

Chapter 5 builds on Chapter 4 in that it assesses the issue of regional and interurban variations in perceptions of the severity of serious violent crime, with a specific emphasis on homicide. This is done by drawing in part on the findings of the *National Survey of Crime Severity,* including the *Sourcebook,* which provides data for metropolitan areas as well as states. In addition, patterns of capital punishment will be related to the geography of perceived seriousness of violence in order to evaluate the extent to which punishment fits perceived seriousness.

Chapter 6 looks at a topic of considerable current concern: homicide patterns within, and to some extent, between cities. Key variables such as race, age, sex, weapons used, and motives, will be reviewed in their geographic context in order to provide a sense of the overall structure of interactions occurring in the urban environment. Particular attention will be given to the reasons underlying changes in patterns of violence *within* cities, and to reasons for variations in patterns of violence *between* cities.

Chapter 7 will focus on two aspects of the ecology of assault: general neighborhood ecology, and the "long, hot summer" issue. An accumulating mass of evidence suggests a link between environmental conditions and patterns of aggravated assault. Data from a series of studies of Dallas will be used to illustrate this strand of violence research.

Chapter 8 addresses the fact that no contemporary discussion of violence in America (or practically anywhere else, for that matter) can be complete without consideration of the interaction between drugs and violence. Drug-related conflict accounts for a considerable proportion of all violence in America. Important, but little understood, spatial dynamics are at work. For example, competition between factions for the lucrative "crack" trade in the Washington-Baltimore area was thought to account for a major component of the high level of violence in that region in the late 1980s and early 1990s. This violence has involved an alarming number of multiple homicides and homicides with juveniles as both victims and offenders, and the escalating use of automatic and semiautomatic weapons aroused great consternation.

Chapter 9 examines the policy implications of patterns of violence, including relationships between violence and poverty, gun control, drugs, public health, and policing. The prospect for coherent and realistic policy is put in the context of the world of the 1990s.

Chapter 2

THE ECOLOGICAL VIEWPOINT, THEORY, GEOGRAPHY, AND VIOLENCE

Crime in general, and violence in particular, may be viewed from a variety of perspectives along a continuum. This continuum may be crudely dichotomized into studies that are either *clinical* or *social* in emphasis. An alternative terminology would use the terms *micro* (individual level) or *macro* (aggregate data) to indicate the scope of analysis. Macro-level analysis is also called *ecological,* and the term *ecological data* is used to refer to information aggregated by geographic units such as census tracts, cities, or states. Brantingham and Brantingham (1984) have used the analogy of a "cone of resolution," to indicate that a phenomenon can be examined in spatial contexts of different levels. Thus the clinical or micro scale would involve the individual or even part of an individual as the subject of study—the tip of the cone of resolution. At the social or macro level, crime within a large area could be investigated—the base of the cone. The clinical approach is the province of psychiatrists, psychologists, and other behavioral scientists. Analysis toward the social end of the continuum is typically the realm of sociologists, criminologists, and other social scientists, including (social) psychologists, social historians and social geographers.

In this chapter, the concept of social ecology and its derivatives is reviewed and considered in conjunction with a brief overview of violence theory, including perspectives from several disciplines. Since terminology has become problematical, a section is devoted to clarification of terms that commonly enter into the language of ecological analysis.

SOCIAL ECOLOGY

The social or macro level approach is more or less synonymous with the *ecological* perspective. "Ecology" in this context has traditionally

incorporated a geographical component as well as concern for identification of causal variables and their interrelationships. While formal definitions of this particular type of ecology are few, Morris (1957) has offered
the following:

> Human or social ecology is concerned with the relationships which exist between
> people who share a common habitat or local territory and which are distinctly
> related to the character of the territory itself; it is a study of social structure in
> relation to the local environment. (p. 1)

The label "ecology" comes from the Greek *oikos* (household or living
place) and was originally a nineteenth century description of organism-
environment interactions used by natural scientists (Hawley, 1968).
According to Morris (1957), the term was used initially in 1878 by the
German Ernst Haeckel, and then to some degree brought into the social
science fold by Eugenius Warming, a Danish scientist, with the publication of his *Plant Communities* in 1895. This book contained a clear
analogue of human communities in the processes of invasion-succession,
and growth and decline. The biological connotation has always been
somewhat unfortunate, however, given that it derived from the assumption that human behavior replicates biological processes.

Distinctly human ecology developed as a branch of sociology through
the influential work of Robert E. Park at the University of Chicago
beginning in 1914. Originally, human ecology incorporated several pos-
tulates drawn from the analogy to natural environment. These included
the underlying theme of *Darwinism,* the *"balance of nature"* concept, and
the notion of *"invasion-succession"* (Hawley, 1968). Modern social ecology,
however, is more sympathetic to McKenzie's interpretation of human
ecology as "a study of the spatial and temporal relations of human
beings, affected by the selective, distributive, and accommodative forces
of the environment" (Hawley, 1968; see also McKenzie, 1925).

Some of the distinctive features of human ecology, as outlined by
Hawley, carry over to contemporary social ecology and are found in
some form in studies of crime, notably *the interaction of population and
environment* and *population as a point of reference.* Useful subsidiary concepts in a discussion of crime and its patterns are *adaptation, survival,*
and *interdependence* (Hawley, 1968).

While ecological studies can be traced to the early nineteenth century,
it was, after Park, the work of Shaw and McKay and others—the
Chicago School of sociology—that is recognized as a major stimulus to

research of the ecological genre. Their research on Chicago and other cities in the 1920s and '30s examined relationships between spatial patterns of juvenile delinquency and neighborhood characteristics (e.g., Shaw and McKay, 1942). Their principal findings were that: (1) Delinquency rates peaked in areas adjacent to Central Business Districts, (2) High rates persisted areally over time in spite of population change, (3) "Social disorganization" explained high delinquency rates, and (4) The spatial correlation of various social pathologies was explained by the social conditions in those communities. The underlying theory was the Burgess concentric zone model of urban structure, rooted in the invasion-succession process from human ecology, and itself the basis for much subsequent work in urban sociology and urban geography. However, the biological analogy was minimal and in this sense the label "ecological" is misleading for the Shaw and McKay work (Baldwin, 1979).

Weaknesses of Early Ecological Research

Baldwin (1979), in a comprehensive review, noted several weaknesses of the Shaw and McKay work: (1) Analyses were based on official crime rates, (2) Such ecological research, based as it invariably is on geographic units of some sort, is subject to the *"ecological fallacy."* The implication of this is that the aggregate characteristics of areas, or of the people in areas, are not necessarily an accurate reflection of the characteristics of *individuals* in areas (see Robinson, 1950). A median family income statistic for a census tract, for example, may misrepresent a bipolar distribution, just as a high homicide rate for a census tract does not necessarily tell us that an individual inhabitant is more prone to violent behavior or to victimization than persons in other locations. It should be noted that a comparable fallacy can operate at the individual level in that relationships at the individual level are not always the product of variables operating at the micro level, what Sampson (1989) has termed the *"individualistic fallacy."* (3) It is difficult to identify causal processes; for example, whether slums produce delinquents or delinquents produce slums by gravitating to them, and, (4) The Shaw and McKay position was politically conservative and failed to account for broad relationships in society, i.e., the possibility that slums neither produce nor are produced by delinquents, but are spawned by regional or national conditions, or some interaction between local and universal processes. Hamnet (1979), for example, has persuasively argued that it is indeed necessary to look for broader causes and avoid the temptation to look at spatial phenomena in isolation from related conditions.

To these criticisms may be added the following: ecological analysis dealt only with street crimes, the relevant processes have changed over time, and, contrary to Shaw and McKay's assertion that densely populated inner cities lacked social organization, some forms of crime need it (McCord, 1989). The underpinning of Shaw and McKay's studies of delinquency, *disorganization theory*, has been criticized by Jackson and Smith (1984) as having declined from the status of "a complex explanatory construct" to "an atheoretical bourgeois value judgement" (p. 166). However, analyses of British Crime Survey data have lent new support to the theory (Sampson and Groves, 1989).

Other Ecological Issues

Another set of issues concerning the ecological approach to crime research has been set out by Byrne and Sampson (1986). These included data sources, context, conceptualization and measurement issues, and research design.

The *data source* issue is a perennial one and concerns the questionable value of official statistics in ecological research, whether from the Uniform Crime Reports (UCR) or the National Crime Victimization Survey (NCVS). The great majority of ecological analyses have used UCR or UCR-type data. Relatively few have employed NCVS or alternative sources for good reason—NCVS data are not available for small areas and are thus not well suited to the areal focus of ecological studies. Other data sources, such as rap sheets or self-reports, are often difficult to access and involve labor-intensive interpretation and concomitant high costs.

While the inadequacies of official data sources are well-known, Smith (1986), in a study of Birmingham, England, found that the creative use of a set of unofficial sources of crime data added only 4.3 percent to the official tally (p. 34). Certainly, the focus of the present book on homicide and assault means that the "dark figure" of hidden offenses is a lesser problem than it would be for an offense such as rape. It must be acknowledged, nevertheless, that assault is subject to a serious degree of underreporting, with only some 58 percent of "aggravated assaults with injury" reported to the police (U.S. Department of Justice, 1988a; p. 34). Homicide, on the other hand, is undoubtedly the most completely reported crime for obvious reasons.

The *context* issue involves the difficulty of obtaining data relating to both *individual* and *aggregate* characteristics for small areas. The census provides aggregate data for blocks and (in greater detail) for tracts, but no individual data owing to privacy constraints. Surveys to obtain such data are usually prohibitively expensive, but both kinds of data are desirable in order to answer the question of whether crime rate variation is due to the aggregate nature of communities, to the characteristics of individuals somehow "sorted" into communities, or to other conditions or processes.

The *conceptualization and measurement* issue relates to the common practice of correlating crime rates with community characteristics and inferring causality. Byrne and Sampson argue, however, that mediating conditions are poorly understood. For example, the process of "alienation" is commonly presumed to mediate between *percent African American* and *crime rate,* providing an explanation of the positive association. Here, they suggest, alienation needs to be measured in order to test the validity of the assumed effect. Furthermore, variables used in ecological analyses are not standardized; thus income, employment, population density, and a host of other conditions can be measured in a variety of ways possibly yielding different results in otherwise comparable models.

Research design is of interest over the question of whether cross-sectional or longitudinal frameworks are most appropriate for research. Most studies have been of the former type, presumably owing to the difficulty, historically, of both obtaining data over time and of analyzing it, since data sets can rapidly become extremely large when both crime-related and social data are cumulated over a period of several years. However, longitudinal studies are vital. As Byrne and Sampson noted, crime is an integral part of the urban change process as well as a product of that change. For example, fear of violence may profoundly change people's behavior in a neighborhood, perhaps contributing to out-migration and vacant housing then occupied by those unable to compete in a more desirable housing market. This population could be more crime-prone than that which it replaced. Thus violence and fear of violence have changed the character of the neighborhood which now "produces" a different complex of crime, both quantitatively and qualitatively, than it did before. This crime complex, in turn, is now itself a neighborhood characteristic and will influence subsequent behavior patterns. In extreme situations, people may acquire conditions comparable to post-traumatic stress syndrome, like battle fatigue (Norris, 1989). For additional discussion, see: Sampson, 1987.

Today, predominantly correlational studies exemplified by Lander's study of Baltimore (Lander, 1954) are widely regarded as unlikely to produce new knowledge, given that many such studies have been done and they are limited in their power by reliance on correlation techniques and aggregated data. The tendency in more recent ecological methodology has been to seek a finer-grained perspective by breaking down problems into smaller pieces, thus increasing chances for the development of new insights. Ecological analyses now often look at specific types of crime or even subcategories within crimes, and attempt, insofar as possible, to bring a broader arsenal of methods into play. (For related discussion, see: Herbert, 1979; Murray and Boal, 1979.)

Sampson (1989), in a review of the shortcomings of macro-level research, suggested four strategies for overcoming the weaknesses of ecological studies: (1) Use survey instruments that capture community concepts such as informal social control and friendship networks. (2) Combine community information with data at the individual level in a merging of the micro and macro levels. (3) A focus on children and families, and (4) Ethnographic analysis. As Sampson put it, "I have learned more about community structure from reading classic ethnographic studies than I ever learned from multivariate analyses of census data."

Research Traditions in Social Geography

Jackson and Smith (1984) have outlined a context of four traditions in social geography, in which the spatial study of crime may be placed. The traditions—*positivist, behavioral, humanist,* and *structuralist*—each have some bearing on how geographers have looked at social problems, including violent crime.

The *positivist* tradition was essentially deterministic and held that problems had definable causes that could be measured, isolated, and used for predictive purposes. Positivism has come to have pejorative meaning given that it historically implied a conservative stance, condoning the political status quo. Positivism was expressed in urban ecology as an emphasis on spatial correlations, implying causal relationships. Most research in the spatial aspects of crime and in criminology has been in this tradition or some variant of it.

However, Gottfredson and Hirschi (1987) have noted that "the history of positivistic criminology is badly in need of revision" (p. 10). Modern positivism no longer separates empirical research and theory, as it once did. Although statistical data are now better than ever before, positivists today are concerned with questions of both meaning and measurement. In general, the contemporary positivist view offers a balanced consideration of both observed patterns of crime and their underlying interpretation, whether that interpretation is to be found in statistics or in more subtle sources. They concluded that "in light of the pervasive distaste for positivism expressed by many modern criminologists, it is surprising to discover that positivistic criminology may today be healthier than ever" (p. 18). Laub (1987), too, has noted the "powerful resurgence" of positive criminology since about 1970.

Behavioral geography arose as a reaction to optimizing "economic man" and put emphasis on individual decisions, human fallibility, and humans as satisficers rather than optimizers. Transposed to the study of crime, this view would oppose interpretations of criminal behavior (particularly property crime) as a rational response to conditions. Herbert (1982) has noted that the tendency of human geography to incorporate behavioral approaches is indeed emerging in work on the geography of crime. Also, efforts are under way to join aggregate and individual levels of analysis and to examine the implications of meanings of place in the analysis of crime. Herbert also saw a growing awareness of the broader social antecedents of crime in social stratification and inter-class conflicts.

Rengert (1989) has argued that considerable scope still exists for the application of concepts from behavioral geography to ecological criminology. These include spatial decision making, subdivisible into *spatial behavior* as distinct from *behavior in space.* The former tries to develop models of, for example, distances traveled to commit crimes, or directions in which criminals travel to indulge in criminal activity. Behavior in space, on the other hand, considers the context in which behavior occurs. Thus the local environment, for example, is seen as providing a set of opportunities or inhibitors vis-a-vis crime. Behavioral geographic perspectives have shown that burglars behave in gender- and ethnic-specific fashions owing to differences in spatial knowledge. Perceptions of spaces apparently skew spatial behavior.

Unfortunately, much of the conceptual framework offered by behavioral geography has only limited or indirect application with respect to the types of violence considered here. Such a high proportion of incidents of violence occur in the home or at other heavily frequented locations, such as neighborhood bars, that the type of behavioral data useful in the study of, say, burglary patterns, is of limited usefulness. However, behavioral perspectives could be useful indirectly in assessments of drug-related movements and displacements, and also with respect to the subset of violent acts (e.g., robberies with injuries or deaths and gang violence) in which responses to environment are integral to the violent act. Yet even gang violence may be *expressive* or *instrumental* and spatial behavior may be less significant for the former than the latter, further reinforcing the complexity of classifications of violent behavior and the danger of adopting standard methodologies. Clearly, some types of crime lend themselves more readily to behavioral analysis than others.

The *humanist* viewpoint, a product of the 1970s in geography, attempts to describe how participants experience social situations. Just as positivism tends to advocate an objective view of the world, the humanist position is subjective and draws on a variety of methods including interviews, census data, other secondary sources, and participant observation. Ley (1974) is regarded as an exemplary study in this genre. In the geography of crime, works focusing on the subjective dimension, such as Carter and Hill (1979) have become more numerous. (For more on this point, see Chapter 7.)

The *structuralist* perspective argues that an understanding of phenomena is found in underlying social and economic organization. From a political left perspective, social problems are essentially reflections of the defects of capitalism. Structuralism is in a sense a counterpoint to earlier correlational studies in criminal ecology which looked for entirely local causes of local problems. The structuralist would see high rates of unemployment among African American youth, for example, as a product of social forces extending through society at large, and merely manifested in distinctive local patterns.

Research Realms in the Spatial Study of Crime

Smith (1986) has presented another perspective from which to view ecological studies of crime. Adopting a framework modeled after Habermas (1968), she examined three realms of research in the spatial study of crime: *empirical-analytical, historical-hermeneutic,* and *critical.* In terms of the earlier classification of traditions in social geography, the empirical-analytical approximates the positivist perspective, the historical-hermeneutic incorporates the behavioral and humanist approaches, and the critical roughly coincides with the structuralist school.

The empirical-analytical view, expressed through quantitative criminology, is also referred to as *direct realism*, often relying rather uncritically on official crime rates and also depending excessively on census measures of social conditions, sometimes at the expense of the rich detail that could be derived from field observation. Smith divides such studies into four classes: nineteenth century cartographic studies of crime in Europe, studies from the Chicago School in the early twentieth century, factor analyses in the 1960s, and econometric studies in the 1970s.

In the historical-hermeneutic tradition, criminology has employed oral-ethnographic methods. Such analyses provide a vivid glimpse of social relationships and permit insights relating to conditions and processes that would not be measured by conventional statistical sources. Among the best known of the earlier workers of this genre were Henry Mayhew (1862) and Charles Booth (1902). Neither was a criminologist as such, but both complied massively detailed observational data on urban life including information on crime. C.R. Shaw, of the Chicago School, exemplified later ethnographic efforts.

Unfortunately, the potential for an oral-ethnographic approach to the study of serious violence is limited by problems of confidentiality, cost, and personal risks to the investigator. It is likely that at no time in history has the personal risk in an ethnographic approach to violence been greater, as the use of automatic and semiautomatic weapons has become commonplace in those environments in which investigation should ideally occur, and the toll of death and injury among bystanders is unprecedented. In addition, ethnographies suffer the drawback that they "provide limited tests of theories because they focus on a single community or, at most, on a cluster of neighborhoods in which community properties do not display sufficient variation" (Sampson & Groves, 1989, pp. 775–776).

Critical, or radical, criminology adopts the position that crime is a product of social inequities. Indeed, laws written by the ruling classes to protect their interests are an expression of that inequity. Crime in this view is a logical expression of class conflict. Property crime is seen as a rational redistribution of wealth. Given that violent crime is disproportionately concentrated among the poor, it can also be seen as a predictable reaction to oppression by the ruling classes.

This view, predominantly sympathetic to a socialist interpretation of social structure and process, overlooks the fact that serious violence is found in all societies; the presence or absence of capitalism is not a reliable predictor as we see when we compare Japan, with its low rates of violence, and the United States, with high rates. Indeed, the racial or religious homogeneity of a society may be a better predictor of levels of serious violence than the presence or absence of predatory capitalism (cf. Northern Ireland, the U.S., Japan). Thus direct and indirect consequences of bigotry and racism may provide more plausible superficial explanations than forms of economic organization.

Each of these perspectives has strengths and weaknesses and none can in isolation provide the all-encompassing interpretation sought by researchers and policy makers. The perspective provided here will attempt to incorporate evidence from a variety of sources with a bearing on the spatial ecology of violence, regardless of the research tradition from which it comes. By default, however, because of the sheer volume of existing work, the bias will tend to be toward the empirical-analytical (or positivist) tradition.

TERMINOLOGY: ECOLOGICAL, ENVIRONMENTAL, AREAL, SPATIAL, SITUATIONAL

In the present work, "ecological," "environmental," "areal," and "spatial" will be used interchangeably and will refer to any study or perspective involving the analysis or comparison of areas, or geographic distributions of violence-related phenomena. "Situational" refers to a closely related concept, that of the time-space contexts in which crimes occur. As such it is essentially a subset of the ecological perspective. The phrase "situational crime prevention" has come to refer to manipulation of certain elements in the environment in order to deter crime in some way. Such control necessitates an understanding of how humans interact with their surroundings in space and time.

Certainly, the concept of *area* is central to the ecological perspective, and Morris (1957) has noted that the *natural area* is one of the most valuable of the tools used in the ecological approach. Indeed, because of confusion over the meaning and implications of the term "ecological," Baldwin (1979) has argued that *areal* is more appropriate. However, the term has not gained wide usage.

The spatial view has been reinforced in recent decades by the isolation of the ghetto underclass in the inner city. African American communities, historically microcosms of the larger metropolis (in that they contained areas representing a partial cross-section of economic status) now have lost many of their more mobile residents to suburbs. The result has been inner cities inhabited by those who are in some respect sufficiently disabled that they are unable to escape.

Given that observations suggest a strong association between the location of the underclass and the presence of serious violence, the areal perspective has recently received new energy. The importance of place, community, general social and economic processes, and the intersection of pathological conditions in an explicitly spatial framework, are currently receiving attention not accorded to such phenomena since the disturbances of the 1960s. Unfortunately, it has taken a stunning toll of death and injury, primarily associated with drug dealing, to achieve this renaissance.

"OFFICIAL" CAUSES OF VIOLENCE

More than twenty years ago, the National Commission on the Causes and Prevention of Violence (National Commission, 1969a), outlined causes of violence and noted that it was concentrated then, as now, "especially among poor black young men in the ghettoes" (p. 47). Drawing on various sources, the Commission listed fourteen urban conditions associated with violence:

- low income
- physical deterioration
- dependency
- racial and ethnic concentrations
- broken homes
- working mothers
- low levels of education and vocational skills
- high unemployment
- high proportions of single males
- overcrowded and substandard housing
- high rates of tuberculosis and infant mortality
- low rates of home ownership or single family dwelling
- mixed land use
- high population density

To this list we would have to add, today, evidence of overt drug trading and use. In a vivid passage, the Commission linked race, poverty, and violence:

> To be young is to be degraded; to be poor is to be degraded more; to be [black] is to be degraded even more; and to be young, poor, and [black] is to be degraded more than any other group in the society. It becomes increasingly understandable, then, why the ranks of young, poor [blacks] should provide proportionally the highest percentage of recruits to criminal violence. (National Commission, 1969b, p. 507).

The Commission interpretation was essentially ecological; indeed, the report cited Shaw and McKay and expanded on the role of various pathologies of home, family, and neighborhood. However, like older, less critical ecological interpretations, it was empirical and associative—certain conditions were seen in the city, violence was associated with those conditions, and a causal relationship was inferred. Citing high population density as a correlate of violence is a case in point. Careful studies of the density issue have shown that the relationship between density and social pathologies is at best quite ambiguous. Density is a two-edged phenomenon; while high density increases the probability of potentially negative social interactions, it also provides surveillance to counter such events (see, for example: Baldassare, 1979; Freedman, 1975).

Although lacking in theoretical rigor and depth, the broad brush approach of the National Commission had the virtues of being comprehensible and plausible in a commonsense way. It is a stance drawing on both the empirical-analytic and historical-hermeneutic approaches to criminology. Insofar as the promise of capitalism has broken down in the slums of the inner city, critical theory, based on the assumption that inequities are incorporated into the fabric of society by various acts of omission and commission, is also recognized.

The most serious weakness of the "laundry list" presented by the Commission (in effect an informal representation of disorganization theory) is that it fails to explicitly recognize fully the factors underlying the symptoms of social collapse, including racism, the failure of democratic processes to redress grievances (through the equitable allocation of resources), and the tacit acceptance of the existence of a permanent underclass. (For a comprehensive analysis with a set of contemporary "problem solving" initiatives, see Reiss and Roth, 1993.)

VIOLENCE THEORY

Violence theory is relatively weak at the macro (aggregate, sociological, or ecological) level. As Gottfredson and Hirschi (1989a) put it:

> An increasingly obvious shortcoming of criminology is that it lacks a general theory to guide social policy in the area of crime treatment and prevention. Since the Great Society programs of the 1960s, and the deinstitutionalization movement of the 1970s, no criminological theory can claim responsibility for important elements of public policy about crime. (p. 57)

It could be argued that theory tends to be stronger at the micro (individual or psychological) level than at the macro level. The basis for the distinction between macro- and micro-theory may be found in a comparison between certain physical and social sciences. Holt-Jensen (1988) has pointed out that theory formulation based on hypothetic-deductive methods evolved into its most advanced state in physics and chemistry. In physics, for example, data are quantifiable, but very abstract; such phenomena as neutrons or atomic nuclei could not be observed directly so processes are hypothesized and verified mathematically. Theory is absolutely critical in order to provide a model for experimentation. In the social sciences, however, including criminology, sociology, and geography, phenomena are frequently observable and the need for theory to provide a model of process, while present, is less compelling. For example, anyone can observe through a moderately close reading of major newspapers that the areal coincidence between the distribution of the underclass and the occurrence of high rates of violent crime is overwhelming; the condition can be verified in the field. Theory is necessary to develop an explanation of underlying processes, but not to provide a picture of the general distribution. Interestingly, those phases of social science with less easily observed phenomena (perceptions, attitudes, motivations of behavior, for example) tend to have better developed theory in a manner analogous to physics. Psychology, including the study of violence from a psychological perspective, fits this pattern.

It is not surprising, therefore, that the empirical-analytical perspective has dominated the study of violence at the macro level, and that theory is relatively weak. This type of weakness of theory does not necessarily mean that we lack knowledge of violence or that the ecological study of violence is devoid of theory. (On this point, see Sampson and Groves, 1989.) It indicates, rather, that:

1. Data gathered at any particular place may or may not represent all places.
2. As statements about violence realities become more specific, they are less likely to contribute to universal theory; they may document the unique but fail to add much to general explanation.
3. Conversely, as statements about violence realities become more general, exceptions are more likely.

The list of violence-related factors generated by the National Commission on the Causes and Prevention of Violence is, in effect, a primitive theoretical statement lacking parameters. In other words, we know that low income and minority concentrations are associated with violence, but we do not have a quantitative model—or any model—with acceptable predictive or even descriptive explanatory capability. This weakness was illustrated in 1989 by a *Washington Post* news analysis seeking to discover why Washington D.C. had a rate of homicide higher than that found in any other city, including some, like Detroit, apparently comparable in many respects. The headline made the problem clear: "The puzzle of D.C.'s deadly distinction: Experts offer theories, but no certainties, on why Washington leads nation in killing." A battery of causal factors was reviewed in a series of interviews with experts: wealth, income differential between rich and poor, bad luck, turf conflicts over drugs, poverty, unemployment, and organized crime (or lack of it). Ultimately, however, experts could not offer a coherent explanation for Washington's preeminent position.

Of course, various researchers have produced quantitative models incorporating the usual array of social and economic variables, but each is essentially unique to the context studied. Furthermore, measures used often vary; hence models are not standardized in any useful way. Given that so many alternative metrics may be used for, say, poverty, it is not surprising that nominally similar models may yield different, sometimes contradictory, results. Furthermore, it can be argued that such mechanistic models are, in any event, not useful as they inevitably rest too heavily on objective data at the expense of subjective phenomena. A mechanical, parametric model is of little use to policy makers who need to have a comprehensive view of processes related to the production of violence.

The study of violence, like the study of other human phenomena, deals with unpredictable human behavior, unlike physics or chemistry where processes are underlain by highly predictable physical laws. But who is to know exactly what will happen in some particular mix of drugs, poverty, law enforcement, and racial discrimination? The possible combinations of behavior and interactions between numerous variables are virtually limitless, and none can be isolated and studied under experimental conditions.

All violence researchers—like other researchers—want theory, but useful theory is hard to come by. Social contexts are often so dynamic and unique that any but the most general theoretical statement may not apply. For example, the arrival of many new immigrants from Southeast Asia, Cuba, Haiti, and Central America in the 1980s created volatile situations in some communities, but each context was different: Cubans and Haitians in Miami, for example, Southeast Asians and Central Americans in Southern California. No one theory specifies whether or how a particular ethnic or racial group will contribute to violence in its community. Each culture is unique and complex, defying a formulaic quantitative indication of behaviors. All we can say with any certainty, in the case of this immigration example, is that if immigrants came from a violent culture, then it is likely that the tendency toward elevated levels of violence will be brought with them. As noted in Chapter 1, it was this type of influence that is thought to have contributed to rising rates of homicide in the U.S. in the first decade of the twentieth century.

Views from Selected Disciplines

An overview of the theory of violence is obliged to look at perspectives from a variety of disciplines. In 1969, the National Commission on the Causes and Prevention of Violence (National Commission, 1969b) provided an unusually comprehensive description of positions taken in a variety of fields, including biology, psychology, psychiatry, anthropology, and sociology. Although dated, this multidisciplinary view provides a basis for appreciation of nuances provided by disciplinary paradigms.

Biology

The essence of the biological interpretation is that nothing conclusive can be said about the role of genes in the development of violent behavior. The heavy involvement of African Americans and the low level of female involvement in violent crime raise the superficial possibility, particularly in the eyes of lay observers, that genetic attributes are implicated. However, blacks and whites cannot be differentiated biologically. Differences between blacks and whites in terms of violent crime have cultural explanations, particularly in terms of lifestyle, pattern, and opportunity. More specifically, high rates of violence among African Americans are apparently linked to deprivation and stress of various kinds. Similarly, male-female differences are due to nurture rather than nature, particularly in terms of the behavioral expectations and models presented to women for their emulation. In short, biological explanations of violence as an innate trait are lacking, and characteristics of groups of people assumed by many to have a biological basis do not.

Psychology

Part of the psychological viewpoint can be understood through a dichotomy between *instigators* and *inhibitors*. Instigators are conditions helping to promote violent behavior by modeling it or explicitly teaching it. Violence in sports and the media or army training could be instigators. Inhibitors tend to reduce violent behaviors and include reinforcing nonaggressive responses through teaching, rewarding, punishing, or the use of appropriate role models.

Another perspective from psychology notes that no apparent relationship exists between mental illness and violence. As the Commission (p. 445) pointed out, murder is distributed unevenly, with higher rates in the South, but "mental illness, contrary to violent crime and other acts of violence, seems equally distributed geographically." The sciences of psychology and psychiatry are unable to predict individual violent acts with an acceptable degree of accuracy. The media are replete with stories about the murderer paroled from prison after having been classified as "not a risk to society", who then murders again. Incidents along these lines were instrumental in the drastic redefinition of Maryland's innovative Patuxent Institution in 1989, for example. However, psychology and psychiatry, while unable to predict individual violence, can identify types of persons or situations with a relatively higher probability of producing or contributing to violence.

Anthropology

The anthropological view sees violence as a trait shared by other organisms. However, our level of involvement with violence is viewed as culturally conditioned and passed from generation to generation. The Commission (p. 481) suggested several sources of violence in the U.S.: the underlying generic existence of violence in all societies, group frustration, territorially based fears, social isolation, belief in the use of violence as a policy enforcement device at home or abroad, war readiness, and experience of violence. The Commission noted that:

> Americans thus are "ready" for violence— as members of the human species, as members of the American culture, and as members of special subgroups. Given such readiness, the problem now is to account for the special and differential use of violence by various subgroups in the country. (p. 482)

Sociology

Only two of the many theories produced in sociology will be touched on at this juncture, but these have received considerable currency in the context of the study of violence: the subcultural and opportunity theses. *Subcultural* theory argues that middle class standards are normative and that lower class individuals develop their own way of doing things, their own values, beliefs and attitudes. Such behaviors as toughness and hustling are accepted as normative in this environment. Rose (1978) asked whether there is "a black subcultural dimension which fosters a resort to violence under a prescribed set of conditions" and noted that the subcultural theory has lent support to the notion that "segments of the black population are practitioners and transmitters of such a subculture" (p. 456). The underlying assumption is that adverse childrearing conditions and a generally stressful environment may lead to "new modal personality types" and the possibility of "regionally distinct black subcultural configurations" (p. 457). Wolfgang (1981) has referred to the subculture of violence as being "congealed in pockets of populations." In the subculture, violence is condoned or encouraged in a variety of settings including play, punishment, and gang behavior (see also Wolfgang and Ferracutti, 1967).

However, it may be argued that lower class persons usually profess an abhorrence of violence and actually have values indistinguishable for the middle class. Given that lower class violence is overwhelmingly a phenomenon of youthful males, there is the likelihood that the subculture is mainly confined to them (see: Curtis, 1975). This assertion also seems to be supported by incidents of the genre of the notorious assault in a Central Park jogger in New York in April, 1989, in which a 28-year-old woman was attacked by a gang of teenagers, beaten, bound, gagged, and raped, as part of a bout of so-called "wilding." Governor Mario Cuomo referred to the incident as "the ultimate shriek of alarm," baffling observers as the suspects lacked the background of poverty and drugs so commonly seen in such situations (Span and Kurtz, 1989; see also Harries, 1989a, and Chapter 9).

Opportunity theory is also founded on the assumption that middle class values are normative. However, opportunities for achieving middle class goals vary from place to place; while some communities have predominantly legitimate means for achieving goals (education, employment), others may have mostly illegitimate avenues, such as drug sales, robbery or theft.

Glaser (1979) reviewed crime theory and suggested that there is a great deal of indifference toward theories explaining crime, owing to their perceived failure in the past. Theories wax and wane in cyclical fashion. For example, up to about 1950, the emphasis on psychiatric theories meant that there was some degree of confidence in rehabilitation, and indeterminate sentencing became fashionable. Subsequently, criminals have come to be seen as "rational calculators" with the result that a utilitarian view has come to the fore, dictating the use of determinate sentencing.

OTHER SOCIOLOGICAL INTERPRETATIONS. Glaser (1979) argues that school performance is critical because of evidence that factors reducing school performance tend to be correlated with delinquency. Two important trends are seen: (1) Children are staying in school longer (about 1 year longer per 10 years), and (2) the existence of more age segregation in society. "Home and workplace" argued Glaser, "have become less influential for adolescents as sources of instruction in conventional adult roles" (p. 217). Hence, positive school experiences are seen as critical. Paradoxically, according to Glaser, children who are arrested do better if they drop out of school and their prospects are better yet if they get a job and get married.

Gottfredson and Hirschi (1989a) have asserted that criminological theories are biased toward traditional sociological variables to the exclusion of contributions from other disciplines. They advocate what they call a "propensity-event" general theory of crime. They contend that their theory would enable the control of crime without, as they put it, "fundamental reconstruction of [society] or the individuals within it" (p. 58). This theory is clearly at odds with the structuralist view advocating such reconstruction, at least of society.

The Gottfredson and Hirschi approach distinguishes between the concepts of *crime,* as an event, and *criminality,* an attribute of people. *Crime* theory informs us about conditions leading to crime; *criminality* theory tells us which people are more likely to commit crimes. Crimes occur at specific places and times and each crime must have certain conditions present before it can occur. These conditions may relate to all manner of social and physical environments, such as the availability of a victim, lack of a controlling agent (police, parents), a suitable physical setting, and the availability of a weapon.

This interpretation is sympathetic to approaches variously labeled "environmental," "ecological," or "routine activity" (Cohen and Felson, 1979). Criminality is seen here as "a consequence of inadequate child rearing practices" (p. 60). The underlying assumption is that criminality is a more or less inherent trait in humans, and it is controlled by socialization through parenting, school, work, and comparable processes and conditions.

SITUATION, ROUTINE ACTIVITY, AND LIFESTYLE APPROACHES

Situational Factors

According to Monahan and Klassen (1982), situational approaches have become more popular owing to the relative failure of individual level analyses leaving a gap into which situational interpretations have moved. Such approaches are seen as promising for predictive purposes since data relating to *situations* may be more readily available than data relating to *individuals*. Monahan and Klassen adopted the Pervin (1978:79–80) definition of situation, as follows: "an organism's engagement with an array of objects and actions which covers a time span. A situation is defined by *who* is involved including the possibility that the individual is alone, *where* the action is taking place and the nature of the action or activities occurring."

Monahan and Klassen (1982) and Gabor (1986) identified several situational correlates (not causes, necessarily) of violence: *family environment, peer environment, job environment, availability of victims, criminal opportunities,* and *availability of drugs and alcohol.* Clarke (1983), noted that there is a general trend in the social sciences to "set greater store by situational determinants of behavior" which are "supplanting predominantly 'dispositional' accounts of social problems with their emphasis on individual malfunction or maladaptation" (p. 226). Individual disposition toward violence will not lead to crime without situational factors such as target and opportunity. Gabor (1986) suggested that situational crime theory should include two elements: "First, a description of the nature and distribution of criminal opportunities and, second, an account of how offenders' decisions are affected, not merely by facts of upbringing and personal history, but also by the circumstances and situations in which they find themselves" (pp. 230–31).

Urban Design as a Situational Factor

Given that the situational concept embodies relationships between individuals and their environment, the physical form of the city is of interest. Clearly, the physical form of local environments may contribute to their propensity to harbor certain kinds of violent or violence-related behavior, although care must be taken to avoid attributing too much influence to urban design alone. The underlying problem is a social one, and urban form is superimposed on the social framework (or vice versa). The literature (for example: National Commission, 1969b; Newman, 1972) has pointed to the importance of a variety of conditions with a bearing on violence: space and location, access to space, visibility and surveillance, scale, ownership and control of property, density, and the overall quality of the urban environment. However, the characteristics of residents of areas or structures are critical as partial determinants of qualitative variation in patterns of crime. Newman (1972), for example, noted that for low-income families with children "the high-rise apartment building is to be strictly avoided" while "for low-income elderly, the high-rise apartment building seems to work very well indeed." (pp. 193–194)

Interestingly, more than twenty years later, some of the predictions of the National Commission on the Causes and Prevention of Violence (1969) have come to have a ring of plausibility to them. These include the suggestions that 1. suburbs would be safe, protected by their racial and economic heterogeneity and by distance from the underclass ghetto, 2. expressways would become "sanitized" corridors connecting safe areas, and 3. streets and neighborhoods would become sharply differentiated—some would be "human jungles" while others would be quite safe. The Commission noted that:

"Space and location permit or limit all human behavior, including crime. When these variables are applied to control crime or violent behavior, distance and access to space are used to separate groups of potential victims from potential offenders" (p. 718).

While safe suburbs are separated from dangerous cities, the separation has occurred by chance; defensibility merely has been a by-product of the development process. The Commission predicted that "if urban crime continues to increase and is not abated by other means, we believe defensive cities will become a reality in America" (p. 722). However, this has not come about for the obvious reason that the population has continued to sort itself into those who could, and did, leave the city, and those who could not, and did not. The city has been abandoned rather than defended.

The underclass inner city then becomes both offender and victim. It lacks the resources to defend itself against itself, and is only reluctantly assisted in this effort when the situation becomes such a political and/or diplomatic liability that "something" has to be done. The adoption of Washington, D.C. by federal drug czar William Bennett in 1989 is a case in point, even though the promises incorporated in the adoption were largely unfulfilled. (For a critical review of the urban design issue, see, for example: Taylor, Gottfredson, and Brower, 1980.)

The Routine Activities Approach and The Lifestyle Model

These concepts are closely related. Both deal with *crime* rather than *criminality* and both deal with "patterned behavior among population aggregates rather than with variability in individual characteristics" and are both, therefore, sociological in character (Garofalo, 1987:27). *Routine activities* (Cohen and Felson, 1979) were taken to include work, school, shopping, and similar actions. It was argued that such activities, over the last 40 years or so, have shifted away from the home toward interactions between unrelated persons. This has made it more likely that the necessary combination of three elements: a likely offender, a suitable target, and an absent guardian, would occur. As Felson (1989) has expressed it, "crime is a routine activity feeding on other routine activities."

Similarly, the *lifestyle model* (Hindelang et al., 1978) regarded school, work, shopping, and leisure activities as "determining the likelihood of personal victimization through the intervening variables of associations and exposure" (Garofalo, 1987:24). The model was based on extensive analysis of NCVS victimization data and the investigators noted that crime does not occur randomly in space or time—both high-risk places and high-risk times can be identified. By the same token, high-risk persons also exist. Lifestyle was seen as influencing exposure to times, places, and persons.

According to Garofalo (1987), the differences between the concepts are based on the longitudinal perspective of the routine activities model compared to the focus of the lifestyle model on one point in time. Either model, however, could be applied longitudinally or cross-sectionally, and both are clearly sympathetic to an approach emphasizing the study and interpretation of patterns of crime rather than of criminality.

SYNTHESIS: A CONTEMPORARY VIEWPOINT

Vila (1994) has proposed an approach to theory that integrates and synthesizes perspectives across disciplines. He pointed out that "no satisfactory unified theoretical framework has yet been developed," a situation that has "diminished the policy relevance of recommendations from even some of the most comprehensive interdisciplinary research on crime" (Vila, 1994:313). As a result, policymakers rely on sharply different crime reduction strategies depending on whether they are attached to the political right or left. The latter will emphasize the responsibility of society (macro-level causes); the former will lean towards placing responsibility on individuals (micro-level). Consequently, policies oscillate with swings in the political pendulum, ensuring long-term inconsistency and ineffectiveness. This impotence of policy is illustrated by the 88 percent constant dollar increase in criminal justice expenditures and the threefold increase in imprisonment rates between 1971 and 1991. During this time, violent crime rates increased 85 percent (Vila, 1994).

Ecological approaches, emphasizing environmental and situational variables, have never been integrated with micro-level (individual) and macro-level (structural) "domains" (Vila, 1994). Defining crime as activity involving *force, fraud,* or *stealth,* Vila develops a model represented by Figure 2.1, incorporating biological, sociocultural, and developmental factors. Biological factors are included not in support of biological determinism, but rather to recognize that an individual's growth and development are affected by conditions such as health care, nutrition, drugs, and pollution. Crack babies and children affected by the ingestion of lead paint chips or dust are obvious examples. The emphasis, then, is on the interaction of the three sets of factors in the context of what Vila calls a *generational time scale,* since it is at that scale that change

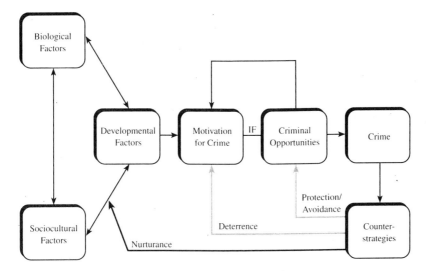

Figure 2.1. Alternative foci for crime control strategies. *Source:* Vila, 1994. Adapted by permission of the author and the American Society of Criminology.

is effected. The developmental context of children is seen as particularly critical—children deprived of appropriate parental influence may be predisposed toward a "strategic style" of criminality, fostering motivation for crime. Then, if opportunity presents itself, the individual may make the necessary decision to behave in a criminal manner.

Counterstrategies (Figure 2.1), argue Vila, should be directed toward each of the incremental stages of which the outcome was crime. Protection/avoidance would involve a combination of staying away from dangerous places (violent crime) and target hardening (property crime). Motivation would (theoretically) be blunted by deterrence, operationalized, perhaps, in the form of harsher penalties. The developmental stage would be remediated through the application of the necessary levels of nurturance.

This integrative approach advocated by Vila is attractive in that it cuts across disciplinary boundaries and brings together relevant factors regardless of source. From a policy perspective, however, the *generational time scale* is a practical problem in that politicians are typically elected in 2, 4, or 6 year increments, none of which approaches the unit of generational time. This makes it difficult, if not impossible, to make the longer term perspective appeal to voters, who are already skeptical of campaign promises framed in terms of the short tenure of officeholders, and who would not be captivated by promises reaching out 20–25 years.

In short, even the most well-meaning and sincere of politicians has no effective mechanism for operationalizing change over a generation. The best that can be hoped for is a kind of "incremental continuity" in which like-minded politicians succeed each other and "carry on the good work."

CONCLUSION

No one theory of violence has been universally accepted. On one hand, we observe clear links between deprivation and violence. On the other, we know that deprivation and violence are not inevitably related, and theory then looks to intervening conditions, such as racism and frustration, to elucidate process. The matrix of situations and relationships soon becomes so complex that the challenge of developing simple, verifiable, universally acceptable theory is daunting if not insurmountable.

Stress, defined as "a state of imbalance between the demands of the social and physical environment and the capabilities of an individual to cope with those demands" (Monahan and Klassen, 1982), may be a useful organizing and unifying concept for the purpose of developing theory. Stress can be considered at both *individual* and *community* levels. Social and economic stresses affecting individuals may be manifested in community level pathology if stresses are epidemic (see also Linsky & Straus, 1986.) The advantage of stress as an overarching theme—that it is inclusive—is also its greatest liability as it is so inclusive, in fact, that it poses the threat of degenerating into what is, in effect, nothing more than a new version of amorphous disorganization theory.

Murray and Boal (1979:147) suggested that one scheme for classifying theories of violence would have two categories. The first consists of *environmental* theories, including the subcultural hypothesis, and interpretations relating to situation, routine activities, and lifestyle. Such theories have been accorded some attention here as they are in harmony with the ecological perspective. The other class of theories is *structural* and deals with hypotheses associated with such concepts as alienation and labeling, having their root in the broader social fabric. Ideally, ecological analysis considers both streams of interpretation, combining an awareness of broader social processes with interpretation incorporating environmental factors. In this way, some of the pitfalls of older ecological approaches may be avoided.

The central question with which this book concerns itself is why certain violent crimes occur *where* they do. As noted in Reiss and Roth (1993:17):

> A promising approach to the understanding, prevention, and control of violence—a perspective with roots in both criminology and public health—is to focus on the places where violence occurs. The incidence of violent events varies widely in space—by city, neighborhood, and specific address. The greatest variation is found across locations within cities; for example, although 97.8 percent of all Minneapolis addresses generated zero robbery calls to police in 1986, 8 generated more than 20 calls each.

The focus is on patterns of crime rather than individual criminal behavior, although the characteristics of the actors in the crime events and some aspects of their behavior patterns are of great interest. No predictive theory is developed; after all, no discipline—not psychology, psychiatry, sociology, anthropology, or criminology—have succeeded in predicting which individuals will become criminals and which will not. The more modest objective is to clarify processes to some extent in an ecumenical framework. In so doing it is hoped to underscore the need for a coherent public policy addressing the violence issue. In the course of this, some emphasis can be placed on elements of theory that are reasonably comprehensible to policy makers. The appeal for policy and the programs and resources to give the policy expression should be linked to a theoretical base. Public policy in the late twentieth century is fragmented and ineffectual, hopelessly distracted by the drug issue toward draconian control measures and away from social policies dealing with underlying conditions.

Chapter 3

CRIME CLASSIFICATION: THE CASE OF HOMICIDE AND ASSAULT[1]

K nowledge about the relationship between homicide and assault is sparse. Studies addressing the question have been based on small samples (or aggregated data) and are quite dated (Pittman & Handy, 1964; Pokorny, 1965; Block, 1977). Although this and related crime measurement issues have significant implications for public policy, social scientists, including geographers, who have involved themselves in policy questions have tended, rather, to focus on such matters as policing and neighborhood crime control (Herbert & Harries, 1986; Smith, 1986).

It is generally understood that homicide rates are lower than assault rates, and research has suggested an inverse relationship between the rates of both offenses and socioeconomic status (SES) (Brantingham & Brantingham, 1984). Other dimensions of possible quantitative and qualitative comparisons between homicide and assault are poorly developed, however, including the concept that the only difference between the crimes is their outcome. Analyses of homicide tend to occur to the exclusion of assault, and vice versa, with the unavoidable implication that each is a discrete category of behavior (New York Academy of Medicine, 1986). The effect of this dichotomy has been to separate homicide and assault in all phases of data gathering, analysis, and public perception.

In practice, media attention is drawn to homicides, which are more

[1]This chapter is an adaptation of material originally published as: "Homicide and assault: A comparative analysis of attributes in Dallas neighborhoods, 1981–1985", *Professional Geographer,* 41(1989):29–38. The research on which the work was based was supported by Contract No. 86M043907901D, Center for Studies of Antisocial and Violent Behavior, National Institutes of Mental Health, Rockville, MD 20875. Findings were originally presented at the Southwest Research Conference on Violence, Dallas, TX, November 7, 1986, and at a conference entitled "Black Homicide", held at The Johns Hopkins University School of Hygiene and Public Health, Baltimore, MD, March 23, 1987.

sensational than assaults. In the first few months of 1988, for example, and again in 1989, much was made, by the *Washington Post* and *Newsweek*, of the extraordinarily high rate of homicide in Washington, D.C., and its relationship to drug traffic (see, for example: Baker & Cohn, 1988; Horwitz, 1988a; Horwitz, 1989). The high rate of aggravated assault in the nation's capital (and other major metropolitan areas) has been virtually ignored, yet it also constitutes a major social problem. The net effect is to place *less* emphasis than is warranted on the degree of pathology present in poor, predominantly African American, central cities. Furthermore, our understanding of small area social processes is impeded by the myopic way in which data about violence are classified.

The general hypothesis of this chapter is that the legal labels "homicide" and "assault" represent essentially similar behaviors differing principally in outcome rather than process. Given that it is well established that poverty areas tend to be associated with high rates of violence, a geographic framework based on neighborhood status provides an appropriate analytical context, relatively disaggregated compared to prior research. Crime is a social problem with a sharply territorial component, in that crime rates can differ substantially over short distances, and people are willing to organize on the basis of neighborhoods in an effort to reduce criminal behavior. However, prior research on the relationship between homicide and assault has been aspatial, and has tended to confine itself to comparisons between offenses solely in terms of highly aggregated basic demographic attributes. The addition of geographic (and temporal) perspectives fortifies comparative analysis and strengthens underlying theory. From an applications perspective, comprehensive comparative analysis will enhance insights relating to the nature, and environmental correlates, of each offense. Ultimately, this may increase the likelihood of appropriate public policy responses—in the realms of criminal jurisprudence, welfare, housing, public health, education, and law enforcement—to the complex of behaviors represented.

Improved knowledge of the relationships between major forms of violence and their local contexts and patterns provides the opportunity to make intervention and prevention programs more effective. For example, the nature of drug use and dealing in a neighborhood may have important qualitative and quantitative implications for patterns of violence. Such patterns may depend on the characteristics of individual users and on the organization of trafficking, including the presence of absence of significant territorial conflicts between dealers (see Nurco, et al., 1988).

DEFINITIONS

The Uniform Crime Reporting program of the FBI defines homicide and assault as follows:

Homicide: "the willful (nonnegligent) killing of one human being by another."

Assault: "an unlawful attack by one person upon another for the purpose of inflicting severe or aggravated bodily injury. This type of assault is usually accompanied by the use of a weapon or by means likely to produce death or great bodily harm" (FBI, 1987).

These definitions are broad enough to include substantial qualitative variation. Among homicides, the distinction has been drawn between "primary", in which personal injury was the immediate objective of the assailant, and "secondary", referring to homicides committed in the course of other crimes (Jason, Strauss, & Tyler, 1983; Jason, Flock, and Tyler, 1983). The latter are also referred to as "felony" homicides. National data show that some 60–70 percent of homicides are of the primary type, not associated with other felonies (Reidel, Zahn, & Mock, 1985; Centers for Disease Control, 1986). Until 1990, it was a truism that at least half of all assaults were committed by acquaintances or relatives, indicating the importance of "primary" assaults (Luckenbill, 1984). However, data specifically for homicide in 1991 indicated that, for the first time, more than 50 percent of murders were committed by strangers or persons whose relationship to the victim was unknown, indicative of a fundamental change in the nature of American homicide. One by-product of this shift is a sharply lower rate of case-solving, down to 65 percent in the mid-1990s from 91 percent in 1965 (Thomas, 1995a).

METHODS

To facilitate this research, a large data base was necessary in order to permit comparisons disaggregated in terms of geography and other attributes, for both offenses. The need to have a large sample of relatively infrequent homicides meant that the data had to encompass several years, even in a city marked by historically high levels of violence. Given a long enough time profile, any major city could have served. Dallas, Texas, was the focus of this case study for two principal reasons: (a) the city has experienced sustained high levels of serious violence, and (b) the author had developed rapport with the Police Department and had considerable experience with the form and content of the data in the course of prior research (e.g., Harries & Stadler, 1983, 1986, 1988; Harries, Stadler, & Zdorkowski, 1984).

TABLE 3.1. TOTAL NUMBER AND PERCENT OF VICTIMS BY OFFENSE AND SES, DALLAS, 1981–85

	HOMICIDE		*ASSAULT*	
SES	*Total*	*Percent*	*Total*	*Percent*
High	111	9.04	4,288	13.36
Medium	515	41.94	13,223	41.20
Low	602	49.02	14,585	45.44
Totals	1,228	100.00	32,096	100.00

Note: SES is based on locations of incidents.

Data describing some 1,200 homicide victimizations and 32,000 aggravated assaults were obtained from the Dallas Police Department. The incidents covered the years 1981 through 1985 (Table 3.1). This was the longest available time series when the request for data was addressed to the Department in 1986. The series permitted comparisons of the temporal, demographic, locational, and weapons contexts of both offenses, within the geographic framework of neighborhood SES. The limitations of the data were that they were victim-based and lacked information describing offenders, victim-offender relationships, or circumstances. Furthermore, no data relating to drug or alcohol involvement were available. Normally, homicides are quite fully reported, while about half of all other violent crimes, including aggravated assault, go unreported. Thus, in spite of the very large number of cases utilized in this analysis, it is possible that systematic biases remained in the data.

In order to construct a socioeconomic context in which to develop more detailed comparisons, all homicide and assault cases were assigned to one of twelve housing areas recognized by the Dallas Department of Housing and Urban Rehabilitation. These areas were then classified according to an Urban Pathology Index (UPI) based on scores on the following variables: substandard housing, African American population, and median household income. A neighborhood score was the inverse of the rank, except for income. Thus high status neighborhood 12 (Northwest Dallas) scored 1.0 for substandard housing, 2.5 for African American population, and 1.0 for income, for a total UPI of 4.5. In contrast, the lowest status neighborhood, number 4, (Fair Park, South Dallas), scored the maximum 35.0. The Index yielded a robust tripartite classification of the housing areas such that they could be designated as High, Medium, and Low SES. The relevant methodology and a map of Dallas with the levels of SES designated has been reported in detail elsewhere and will not be reproduced here (Harries, Stadler, & Zdorkowski, 1984). Following the allocation of incidents to the appropriate areas, detailed cross-tabulations were developed of several classes of attributes, in addition to time-series analyses of each offense.

It should be noted that SES is based on the characteristics of locations of incidents and is not necessarily an indication of the traits of either victims or assailants. In general, however, it is reasonable to assume strong correlation between generalized neighborhood SES and the attributes of victims and offenders, given that homicide and assault are so frequently domestic or local in nature (see Wolfgang, 1975, Table 20, p. 378; Block, 1987, p. 6; O'Carroll & Mercy, 1986, Table 3, p. 37).

RESULTS

Over the five-year study period, homicide incidents averaged 0.66 per day, while the risk of assaults was some 27 times higher for a mean of 18 incidents per day. Population-based rates were developed for each SES level for each offense (Figures 1 and 2). For both homicide and assault, SES was inversely related to rates throughout the series. In Low SES, relative homicide risk was some eight times greater than in High SES. For assault, relative risk was on the order of six times greater.

Temporal Relationships

Three types of periodicity were evident, particularly in the assault series: distinct peaking in summers, on weekends, and in evening and night hours. Summer peaking was most accentuated in Low SES.[2] Summer was defined functionally rather than astronomically to cover the months May through October, in which daily maxima of at least 80°F (27°C) occur. Summer peaks were consistent with the increased probability of social interaction in the warmer months, and with heightened

---

[2]For further discussion of the relationship between violence and the long, hot summer, see Chapter 7.

aggression due to heat stress and increased consumption of alcoholic beverages (Figure 3.1) (Harries and Stadler, 1983). In general, the relative relationships of the curves by SES and offense were quite similar. Seasonality was most clearly evident in the assault series, although the highest rates in the homicide series also occurred in the summers, as defined here. Both series showed some evidence of perturbation in the Christmas periods, times of relatively intense social interaction.

More rigorous investigation of the seasonality issue suggested that assault had a stronger seasonal component than homicide. For the aggregated assault data, the U.S. Census Bureau's X-11 Seasonal Adjustment Program was utilized; it has been employed for other analyses of seasonality in crime series, e.g., Block (1984), Bureau of Justice Statistics (1980), and Cheatwood (1988). One product of the procedure is a "test of stable seasonality" based on computation of the ratio of variance "between months" to residual variance. A significant F statistic suggests that seasonality is present (Shishkin, et al., 1967). In the present analysis, the test of stable seasonality for assault yielded $F = 13.35$ ($p = 0.0001$). The comparable statistic for homicide was $F = 0.80$ ($p = 0.64$). Tests of stable seasonality across neighborhoods were significant for all three SES levels for assault, but not significant for homicide (Table 3.2). Although this does not prove lack of seasonality in homicide, it suggests (in concert with Figure 3.1) that homicide periodicities are asymmetrically phased, highly variable, and poorly autocorrelated (i.e., the incidence of homicide in a given month was a relatively poor predictor of the level in the following or preceding month). Recent analysis by Cheatwood (1988) also failed to detect a seasonal component in homicide. (See also Cheatwood, 1995.) While assaults are rare events (18 per day in a city of some 900,000), homicides, in comparison, are extremely rare, an observation that probably does not correspond to public perception. With such low frequencies, it is not surprising that a local series is highly variable—one multiple murder will produce a peak overwhelming underlying seasonality or other cyclical components.

Analysis of the dichotomy between "summer" and "non-summer" patterns showed that more than 50 percent of incidents for both crimes, regardless of SES level, occurred in the summers as defined for this analysis. The difference was somewhat more pronounced for assault, as the discussion of seasonal stability implied. This mirrored the national experience, which indicated evidence of summer peaking in both homicide and assault, with the peaking for assault more accentuated and

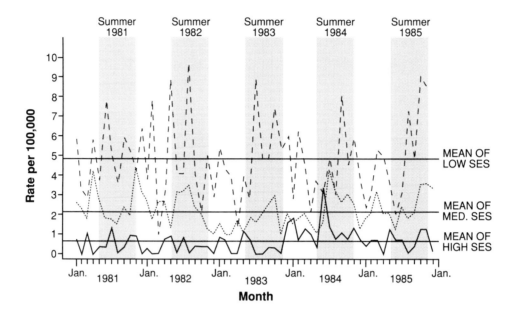

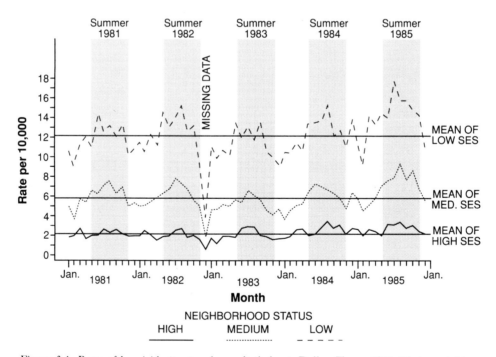

Figure 3.1. Rates of homicide (top) and assault (below), Dallas, Texas, 1981–85, by neighbor-hood status and season.

TABLE 3.2. TESTS OF STABLE SEASONALITY

| | *HOMICIDE* | | | *ASSAULT* | |
SES	*F*	*P*	*SES*	*F*	*P*
High	1.28	0.27	High	8.79	0.0001
Medium	1.32	0.24	Medium	12.53	0.0001
Low	1.02	0.44	Low	7.30	0.0001
(Overall)	0.80	0.64	(Overall)	13.35	0.0001

Note: SES is based on locations of incidents.

more consistent. Review of national seasonal variation for the decade 1976–85 revealed a mean summer peak for assault some 17 percent above the annual averages. For homicide, the summers exceeded annual means by about 8 percent (FBI, 1987). Homicide trends were distinguished by sharper December peaks compared to assault. The latter would seem to be associated with intensified social interaction during the holiday season, in combination with an increase in robbery-homicides.

In theory, periodicities of assault-homicides and assaults should be similar. An assumed distinguishing feature of homicide—the use of more lethal weapons—is unlikely to be affected by purely temporal considerations. A secondary issue, also with ramifications for the understanding of processes, is whether periodicities differ across neighborhoods. Of particular interest from a geographic perspective is the question of whether the amplitude of trends is relatively accentuated in Low SES environments, a finding that would suggest less capacity to deal with cyclical stresses. Inspection of Figure 1 suggests that this may be the case.

If seasonality is the primary periodicity of the series, then a secondary source of cyclical fluctuation lies in the dichotomy between weekends and nonweekends. *Weekends* are defined here as Fridays, Saturdays, and Sundays, the days with clearly highest frequencies. *Nonweekend* refers to the other days of the week. Fifty-four percent of both homicides and assaults occurred on the three weekend days, suggesting that leisure time and social interaction play crucial roles in the epidemiology of both offenses.

A third source of temporal fluctuation was found in the *diurnal cycle*, which was disaggregated by four-hour blocks. The daily rhythms for both offenses were almost identical, with some 20 percent of incidents occurring between 4 P.M. and 8 P.M., 29 percent between 8 P.M. and midnight; and 26 percent between midnight and 4 A.M. The fact that about 75 percent of the incidents occurred in the 12 hours between 4 P.M. and 4 A.M. is not remarkable, given that crimes of violence will tend to occur when (and where) opportunity is maximized—the hours of leisure. However, the degree of congruence between the offenses is especially strong. The temporal pattern for all the so-called *Index* crimes of the FBI tends to be quite similar at any given location; the data available here did not permit this assessment.

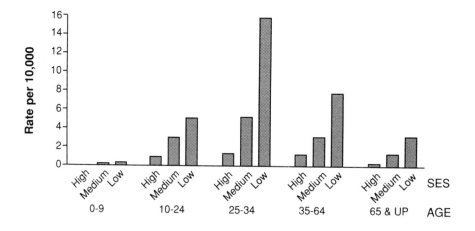

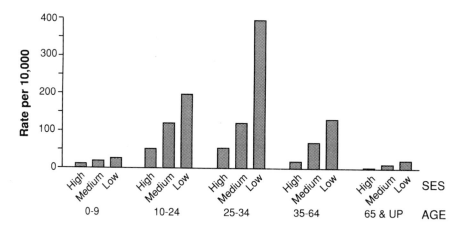

Figure 3.2. Rates of homicide (top), and assault (below), Dallas, Texas, 1981–85, by neighborhood status and age cohort.

Demographic Relationships

Victim age, race, and gender were also compared. Consistent with the earlier finding of inverse relationship between rates and SES, this correlation held within all age categories for both homicide and assault (Figure 3.2). For both offenses, the absolute peak in rates was seen in the Low SES 25–34 age category where the relative risk of homicide was about 13 times that of the High SES in the same age cohort, and about 8 times that of the High SES for assault. One clear difference between homicide and assault in this comparison appeared in the 10–24 and 35–64 age groups. For homicide, the 35–64 Low SES exhibited sharply higher rates as compared to the 10–24 cohort. The reverse was obtained for assault.

These findings are quite consistent with national norms. A factor in the relatively low rate of homicides in the younger age group may be the distribution of firearms in this cohort. Some poll data suggest that younger persons are less likely to own guns (the recent upsurge in firearm violence associated with drugs excepted). In a 1983 Gallup report, 33 percent of respondents under the age of 30 reported that they had a gun in the house, compared to 44 percent for the 30 to 49 cohort and to 45 percent for those aged 50 to 60 (McGarrell and Flanagan, 1985). Data collected in 1994 suggested that these percentages have remained fairly stable, although it is unlikely that persons with unlicensed or other illegal weapons in their homes would admit to such possession, thus deflating the data to some—unknown—extent (Maguire and Pastore, 1995). Another contributing factor may be differentials in the mix of *expressive,* or emotional, violence versus *instrumental* violence, for material gain (see McClain, 1984). Lacking details of the circumstances of each victimization, it has not been feasible to assess this issue.

Consistent with the implied inverse correlation between percent black and SES, white victimization was greatest in High SES, black in Low SES (Table 3.3). Blacks and whites were victimized in proportion to their presence at each level of SES. This was to be expected, given that the data were fundamentally an expression of the racial composition of each area. With respect to gender composition, risk varied across SES levels (Table 3.4). About 30 percent of both homicide and assault victims were female in High SES, but the proportions shifted to 16 percent for homicide and 35 percent for assault in Low SES neighborhoods. The dominance of males in homicide victimization, particularly in Low SES

TABLE 3.3. RACE OF VICTIMS, OFFENSE, AND SES (%)

	RACE			
SES	*White*		*Black*	
	Homicide	*Assault*	*Homicide*	*Assault*
High	85.59	86.99	14.41	13.01
Medium	77.67	73.14	22.33	26.86
Low	30.07	27.75	69.93	72.25

Note: SES is based on locations of incidents.

TABLE 3.4. SEX OF VICTIMS, OFFENSE, AND SES (%)

	FEMALE		*MALE*	
SES	*Homicide* (1)	*Assault* (2)	*Homicide* (3)	*Assault* (4)
High	31.53	30.46	68.47	69.54
Medium	19.03	29.38	80.97	70.62
Low	15.61	34.68	84.39	65.32

Notes: Columns 1 + 3 = 100%. Columns 2 + 4 = 100%. SES is based on locations of incidents.

areas, is consistent with the established link between maleness and aggression (accentuated in stressful environments), and violence that is victim-precipitated (Block, 1977). Furthermore, Low SES is characterized by greater lethality, as represented by patterns of weapon use, a finding consistent with the Welte and Abel study of Erie County, New York (Welte & Abel, 1986).

TABLE 3.5. WEAPON TYPE, OFFENSE, AND SES (%)

	WEAPON							
SES	*Firearms*		Knives/*Cutting* *Instruments*		Hands, Feet Fists		*Other*	
	H	A	H	A	H	A	H	A
High	69.37	29.38	18.92	23.13	1.80	19.38	9.91	28.10
Medium	70.10	32.41	19.81	30.13	3.88	12.80	6.22	24.66
Low	72.43	36.49	19.44	34.62	3.49	8.08	4.66	20.81

Notes: Row X Offense cells may not sum to 100 due to rounding. SES is based on locations of incidents.

Weapons

The distribution of firearms across offenses and SES levels showed the anticipated dominance of firearms in homicides across all three neighborhood types (Table 3.5). Overall, more than 71 percent of the homicides involved firearms and about 20 percent knives or other cutting instruments. However, differences were evident between SES levels. Although the percentage of incidents involving firearms was about the same across SES for homicide, the danger of assault incidents, as measured by firearm involvement, increased from 29 percent in High SES to 36 percent in Low SES. Similarly, the use of the second most lethal class of weapons, knives and other sharp instruments, was also comparable across SES for homicide, but much greater in Low SES compared to high (35% versus 23%) for assault. The level of use of less effective weapons—hands, fists, feet ("personal weapons") and *other weapons* (which includes motor vehicles, poison, and "abuse") correlated inversely with SES. Thus, events classified as assaults in Low SES are relatively more harmful and will make greater claims on emergency care systems and result in more serious social and economic ramifications, compared to higher SES levels. Many assaults probably remain classified as such owing to the effectiveness of emergency care.

TABLE 3.6. SITES OF VICTIMIZATION, OFFENSE, AND SES (%)

					SITE & OFFENSE							
	Res		*Street*		*Bar & Bar Parking Lot*		*Park, Playground*		*Other*		*Totals*	
SES	H	A	H	A	H	A	H	A	H	A	H	A
High	6.43	6.59	0.49	2.40	0.90	1.57	0.08	0.04	1.14	2.74	9.04	13.34
Med	21.74	19.17	6.60	10.13	4.64	3.71	1.47	0.76	7.49	7.39	41.94	41.16
Low	26.79	23.55	9.36	11.57	3.34	3.23	0.33	0.34	9.20	6.74	49.02	45.52

Notes: Totals may not sum to 100 due to rounding.

SES is based on locations of incidents.

"Residence" includes apartment parking lots, yards and driveways of homes.

"Other" category cumulates sites with <1 percent of the incidents.

Sites of Incidents

Data relating to the sites of incidents were collapsed from their original 175 classes to the 5 seen in Table 3.6. Residences and their related land uses accounted for the bulk of incidents of both homicide and assault. Overall, the locational distributions of both offenses were quite similar. Two principal differences were evident: (a) well over half the homicides, but somewhat less than half the assaults, occurred in residences, and (b) assaults were more likely to occur in street settings. This locational dimension serves to draw attention to the relative privacy of the environments in which a large proportion of incidents of serious harm occur. Unless public argument is a precursor of violence, the probability of intercession by law enforcement or other emergency personnel is minimal. On the other hand, about half the incidents occurred in public or quasi-public locations where the chances of successful interdiction were greater, if citizens were willing to report. Even so, violent incidents have low space-time density, and can elude purposeful searchers.

IMPLICATIONS

Our perception and understanding of violence is strongly affected by the way in which incidents are classified by authorities, including police and emergency medical personnel. The normal legal practice of discriminating between homicide and assault as discrete categories of behavior appears to be of questionable validity, based as it is on classification by outcome rather than by process. In contrast, robbery, burglary, and larceny are each differentiated on the basis of the method used to separate property or money from their owners, not by outcome. Rape and vehicle theft are treated differently owing to the unique nature of the crime (rape) or the specialized target (auto theft). While classifying criminal incidents by outcome may have its uses, process-based definitions are intuitively more appealing as they are more hospitable to cause-oriented analyses.

The typical homicide is most appropriately considered a fatal assault. Except for their fatality, homicides share socioeconomic, temporal, racial, age, and gender characteristics of assaults. Differences between homicide and assault are due primarily to (a) variations in the lethality of weapons, and (b) the analytical mixing of primary and secondary homicides.

The weapons issue implies that if numbers of privately owned firearms were to be reduced, the frequency of violent acts would not necessarily be affected, but mortality may be reduced. Violence would, in effect, be displaced into less lethal weapons categories, increasing chances for victims' survival.

Incidents in which the offender apparently intended to inflict injury (primary homicides and primary aggravated assaults) should be combined into a single (subdivisible) category in crime statistics, given the apparent similarities of their dynamics. Homicides and assaults occurring in the course of rapes, robberies, and burglaries (secondary events), should be separately identified in order to permit a more sophisticated system of classification and analysis. Parallel examination of homicide and assault data would permit local, discrete analyses of the demographic, temporal, and spatial dimensions of either type of crime in order to identify relevant social, temporal, and spatial modalities. Given recent initiatives to treat violence as a public health problem, recognition of the general need to regard homicide and assault as a continuum will result in more coherent, area-specific, policy responses. This position has found support in Greenberg, Carey, & Popper (1987), who noted that "we believe that all the major types of violent death ought to be studied together as alternative responses to stress rather than—as they usually are—separately (p. 47).

Insofar as every assault is a potential homicide, assault prevention may be the most practicable way of limiting the occurrence of homicides. Detailed small area analysis based on the revised categorization advocated here could help develop more meaningful patterns and trends of violence. Thus policy formulation could be focused qualitatively and geographically in a manner currently inhibited by the crudeness of data classification.

Chapter 4

HOMICIDE: REGIONAL PATTERNS[1]

Many scholars (e.g., Lottier, 1938; Shannon, 1954) have noted the existence of high rates of homicide in the American South. This phenomenon has begged the question whether the region is really different from the rest of the United States with respect to violence and its determinants. Is southern violence only a manifestation of southern poverty, for example, or are subcultural processes influential? Indeed, are rates of violence really higher in the South?

From the debate emerged a phenomenon variously referred to as "the southern subculture of violence" (O'Connor & Lizotte, 1979) and the "Southern Violence Construct" (SVC) (Hawley, 1987). This perceived regional attribute became institutionalized in the late 1960s and early 1970s and is exemplified by the work of Hackney (Hackney, 1969) & Gastil (Gastil, 1971; 1975), who interpreted southern violence as a subcultural phenomenon. Hackney evoked images of dueling, lynching, police brutality, assassination, and arson, and cited evidence relating to gun ownership and the impact of economic colonialism in the South. Gastil argued that after basic socioeconomic conditions were controlled, southern states had higher-than-expected rates of violence, attributable by him to the degree of southernness. As the discussion below will demonstrate, subsequent research has cast serious doubt on the reality of the subculture of violence.

The purpose of this chapter is to provide an overview of the relationship between violence and the South. This is done in two parts. First, a longitudinal perspective is provided in the form of an historical geography of homicide. The historical perspective is developed through the mapping of homicide patterns at five-year intervals from 1935 through

---

[1]This chapter is based in part on: K.D. Harries (1985), The historical geography of homicide in the U.S., 1935–1980, *Geoforum* 16: 73–83. Excerpts are reproduced or adapted here by permission of Pergamon Press Ltd.

1980. On the basis of these patterns, the states are allocated to regions based on their historical homicide rate profiles. Then, several social indicators are plotted against homicide rates in the constructed regions in order to illustrate the broad pattern of regional social change in the time period under review. Second, the issue is put into contemporary focus through a discussion of findings drawn from literature touching on the regional issue.

BACKGROUND: HOMICIDE PATTERNS, 1935–1980

The persistence of high southern rates is evident in a map series showing state-based rates for the period 1935–1980 (Figure 4.1). Nineteen thirty-five, the base year, was the first year that the *Uniform Crime Reports* of the Federal Bureau of Investigation became available. Though the reliability of the data have been questioned, it is generally accepted that homicide is probably the most dependable of the *Uniform Crime Reports* series owing to the seriousness of the offense, the relative difficulty of concealment of the act and the relatively low probability of nonreporting. The maps are based on quartile divisions such that the median observation, by definition, is at the boundary between the second and third quartiles.

The beginning of the series suggests that the southern high homicide region was actually somewhat less contiguous in 1935 than in the period 1940–60, when the homicide South was contiguous and relatively unchanging. In 1955 Nevada emerged as an anomalous case in the top quartile, but not contiguous with the South. Nevada remained a top quartile state in the period 1955–1980, with the exception of 1970. In 1965, increased variability began to appear in the regional pattern, though the South continued to dominate the top quartile, which was entered by Missouri in 1965, Illinois in 1970, New Mexico (returning for the first time since 1935) and Michigan in 1975, and California and New York in 1980. Southern states dropping in and out of the top quartile in recent quinquennia have been border or near-border states such as Kentucky, Tennessee, Virginia and North Carolina. Five states, Texas, Florida, Louisiana, Alabama, and Georgia, are in the top quartile in all ten quinquennia. The exclusions of Mississippi and South Carolina in 1935 may have been artifacts of reporting deficiencies as they have been consistently included for every subsequent quinquennium, and it

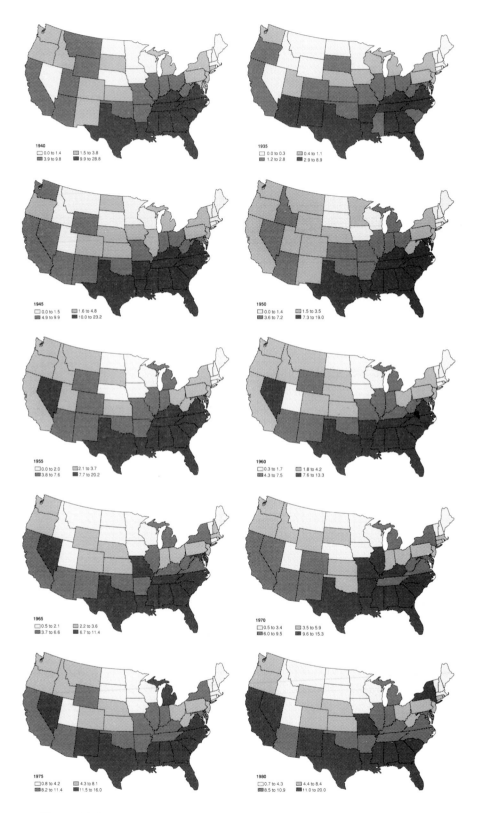

Figure 4.1. State-based homicide rates per 100,000, by quartiles, 1935–1980.

is not unreasonable to suggest that the latter seven states constitute the core of the homicide belt.

Although 1965 saw the beginning of increased variability, the 1980 map still retains the seven core states in the top quartile, and the map is far from the random spatial distribution that a condition of "behavioral entropy" would demand. Even a casual comparison of the 1935 and 1980 patterns suggests that the similarities are more striking than the differences, in spite of some evidence of decay of the pattern of the 'forties and 'fifties. A review of 1987 rates, the most recent available at the time of writing, indicated that traditionally high-rate states, including Georgia, Alabama, Texas, Florida, Louisiana, Mississippi, and South Carolina, were still in the top quartile. Furthermore, the difference between the top and bottom quartiles continued to be substantial. The mean rate for the top quartile was 10.7/100,000, compared to 2.6 for the bottom.

Regionalization Based on Historical Rate Profiles

In order to generalize the regional trends, the 48 states were clustered using Ward's method, generally recognized as a versatile clustering algorithm (Anderberg, 1973). The raw data were the quinquennial homicide rates. At the three-cluster level some 77 percent of the variance in the matrix was accounted for, and subsequent steps resulted in small increments in explained variance, with $R^2 = 85$ percent at the five-step level. The three-cluster regionalization is the best generalization, but the five-region solution provides insights relating to two subregions of some interest. These two minor clusters consist of the Alabama-Georgia dyad (historically very high rates) and Nevada, which sets itself apart with rates characterized by variability and high level. This variability of Nevada is presumably due in part to the small base population upon which rates are calculated, with the effect that a small absolute change in the frequency of homicides will result in a substantial fluctuation in rate.

The principal division of the states reveals three regions, with homicide rates that may be regarded as having been low (region 1), intermediate (region 2) and high (region 3), over the ten reference points of the study period (Table 4.1 and Figure 4.2). When Alabama and Georgia (region 4) were combined with region 3, and Nevada (region 5) was dropped from consideration, the differences between the regional rates were found to be significant ($F = 414.89$, $P < 0.0001$), suggesting that the regionalization is quite robust. As Figure 4.1 had suggested, the major regions consist of three belts trending approximately east-west and

TABLE 4.1. DESCRIPTIVE STATISTICS FOR REGIONS

REGION	NO. OF STATES IN REGION	MEAN RATE PER 100,000	STANDARD DEVIATION
1	20	5.06	1.82
2	16	5.95	2.01
3	9	7.08	1.88
4	2	8.05	1.65
5	1	6.76	2.66

Notes: See Figure 4.2 for map of regions. Each mean shown here is the mean of the ten quinquennial means (1935–1980) for each region. The N for each mean shown is 10.

Source: Calculations by author.

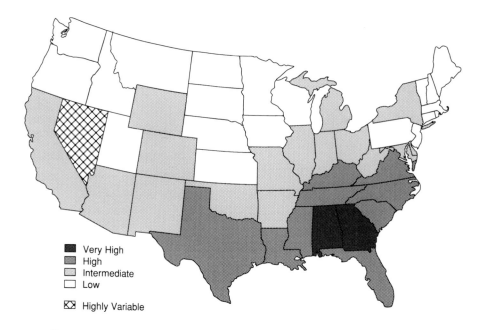

Legend:
- Very High
- High
- Intermediate
- Low
- Highly Variable

Figure 4.2. Regionalization based on quinquennial homicide rates, 1935–1980.

graduating from lowest rates in the northern tier to highest in the southern.

Social Trends in the Regions

To permit interpretation of social trends within the regional clusters, seven demographic indicators, plus the homicide rate, were plotted for the decennial census years 1930–1980. The seven indicators, selected for their relevance in the explanation of crime as well as their historical availability, were populations classified as white, black, rural, young (24 and under), middle aged (25–64) and old (65 and over). These population counts were then converted to percentages, which were transformed into conventional standard (Z) scores in which data values are expressed in standard deviation units, with mean = 0.0 and standard deviation = 1.0. Mean Z scores were then computed for each cluster of states. The original five clusters were reduced to three to allow comparable levels of generalization by eliminating or combining regions 4 and 5 as noted above. The Z scores were calculated across 47 states, and the means of these values were plotted for the three regions. The resulting plots are shown in Figures 4.3–4.5. Though the plots are separated for clarity, all three are scaled identically. Each is a subset of the 47 states for which the Z scores were calculated; hence the three plots may be compared directly. The zero line on each plot is the mean for 47 states. Each plot provides a direct comparison between the region it represents and the national context for any of the six census years.

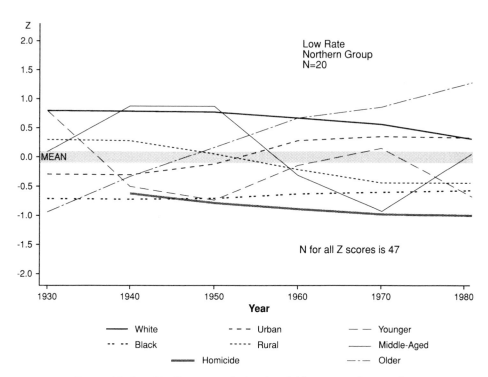

Figure 4.3. Social indicator trends, low homicide rate, northern region.

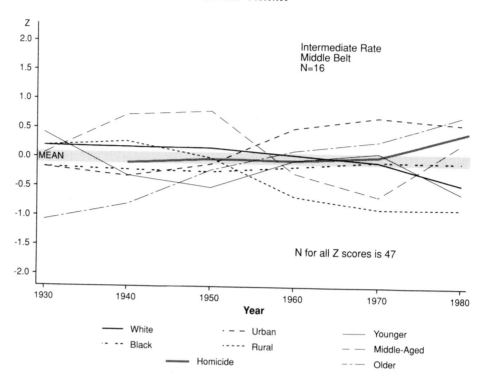

Figure 4.4. Social indicator trends, intermediate rate, central region.

Region 2, geographically intermediate between regions 1 and 3, is also intermediate in terms of its homicide rate history, with Z scores close to the mean for all census years (Figure 4.4). Visual inspection of Figures 4.3–4.5 suggests that region 2 is closer to the mean for all variables and all census years, than regions 1 or 3. The principal trends suggest that region 2 remained close to average in terms of racial composition, while sharing the general trends of urbanization and population aging.

Region 3 is the southern cluster of high homicide rate states (Figure 4.5). A general trend of convergence toward national averages is apparent, lending some support to the positions of McKinney and Bourque (1971) and Jacobson (1975). In 1930, region 3 was relatively rural (Z = 1.33), young (Z = 1.61) and African American (Z = 1.86). The homicide Z-score was 1.55 in 1940. Comparable data for 1980 illustrate the persistent trend toward the national mean, with a dramatic relative decline in rural (Z = −0.29) and young (Z = 0.45), and less striking relative declines in African American (Z = 1.10) and the homicide rate (Z = 1.10). Setting region 3 apart from the others in 1980 was its high

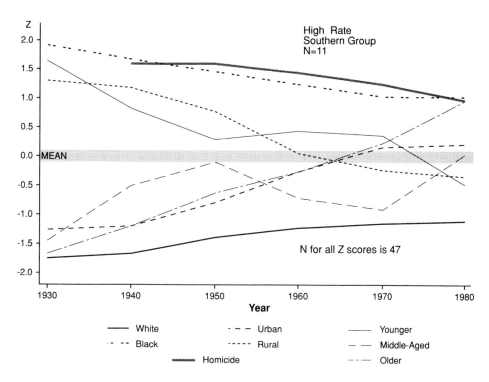

Figure 4.5. Social indicator trends, high rate, southern region.

homicide score and its relatively low white-to-black population ratio. If it were not for these characteristics, region 3 would be virtually indistinguishable from regions 1 or 2, based on this limited set of indicators.

THE REGIONAL ISSUE IN THE LITERATURE

The Case for a Southern or African American Subculture of Violence

Although some work on the regionalization of U.S. crime patterns had been done in earlier decades (Lottier, 1938; Shannon, 1954), a significant stream of research was apparently triggered by Hackney's (1969) paper advocating a cultural explanation of high rates of homicide in the South. The South was seen by Hackney as a region in which violence is a way of life, passed from generation to generation. Incorporated in this culture is a sense of inferiority, of being manipulated by outside forces. In a regression analysis, the South/nonSouth dichotomy provided significant statistical explanation of the high rate of Southern homicide, after various demographic and socioeconomic factors were controlled.

Another cultural interpretation followed (Gastil, 1971), arguing that southern violence has diffused spatially and temporally. Southern homicide was seen as having distinctive character, with its history of street duels and a generally exaggerated sense of honor. In the context of multiple regression analysis, southernness was measured with a more sophisticated Southernness Index, based on a set of criteria relating to the presence of southern influence as perceived by Gastil. For example, "core" Southern states such as Alabama and Georgia received the maximum score of 30. California scored 20, New York 10, and North Dakota 5 (Gastil, 1971; 1975).

Reed (1971) also drew attention to the "peculiarly Southern disposition to use force to settle personal, sectional, and national grievances" (430). The duel, lynching, civil rights murders, school and church bombings, and the southern tendency to high rates of interpersonal violence were all cited in support of the distinctiveness of southern culture with respect to violence. Reed examined public opinion poll data with respect to two issues bearing on the culture of violence: private gun ownership and use and corporal punishment of children. He found that southerners were more likely to own guns and were more accepting of corporal punishment. Data standardization had little effect on the interpretation of results: "Educated, urban business and professional people in the South differ from educated, urban business and professional people in the North to about the same extent as uneducated farm people in the South differ from their northern counterparts. Most strata show regional differences of around 10 percent" (p. 439).

Overall, Reed argued, "demographic convergence" could not be linked to interregional differences in attitudes relating to firearms and corporal punishment. (For further discussion on the gun issue, see below under "Gun Ownership and Region.")

Messner (1982) reported for 204 SMSAs that the size of the poverty population was negatively correlated with the homicide rate, a finding inconsistent with most other research. The same study reported moderate correlation between family income equality and the homicide rate, and strong partial effects for measures of southern regional and racial composition, leading to the conclusion that subcultural interpretations of southern violence could be supported. Further research by Messner

(1983a) found that the effect of minority proportion on the homicide rate varied considerably between regions, from a strongly positive relationship in the nonSouth to no significant effect in the South. Messner felt able to confirm the existence of a southern regional effect, noting: " . . . regional differences in the importance of racial composition, combined with the significant net effects of region in all the models . . . strongly suggest that there are important cultural differences between regions that bear on the homicide rate" (p. 1005).

Follow-up work tested the hypothesis that poverty and inequality should have a stronger positive effect on crime in the non-south than in the South, owing to value differences. If economic success is defined *universalistically* (the individual compares him/herself to all others), economic deprivation will be frustrating and is more likely to lead to aggression. If economic success is differentiated on a class basis, however, low incomes can be legitimated and frustration is limited. In a regional context, the non-South was seen as universalistic, while the South was characterized as *particularistic,* with its greater emphasis on kinship networks, local loyalties and attention to particulars in other realms of life, including country music lyrics, jokes, and favored southern intellectual pursuits such as journalism, history and literature. Using poverty and inequality as key independent variables, a significant positive relationship was found between poverty and non-southern urban homicide, but inequality failed to discriminate between the regions. Regional context was suggested as a key to understanding the interaction between values and economic conditions in the etiology of violence (Messner, 1983b).

The Case Against a Southern or African American Subculture of Violence

The Poverty Issue

In 1974, Loftin and Hill presented the first rigorous test of the Gastil-Hackney model using a paradigm differing from the originals in three respects: only lowest-level socioeconomic status was measured, the number of situational variables was increased to improve reliability, and the situational variables were combined into a Structural Poverty Index. This was the best predictor of homicide rates, even with the inclusion of Hackney's Confederate dummy or Gastil's Southernness Index. It was concluded that state-level homicide rates are a function of situational rather than cultural variables, the reverse of the Hackney and Gastil findings.

Smith and Parker (1979) and Parker and Smith (1980) also found support for the contribution of structural variables in their analyses of *primary* (those involving family and friends) and *nonprimary* (stranger) homicides. Using 1973 FBI data for 16,163 homicides and a set of independent variables based on Loftin and Hill (1974), including their Structural Poverty Index, it was found that structural variables absorbed the regional measure. However, poverty was more important in the prediction of primary than nonprimary rates. Apart from its failure to support the subculture thesis, this study demonstrated the importance of qualitative differences within categories of violence. An additional replication of Gastil, forcing the Southernness Index last in a regression model, found that the South accounted for only about 4 percent of the independent variance in rate. Gastil's attribution of significance to the Southernness Index was regarded as being due to his misinterpretation of partial correlation results (Bailey, 1976).

Bailey (1984) took issue with Messner's 1982 study using SMSAs as units of observation. SMSAs tend to statistically dilute the influence of the inner city, so that data for entire SMSAs fail to adequately represent the polarity of inner city and suburb. Bailey noted that, contrary to Messner's (1982) findings, many studies have shown links between poverty and homicide at various geographic scales, including the social area, community, city and state. Replicating Messner, but using cities instead of SMSAs, Bailey found a positive and consistent relationship between poverty and murder rates, but not between violence and income inequality. He noted that theory would suggest that it would be property crime, not violence, that would be related to income inequality. Specifically with respect to the South, Bailey found that "when both poverty and income inequality are controlled, there is only a chance relation between region and homicides for 1960 and 1970" (542).

Huff-Corzine et al. (1989), too, found that severe poverty was associated with deadly violence for both blacks and whites; percent born in the South, their regional measure, did not significantly affect lethal violence rates. Humphries and Wallace (1980), viewed crime as a product of withdrawals of capital leading to the out-migration of higher paid workers and the "marginalization" of those remaining, leading in turn to distress in the inner city and conflict over increasingly scarce resources. They felt able to conclude that "We can dismiss explanations such as the "southern culture of violence" thesis . . . on the grounds that urban violence is not a function of region."

Loftin and Parker (1985) responded to inconsistencies in the relationship between poverty and violence by arguing that errors in the measurement of poverty have led to the construction of erroneous models. Measures of persons below the poverty threshold, they noted, exclude payments received for medical care, school lunches, public housing, or other forms of assistance. The infant mortality rate (IMR) was suggested as a relatively satisfactory measure of poverty owing to its established correlation with poverty and the reliability of IMR statistics. Models incorporating IMR led to the conclusion that "poverty has a significant and positive effect on the homicide rate" (281). Of the 49 largest cities in the U.S. in 1970 used for the analysis, a quarter were in the South, yet a *region* variable (dichotomized as South/Other) was not significant in any model.

Gun Ownership and Region

Another attack on the culture model used 1973 Roper Poll data to examine regional differences in attitudes, and found that southern residency increased the probability of gun ownership and of opposition to gun control, while non-southern residence increased the likelihood of being assaulted (Doerner, 1978a). This study, however, did not focus on homicide, but rather on the very broad "assault" category, which may include behaviors ranging from trivial to severe. Doerner was able to conclude that "if a regional culture of violence once existed, it has vanished over the years." Furthermore, Doerner claims that a southern subculture of violence has not been substantiated either at the *ecological* or *individual* levels (Doerner, 1978b).

O'Connor and Lizotte (1979) looked specifically at the issue of gun ownership in response to the assertions of Reed (1972) and Hackney (1969), to the effect that guns are more accepted and more likely to be used in the South than in other regions, with the implication that higher levels of ownership are then linked to higher levels of violence. Using data on the Census South from the 1973–74 Social Survey (for whites only), it was found that growing up in the South had no statistically significant effect on *handgun* ownership. O'Connor and Lizotte pointed out that their research did not deny the existence of a southern subculture, only that subculture does not affect this particular dimension of violence.

Wright, Rossi, and Daly (1983) noted the consensus that: "Private weaponry is more prevalent in the South (and West) than in other parts of the nation . . . the regional effect is also sizable" (106).

Given the high rate of violence in the South and the high level of private weapon ownership, observers have been tempted to see cause and effect. However, gun ownership, including handguns, is higher in the rural than urban areas, yet rates of violence are higher in urban than rural settings. Wright, Rossi, and Daly (1983) concluded that " . . . the effect neither of region nor city size says *anything* about the possible causal relationships between private weaponry and criminal violence, a large number of assertions to the contrary notwithstanding" (107).

Along similar lines, Dixon and Lizotte[2] (1987), using a direct measure of subculture of violence separate from measures of region or gun ownership, suggested that gun ownership is independent of values associated with subcultures of violence. Furthermore,

> . . . both region and gun ownership are related to defensive attitudes that are not indicative of a subculture of violence. These results cast doubt on the validity of the reformulated subculture-of-violence thesis that emphasizes a regional subculture of violence with guns as a central feature. While interpersonal violence, such as homicide, may be a function of subcultures of violence, these subcultures operate independently of region and may be associated with, but are in no way dependent on, firearms. (p. 383)

Historically, firearms have been more likely to be used for homicides in the South than in other regions. However, the differential diminished in the period 1970–87, during which time the level of firearm involvement has stayed fairly flat in the West (range = 8%) and Northeast (range = 6%), but trended downward in the South (range = 13%) and North Central (range = 15%) regions (Figure 4.6). Over the 18-year period from 1970 through 1987, the South and North Central regions were quite close in mean percentages of firearm use in homicides (69 and 66 respectively). While this limited evidence tends to support the position that interregional differences have tended to diminish in recent decades, the observed trends may be dramatically altered when data become available reflecting the surge of drug-related inner city firearm homicides in the late 1980s.

---

[2]However, the Dixon and Lizotte article attracted dissenting views in the *American Journal of Sociology.* See volume 95 (1989), number 1, pages 174–187.

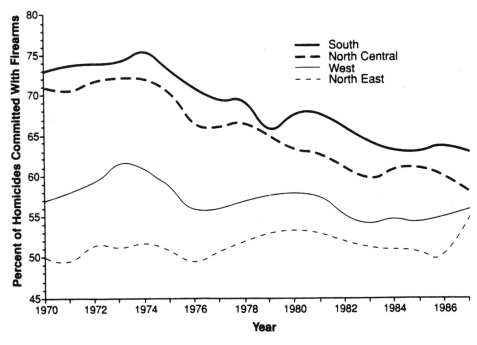

Figure 4.6. Firearm homicide trends, by region, 1970–87. *Source:* Data from FBI, *Uniform Crime Reports,* Washington D.C., 1971–88.

Race and Region

Blau and Blau (1982), like Messner (1982), elected to use SMSAs for research testing the hypothesis that "variations in rates of urban criminal violence largely result from differences in racial inequity in socioeconomic conditions" (114). Three variables constituted the focus of the study: location in the South, percentage of African Americans, and poverty. When economic inequality was controlled, neither poverty nor southern location affected rates of violence, and percent African American had little influence. Interestingly, a rather notable exception to their findings was murder, "which reveals higher rates in the South even when inequalities are controlled" (122).

Sampson (1985a,b) examined determinants of violence, including region, in considerable detail, using cities as units of observation. Sampson took issue with the subculture of violence, particularly as formulated by Curtis (1975) and Spilerman (1971), who argued that the size of the African American population in a given city is critical. Once the African American population exceeds some threshold, they suggested, a kind of "critical mass" exists for the reinforcement of black subculture. Thus the subculture argument could be tested by examining the relationship between rate of violence and percent African American, controlling for other conditions such as poverty and inequality. Sampson used data for the 55 largest cities for 1970 and age-sex, age-race specific arrest data, using a dichotomy between those over and under age 18. Overall, the strongest predictor of homicide was percent African American, followed by poverty. However, when rates were disaggregated by race, percent black was not significant for either blacks or whites. Substitution of absolute size of the African American population also failed to yield a significant relationship, and the use of the South/nonSouth indicator also had no influence on race-specific homicide.

Clearly, the subculture thesis was not supported by these findings. Sampson commented specifically on the popular tendency to view certain cities as the national homicide capital. When Detroit achieved this dubious distinction, its high rate was due solely to the *size* of the black population, given that homicide rates are higher among blacks than whites. However, the *rate* among African Americans in Detroit was about the same as among African Americans in other cities.

In another study undermining the subculture thesis, Sampson (1985b) examined a broader set of crimes (for approximately the same set of large cities), including murder and assault, and found that, for white juveniles and adults, poverty was a significant correlate, while income inequality was not. The reverse held for black juveniles and adults. In ten of twelve regression models, income inequality was positively related to African American offending, "net of the influence of region, racial composition, poverty, and structural opportunity" (667). South region was significant for both white and black juveniles, but was negative. This meant that nonsouthern cities had *higher* rates of juvenile violence than the South. For adults, South was not significant. In general, this research supported the argument that structural economic factors are important predictors of offense patterns.

OTHER PERSPECTIVES

Measuring Legitimate Violence

Baron and Straus (1988), directly addressed the question of whether high homicide rates are better explained by cultural or economic factors and noted that, in prior work, cultural support for violence had never been separated. In other words, it had never been verified that the South represents a constellation of traits supportive of violence. To this end, a *Legitimate Violence Index* (LVX) was constructed, measuring *non-criminal* violence. A dozen indicators represented *mass media preferences* (violence in TV or magazines), *governmental use of violence* (e.g., corporal punishment, executions), and *participation in socially approved violent activities* (e.g., hunting, college football, lynching). Western and southern states scored highest; the top six were Wyoming, Montana, Mississippi, Idaho, Utah, and Georgia. This casts further doubt on the validity of the stereotypical notion that the culture of violence is a dominantly southern trait. Regression analysis at the state level supported the proposition that legitimate violence, poverty, and inequality, are all significantly related to violence. However, the "Confederate South" "did not attain a greater than chance association in the regression analyses" (382).

Diffusion

Another issue relevant to the discussion of regional influence touches on the issue of diffusion of high homicide rates outside the South as a function of interregional migration. Block (1979) found that two variables were clearly related to violent crime rates in community areas of Chicago; percentage of residents from the South and the residential proximity of poor and middle-class families. Percentage of residents southern born was the only variable significant in models of homicide, robbery and aggravated assault rates, and it was most important in the homicide model. Even then, however, it added only 10 percent to the R_2 and was distinctly secondary to residential proximity ($R^2 = 0.56$). Overall, southern origin did not make a convincing contribution to the multivariate models. Other work has attributed increasing levels of homicide in northern cities to the immigration of southern African Americans. In Detroit and St. Louis many black homicide victims had been born in another state, and they tended to fall in the over-30 age group (Rose, 1978).

Other Factors

Linsky and Straus (1986) developed a *State Stress Index* (SSI) incorporating stressful conditions thought to be associated particularly with crime and illness. Various life events were translated into macro indicators. For example, the event "Lost a home through fire, flood or other disaster" was measured by the surrogate "Disaster assistance per 100,000 families" from the American National Red Cross. *Economic, family* and *other* (e.g., welfare recipients, high-school dropouts) stressors were combined in the SSI, which, overall, was heavily weighted toward variables with a direct or indirect economic connotation.

Literature reviewed by Linsky and Straus indicated that marital assault and homicide both correlated to some extent with stressors. The theoretical rationale for links between stress and crime were based on several factors. First, is the *fight or flight* reaction to threatening situations, a physiological response caused by changes in adrenal secretions. Second, interaction between social control and stress may lead to disease (when social control is strong and physiological arousal is constant), or to behavioral reaction in the form of suicide or depression. When social control is weak, aggression may be the direct product of arousal. Third, stresses may be legitimized over time by the culture of a group, as some would argue is the case with respect to the southern violence phenomenon. Fourth, the process of change and destabilization in the course of such events as divorce and migration has the effect of stressing individuals and removing informal social controls. Fifth, law enforcement may be affected by the accumulation of stressful events, in that it may react selectively to groups or situations that have become the focus of public concern, such as the "mod and rocker" phenomenon in the UK in the 1960s (Cohen, 1980) or bikers and skinheads in the U.S. (Linsky & Straus, 1986:69–71).

Linsky and Strauss felt able to conclude that: "stressful life events are positively correlated with all seven of the so-called 'index crimes'... cumulative stressful events are causally related to each of these crimes" (p. 77).

A regression model of state level murder/manslaughter rates incorporating the SSI, and other selected variables achieved an R^2 of 0.78. The regression coefficient of the SSI alone was 0.20, indicating that for each increase of one point in the SSI, the homicide rate increased 0.2/100,000, or some 2.7 percent of the average state murder rate in 1976. A comparable result was found for assault, with a regression coefficient of 7.39, indicating an increase of >7 assaults per 100,000 population for each one point increase in the stress index (Linsky & Straus, 1986:81–82). The results of this state level approach were consistent with other research done at the state level suggesting the importance of economic factors in violence and implicitly failing to lend support to the subcultural interpretation. Given that the major component of violence at the state level is in fact urban, we can infer that variables explaining state level violence have relevance at the urban scale (see Chapter 6). For example, of the 153,268 homicides reported in the United States from 1976 to 1983, 40,797 (26.6 percent) occurred in the ten *cities* (not metropolitan areas), discussed in Chapter 6, containing only 8.2 percent of the nation's population.[3]

Williams and Flewelling (1988) argued that prior regional and comparative urban analyses of homicide had relied on total homicide rates; they argued that homicide rates should be disaggregated into more refined categories in order to permit the testing of hypotheses about particular types of homicide. Inconsistencies in prior research, they suggested, might be attributable to this use of the total homicide rate.

Based on previous work, it was suggested that three theoretical constructs had reflected sources of homicide in prior studies. These were: *social disintegration, resource deprivation,* and *violent cultural orientation.* Interpersonal incidents were regarded as more important than felony-type events, and rates of homicide by family members, acquaintances, and strangers were analyzed using a sample of incidents for cities over 100,000 for the years 1980–84. Region was measured using a dummy variable based on South/Nonsouth. The total (nondisaggregated) rate was significantly related to all variables *except* southern location. Also, the total rate correlated only inconsistently with the disaggregated rates, suggesting that the total rate fails to adequately represent disaggregated rates. Variations observed in relationships between independent variables and the disaggregated rates were as expected on the basis of theory. This research, too, failed to lend support to the southern subculture of violence position.

In a different approach to evaluation of the culture model county level data were used to test two hypotheses: that southern census regions, in terms of homicide rates, were (a) *relatively homogeneous* and (b) *significantly different* from nonsouthern regions (Doerner, 1975). The Northeast and South regions were internally homogeneous. Within the South only one of the three subregions (the East South Central) was found to be homogeneous, suggesting the inherent inappropriateness of census regions for the analysis of cultural hypotheses.

Trend-oriented studies offer insights relating to changing cultural patterns in the South and homicide trends. McKinney and Bourque (1971)

---

[3]The U.S. Population in 1980 was 227 million. The ten cities accounted for 18.7 million.

identified *convergence* between the South and nonsouth as southern traditions fade and the social systems of the regions become integrated. The South was seen as having changed more rapidly than the rest of the U.S. since 1930, through the influence of modes of exchange (particularly transportation and communication), Supreme Court decisions (school integration, 1954; urban representation, 1962) and the civil rights movement of the 1960s.

Analysis of crime trends in 467 U.S. cities between 1951 and 1970 hypothesized (a) *converging crime rates* between South and nonSouth and (b) *regional effects* decreasing in influence on property crimes over time and not significantly related to personal crimes, owing to the greater responsiveness of property crimes to regional structural change. It was concluded that homicide and assault were the only offenses with persistently high rates over the study period. With respect to homicide, "the long-range evidence favors a narrowing gap between North and South" (Jacobson, 1975).

In conclusion, Hawkins (1986) brought together several arguments to the effect that the subculture of violence concept is severely limited, by factors including *lack of empirical grounding*, underemphasis on *structural, situational,* and *institutional* variables, and the availability of *alternative interpretations* of high rates of homicide among African Americans. The "crucial ideological bias of subculture of violence theory," wrote Hawkins, "is the lack of a full consideration of economic factors" (219). To this interpretation might be added the finding that violence is only weakly associated with *attitudes* and has little or no association with *values* (Ball-Rokeach, 1973).

AN ALTERNATE VIEW OF REGIONAL VARIATION

O'Carroll and Mercy (1989) examined the idea that "regional differences in age structure may have accounted for or altered regional differences in homicide rates" (18). They found that, although *crude* rates are higher in the South than elsewhere,

> for all races taken together, both crude and age-adjusted rates are highest in the South. For *each* race group considered separately, however, both the crude and age-adjusted homicide rates are highest, not in the South, but in the West . . . among blacks, the risk of homicide victimization is actually *lowest* in the South . . . For whites, the homicide rate is quite high in the South . . . second only to the rate in the West . . . (19)

O'Carroll and Mercy argued that census regions *should* be used for regional analyses of homicide unless clear evidence can be presented to show that they are inappropriate. (On this point, see: Doerner, 1975.) Furthermore, they suggested that researchers may be asking the wrong questions. Instead of "Why is the crude homicide rate so high in the South?" we should ask, for example, "Why does the South have the *lowest* homicide rate among blacks?" or "Why is the *West* so violent?" Similarly, in a study of youth including *all* forms of violent mortality, Greenberg, Carey, and Popper (1987) found the highest death rates to be in western states, with " . . . the highest rates for rural Western whites . . . even higher than those for inner city blacks! . . . The rural areas of the West, rather than the American urban ghetto, is where youth is far more likely to suffer violent death (pp. 42, 43)."

AN INTEGRATED MODEL

In a reconceptualization of regional variations in violence, Whitt, Corzine, and Huff-Corzine (1995) suggested an integrated model of homicide and suicide on the ground that both are forms of violence, with outward expression in homicides, inward in suicides. Following Swidler (1986), culture was seen as a "tool kit," resources used to develop "strategies of action." Thus men tend to have more knowledge of firearms, perhaps due to the predominance of men in the armed forces, including police, and are more likely to employ firearms in crimes. The link between culture and regional variations in violence was seen in *attribution theory.* All violence could be seen as being produced by *Forces of Production* (poverty, frustration, etc.). This "stream" of violence is then influenced by *Forces of Direction* (e.g., cultural influences) determining whether a violent event is a homicide or suicide (or attempt). Attribution theory suggests that southerners tend to externalize blame for personal difficulties and are therefore more likely to respond homicidally than suicidally.

Using counties as their region building units, Whitt et al., found high mean homicide rates in the South (Table 4.2). Mean suicide rates tended to be highest in the West and "Interior Southwest," while "Mean Lethal Violence" rates, integrating homicide and suicide, peaked in South Florida (arguably not "southern" in its culture), but with high values in both South *and* West. This suggests that social scientists may have been overconcerned with *southern* violence (defined only in terms of homicide) given that the integrated perspective draws attention also to the West.

TABLE 4.2
MEAN HOMICIDE RATES BY REGION, UNITED STATES COUNTIES, 1988–89

Region	Non-Metropolitan Counties	Metropolitan Counties	All Counties	Number of Counties
South				
Eastern South	8.86	8.76	8.83	1,240
S. Florida	13.10	10.27	11.32	27
Other	8.82	8.67	8.78	1,213
Western South	6.64	8.69	7.02	282
Interior Southwest	9.80	9.07	9.73	61
Northeast				
Greater New England	2.29	3.09	2.62	125
New York Metro	—	8.55	8.55	25
Pennsylvania	2.30	3.97	3.38	68
Midwest				
Central Midwest	1.90	4.70	2.41	513
Upper Midwest	2.43	4.40	2.69	458
West				
Rocky Mountain	3.45	4.68	3.58	111
Mormon	3.28	3.09	3.27	49
Pacific Southwest	6.02	7.51	6.70	70
Pacific Northwest	4.10	5.22	4.33	100

CONCLUSION

By and large, the concepts of an African American or of a regional subculture of violence have not fared well over the last decade or so. In study after study, regional and racial effects have been insignificant when various structural conditions have been controlled. However, a number of weaknesses remain in the regional studies done to date. Some rely on the use of the Census South for a cultural definition, a geographic division probably too coarse to offer a reliable surrogate for southern culture. Also, it may be suggested that the state is an excessive level of aggregation for ecological analysis. Some analyses have used SMSAs, also inappropriate for the type of work attempted.

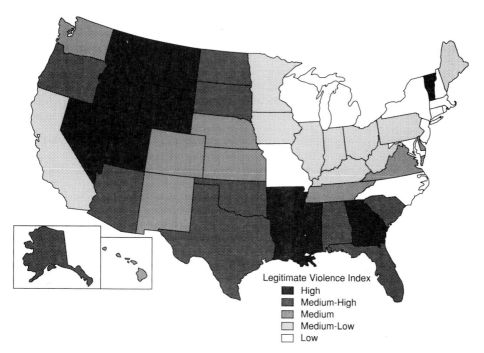

Figure 4.7. Regional distribution of the Baron and Straus Legitimate Violence Index, by quintiles. *Data source:* Baron and Straus, 1988, Table 1, p. 378.

While rigorous analysis has been unable to lend support to the concept of a distinct regional or racial subculture of violence, longitudinal perspectives suggest that measurable (or, perhaps more accurately *measured*) attributes of regions of the United States have tended to converge in recent decades, as demonstrated by Figures 4.3, 4.4, 4.5, 4.6, and 4.8. Some survey data, too, suggest that some regionally measured attitudes have, at least sporadically, tended to move closer together (Table 4.3). In Table 4.3, attitudinal data were abstracted from the *Sourcebook of Criminal Justice Statistics* on questions relating to neighborhood fear, the death penalty, gun ownership, gun control, the televising of executions, and the relationship between violence on television and crime. As indicated, some issues demonstrate fairly sharp regional divisions, while others suggest more homogeneity. In Figure 4.8, showing gun ownership data for 1973 through 1994, the interregional range in the percentage reporting having guns fell from 40 in 1973 to the low 20s, suggesting convergence consistent with that illustrated elsewhere. (See also Harries, 1995a.)

As Hawley (1987) has pointed out, the "Southern Violence Construct"

TABLE 4.3. REGIONAL VARIATIONS IN ATTITUDES RELATING TO VIOLENCE (%)

TOPIC	REGION				YEAR	SOURCE
	EAST	MIDWEST	SOUTH	WEST		
Afraid to walk alone at night in own neighborhood	44[A]	39	54	46	94	N
Favor death penalty for persons convicted of murder	75	78	77	78	95	G
Personally owns a gun	22	35	46	35	95	G
Favor law requiring police permit prior to gun purchase	85[A]	78	77	74	94	N
Executions should be televised	20	22	24	22	93	T
Relationship between television violence and crime	74	78	73	78	93	G

[A]*Data* from region defined as "Northeast."

Source codes: G = Gallup Poll; N = National Opinion Research Center; T = Times Mirror Center for People and the Press.

Data source: Compiled from Maguire and Pastore, 1995.

(SVC) is "almost an article of faith today in the social sciences and history" (29), in spite of a substantial amount of evidence questioning the phenomenon. He attributed this situation to:

> prevalent intellectual sensitivity to pejorative stereotypes of the South, southern institutions, and Southerners themselves . . . the product of the historical, political, economic, and cultural rivalry between North and South . . . the uncritical acceptance of the [SVC] by the academic community suggests that the construct serves latent functions that are more ideological and normative than illuminative and substantive (29).

On the basis of a wide-ranging review of the literature, Hawley concluded that "the SVC, if ever valid, may now be an anachronism" (48). Actually, the SVC has not been accepted uncritically, as the literature cited here indicates, and the credibility of the construct has steadily eroded since it was first advocated in a formal way in the late 1960s and early 1970s.

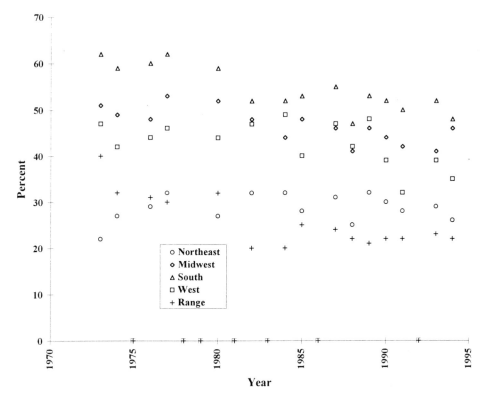

Figure 4.8. Regional variations in percent reporting having guns, 1973–94. *Data source:* Maguire and Pastore, 1995, Table 2.63, p. 186. *Note:* Data are percent reporting having guns in response to the question "Do you happen to have in your home (or garage) any guns or revolvers?"

Chapter 5

PERCEPTUAL DIMENSIONS:
PUNISHMENT AND SERIOUSNESS[1]

Models of the geography of deviance at all scales have tended to emphasize explanation of crime incidence, to the exclusion of other criminal justice system elements. Such exclusive emphasis on the interpretation of *crime* patterns, whether at the neighborhood, interurban, or regional levels, leaves important dimensions of the recursive relationship between deviant behavior, perceptions of that behavior, and various political and legislative responses, unaccounted for. In this chapter, a connection is made between the regional geography of homicide, outlined in Chapter 4, and (a) the geography of a sanction directed against that offense, and (b) public perceptions of the severity of serious violence. This provides a systemic perspective on the criminal justice system in contrast to normative, cross-sectional (pattern) analysis. With respect to any crime, an appropriate question in the context of public policy is whether its perceived severity is congruent with the associated pattern of punishment. The answer to this question may also assist our understanding of both the cultural geography of crime and of the spatial processes underlying the production of legal sanctions. Furthermore, new topical explorations in geographic questions on crime may be encouraged.

OBJECTIVE VERSUS PERCEPTUAL PERSPECTIVES

In the last couple of decades, geographers' interests in the spatial patterning of deviance-related phenomena have led to several general interpretations (e.g., Brantingham & Brantingham, 1981; Davidson, 1981; Georges-Abeyie & Harries, 1980; Harries, 1971; 1974; 1980;

---

[1]This chapter is adapted in part from an article originally published as: Regional variations in homicide, capital punishment, and perceived crime severity in the United States, *Geografiska Annaler* 70 B (1988): 325–334. Adapted by permission of *Geografiska Annaler.*

Herbert, 1982; Pyle, 1974; Shannon, 1986; Evans & Herbert, 1989) as well as more specialized investigations. An overview of the extant research suggests that the geography of crime is divided into two related fields: the study of *objective* and *perceptual* crime patterns (Brantingham, Brantingham, & Butcher, 1986). Analyses of objective patterns are fueled by data sources which are themselves sustained by the need for operationally-oriented data to provide yardsticks of law enforcement resources and performance. Perceptual analyses, on the other hand, have been prompted by the realization that "hard" data (i.e., records of observed or observable phenomena) may obscure as much as they reveal and that such data fail to touch important facets of behavior. Much geographic research on crime has dealt with objective pattern analysis, owing to the ready availability of crime rate data from sources including the *Uniform Crime Reports* (UCR) (FBI, 1986) and the *National Crime Survey* (NCS) (Bureau of Justice Statistics, annual [a]). (For a brief comparison of the two reporting systems, see: Bureau of Justice Statistics, 1983, p. 6.) In this respect, crime research has paralleled work on other quality of life indicators, overwhelmingly dominated by inquiry based on "hard" data. However, objective data are biased toward the crime incident environment, to the exclusion of other stages in the criminal justice process. (For a comprehensive critique of the UCR, for example, see: Hindelang, 1974.) Although prisoner data are available (Bureau of Justice Statistics, annual [b]), no data base permits a comprehensive national or regional view of the tracking of criminal incidents, in geographic context, from occurrence through imprisonment.

In spite of the inherent "user attraction" of objective data, some geographic research has departed from the objective model and has attempted to investigate perceptual crime patterns. Such studies have included criminals' perceptions of crime target areas and police (Carter & Hill, 1979), burglars' target selection strategies (Rengert & Wasilchick, 1985), fear of crime (Smith & Patterson, 1980), and perceived crime risks and seriousness (Brantingham, Brantingham, & Butcher, 1986; Shannon, 1986; Pyle, 1980).

Although the swath of research on the social geography of crime has widened considerably, significant crime-related perceptual issues have been little studied from a geographic perspective. Among the topics neglected by geographers is the *perceived severity* of crime. While perceived severity has clear geographic ramifications, usable data have been difficult to collect, usually necessitating the employment of expensive survey instruments. Even the massive efforts of the U.S. *National Crime Survey,* based on interviews with a large rotating panel of respondents, have not elicited data useful in an explicitly geographic framework.

While the regional tradition is firmly embedded in geography, studies of perceived severity at the regional level are nonexistent; indeed, regional perspectives of any sort have been few and far between. By and large, regional research has been regarded, pejoratively, as empirical, and has been largely superseded by studies at the intraurban scale. Apart from the general decline of regional approaches, lack of interest has been attributed to other factors: the inadequacy of official statistics, and the entrenched assumption that regional variations in crime are explicable only in terms of urbanization (Smith, 1986).

The implication of the latter point is that *regions,* as such, are really devoid of unique crime characteristics—it is, rather, the major cities within the regions that impart whatever regional flavor there may be. Smith, however, found evidence in the *British Crime Survey* (BCS) leading her to question the validity of these perceptions (Smith, 1986). Analysis of the BCS suggested that urbanization did *not* adequately account for regional crime patterns in England and Wales. Even with inner city effects removed, significant regional variation was seen in five crime types (vandalism, burglary, theft from the person, and wounding and robbery). Smith concluded: "In general, then, it seems likely that regional differences in the crime rate do exist which are neither an artifact of official statistics nor a simple reflection of different degrees of urbanization" (p. 59).

It is reasonable to infer the possibility, at least, that regional variations in values, expressed as differential attitudes toward deviant behavior, are a component of such regional variations in the U.S. as well as the U.K. This is not to argue for cultural determinism, but rather to admit the possibility that amorphous "regional culture" may play a role in the formation of attitudes toward crime.

The regional geography of homicide was reviewed in some detail in Chapter 4. What is the social response to this geography? How do public perceptions of serious violence relate to patterns of violence and sanctions directed against it? Capital punishment is a simple, measurable sanction lending itself to comparisons with patterns of violence.

CAPITAL PUNISHMENT, 1930–86

Consideration of capital punishment in a spatio-temporal context must necessarily broach the subject of lynching, which accounted for some 3,724 deaths between 1889 and 1930 (Raper, 1933). However, the point should be made that the practice was almost extinct by the beginning of the time period considered here; by 1935, only a handful of lynchings were occurring annually, compared to an average of about 90 per year at the peak (McGovern, 1982). Thus lynching may be dismissed as a significant direct component in the discussion that follows.

Capital punishment is perhaps the most dramatic evidence of regional variation in social values finding expression in the form of legal sanctions (see: Elazar, 1972; Harries & Brunn, 1978). Data are available for two execution "eras", pre- and post-*Furman v. Georgia* (1972). The first era actually spanned 1930–67, when the Supreme Court placed a moratorium on the practice. The second era was 1977–86, the most recent year for which data were available at the time of writing. In the first era, nearly 4,000 persons were executed, with the South heavily dominating per capita rates. In the second era, following reinstatement of capital punishment, 68 executions occurred. The distribution was still heavily dominated by southern states. Of the 68 executions, only 5 occurred in the nonsouth, in Indiana, Nevada, and Utah. While the South has executed apace, however, several north central and northeastern states have had no death penalty (Figure 5.1). Strikingly, it should be noted that this durable southern emphasis on execution mirrors persistently high homicide rates in the South. Not surprisingly, "cross-sectional analyses have produced results that are not consistent with the hypothesis that capital punishment deters homicide" (Klein, Forst, & Filatov, 1978). For more detail on the geography of capital punishment, see Harries and Cheatwood, 1996.

Just as executions have had their distinctive geography, so have qualifying conditions and methods, suggesting intricate cultural conditioning in the evolution of capital punishment. In Indiana, for example, 10-year-olds may be executed, at least in theory. In 14 states, no minimum age is specified directly. Five methods of execution are specified among the states: lethal injection (most numerous), electrocution, lethal gas, hanging, and firing squad (Idaho and Utah only). Capital punishment epitomizes regional variation in laws. Substantial differentiation is seen with respect to the definitions of, and sanctions for, a variety of

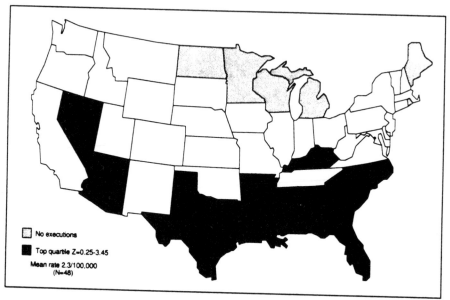

Figure 5.1. Per capita execution rates, 1930–86. Rate calculated on the basis of 1960 population. *Source:* Data from Bureau of Justice Statistics, 1987a.

criminal behaviors. To cite but one example, data for robbery convictions in three states showed mean sentence lengths of 56 months (California), 89 months (Illinois), and 135 months (North Carolina), for large samples of cases (Bureau of Justice Statistics, 1984). Given that each state writes its own criminal laws, any influences affecting legislative behavior, including special interests, public opinion, media coverage of heinous crimes, the local religious milieu, and political posturing by legislators, all constitute part of the cultural conditioning process. Regional variations in values are illustrated clearly by the extraordinary patchwork of abortion laws, a pattern that will probably become even more diverse given the transfer of more powers to the states in the course of consideration of *Roe v. Wade* by the U.S. Supreme Court in 1989 (Reid, 1989).

CRIME SEVERITY

Severity provides a qualitative dimension to the statistical picture of crime, normally expressed in terms of population-based occurrence rates. Enhanced understanding of perceived crime severity is important at two scales: *neighborhood* and *region*. At the neighborhood level, perceived severity is intimately related to fear of crime, which in turn may lead to modified behavior. In July, 1989, for example, a woman sitting on the porch of her home in Hanna Place, Washington, D.C., was killed by a stray bullet from a fight, apparently over drugs (LaFraniere, 1989). A nearby resident interviewed on television in connection with the incident vowed that she would move out of the neighborhood as soon as possible, clearly illustrating the connection between crime, fear of crime, and (potential) behavior. Numerous comparable anecdotal responses to high rates of violence appear in the media (e.g., Nelson, 1989).

At the regional level, the focus of this discussion, perceived severity and fear find political expression through the legislation of penalties for crimes, and also in sentencing inequalities between local jurisdictions. In a nebulous process of creative plagiarism alloyed with the values of population groups dominant at the time the laws were written or amended, states have developed criminal laws which resemble each other in general terms, but differ greatly in detail (Bureau of Justice Statistics, 1987b). As Galliher and Pepinsky noted in a meta-analysis of the social origins of criminal law, "it appeared equally plausible that individuals, monolithic groups, and pluralistic forces had moved the legislators to act" (Galliher and Pepinsky, 1978).

Severity and Law Production

Perceptions of crime severity are conveyed to legislators by grass roots processes; if citizens believe sanctions to be too severe or not severe enough, they are free to petition lawmakers to make corrections. Legislators, in turn, react to public opinion and special interest group pressures, mediated by their own values and preferences. The result is a crazy quilt of sanctions lacking consistency between states (see Harries & Brunn, 1978). This patchwork of laws is, theoretically, a "just desserts" response to perceived crime severity. The pattern is so complex, however, that subtleties are incomprehensible.

Understanding of U.S. culture would be enhanced if it were possible to delve into the confusing morass of state laws and trace the sociopolitical antecedents of major categories. Such work, in effect, would extend concepts advanced by Elazar, who linked regional attitudes to the attributes of incoming migration streams (Elazar, 1972). Unfortunately, to survey state laws in the manner suggested would be a monumental undertaking, and inferences about the attitudes that led to the sanctions observed would be largely speculative. Even a skeletal summary of *sentencing* provisions, alone, of the states, takes more than 200 pages (Bureau of Justice Statistics, 1984; Cooper, Kelley, & Larson, 1982). The evaluation of regional or local perceptions in order to assess the degree of congruence with state or local laws, is also difficult in that survey data of sufficient detail have been lacking.

The National Survey of Crime Severity

Some survey data suggestive of public perceptions of crime severity and related issues have been gathered by various public opinion polls, but the instruments have lacked detail in terms of the scope of their questions and their geographic scale (e.g., Jamieson & Flanagan, 1987). However, a new tool has become available, permitting a more rigorous view of perceived crime severity at the regional, state, and metropolitan levels. The U.S. *National Survey of Crime Severity* (NSCS) (Wolfgang et al., 1985a) was piggy-backed to the ongoing U.S. *National Crime Survey* in July through December, 1977. Following lengthy delays due to the complexity of the analysis (Klaus, 1988), the *Survey* report appeared in June, 1985.

A fundamental defect of both the *Uniform Crime Reports* and the *National Crime Survey* is that they treat crimes as "equal" in the sense that events are unweighted; in frequency counts and rate calculations, a murder counts no more than a pocket-picking. The NSCS was an attempt to evaluate relative seriousness in order to permit a more realistic assessment of crime impacts and to facilitate, for example, work assignments for detectives, evaluation of clearance data, and the assignment of police patrols to shifts based on higher levels of seriousness. At the prosecutorial level, cases may be prioritized on the basis of their seriousness scores. In judicial proceedings, penalties may be assigned on the basis of seriousness where indeterminate sentencing is permitted. Legislatively, seriousness scores could be used to specify punishments congruent with public perceptions of harm.

Wolfgang et al. argued that crime severity is determined by cultural conditions interpreted broadly to include economic status, and that perceptions will change across cultural boundaries (Wolfgang, et al., 1985a). One of the purposes of the survey was "to determine the perceived severities of various crimes according to regions, states, size of place, and other demographic characteristics of the population"; indeed, a substantial part of the NSCS report looked at differentials in perceived severity by subgroups and regions.

In order to arrive at a reliable index of crime severity, it was determined that a ratio scale should be used in order to provide a zero point and an indication of distances among items. Pilot studies established the validity of proposed scales. It was also determined that the most appropriate measurement of central tendency for the ratio judgments was the *geometric mean,* defined as the antilog of the arithmetic means of logarithms of response values. (The advantage of the geometric mean over the other measures of central tendency is that it effectively damps the effect of skewness.) A prescored modulus, or reference item—"A person steals a bicycle parked on the street"—scored 10 and was used as a basis for comparison with, and scoring of, other incidents.

Data were collected in July through December, 1977, as an add-on to the *National Crime Survey.* Sample areas covered all 50 states and the District of Columbia. Groups of counties were the primary sampling units and accounted for all U.S. counties (1,930 units were combined into 376 strata). At the second stage of sampling, census enumeration districts were selected with a probability proportional to their 1970 population size, with further selection of clusters of about four housing units in each enumeration district. Some 32,034 housing units were selected in this manner. Ultimately, 51,623 interviews were obtained, or 87 percent of the theoretical sample. Over 250 offense items were included in the survey, but the burden on respondents was minimized by distributing the questions among 12 different versions of the questionnaire. National geometric means varied from 5.4 for "a person under 16 years old plays hooky from school" to 1,577.5 for "a person plants a bomb in a public building. The bomb explodes and 20 people are killed" (Table 5.1).

Perceived Severity

Perceived severity varied according to the demographic and geographic attributes of respondents. Whites generally reported severity scores twice those of nonwhites for serious injury offenses. Socioeconomic status, as measured by income, occupation, and education characteristics correlated positively with perceived seriousness, particularly with respect to violent incidents; illustrative relationships for occupation and income classes are shown in Table 5.2. In Table 5.3, severity ratios

TABLE 5.1. GEOMETRIC MEANS FOR SELECTED OFFENSES

ITEM	GEOMETRIC MEAN
A person under 16 years old plays hooky from school	5.4
A person has some marijuana for his own use	29.3
A person knowingly carries an illegal knife	53.4
A person carries a gun, illegally	101.6
A person threatens to seriously injure a victim	203.3
A man beats his wife with his fists. She requires hospitalization	400.8
A woman stabs her husband. As a result, he dies.	611.1
A person robs a victim at gunpoint. The victim struggles and is shot to death.	946.1
A person plants a bomb in a public building. The bomb explodes and 20 people are killed.	1,577.5

Source: Wolfgang, et al., 1985a, Table 29, pp. 47–50.

for the West region and for the state of California, are shown for "Injury resulting in death" broken down by demographics, including victimization experience. Table 5.4 compares the states of California and Maryland and the cities of Sacramento, CA, and Washington, D.C. for the same injury category.

TABLE 5.2. "SOUTH" CENSUS REGION:
GEOMETRIC MEANS FOR PERCEIVED SEVERITY OF CRIMES CAUSING
DEATH, BY INCOME AND OCCUPATION CLASSES

OCCUPATION	INCOME CLASS					
	Under $3,000	$3,000–7,499	$7,500–9,999	$10,000–14,999	$15,000–24,999	$25,000+
White collar	666.24	783.01	643.71	888.09	941.90	1577.27
Blue collar	443.41	494.21	488.51	498.85	761.46	1050.31
Farm	255.93	206.07	325.13	422.76	780.91	1808.30
Service	474.48	291.57	682.26	687.76	526.30	958.58
Not available	223.24	502.17	809.55	865.69	680.84	723.83

Source: Wolfgang, et al., 1985a, Tables 126–130, pp. 102–104.

Note: Comparable U.S. geometric mean = 778.37.

Following a comprehensive review of the survey *Sourcebook* (Wolfgang et al., 1985b) and the survey report proper, one survey offense representative of homicide was selected for more detailed investigation. The survey description was "a person stabs a victim to death", which recorded a national geometric mean of 781.37. The geographic scale selected was the federal region, essentially a compromise between the state level,

TABLE 5.3. SEVERITY RATIOS: WEST CENSUS REGION AND CALIFORNIA (ITEM: "INJURY, DEATH")

RACE

	White	Black	Other
West	54.8	27.9	27.7
CA	63.7	25.5	47.2

AGE

	18–19	20–24	25–34	50–64	65+
West	39.5	48.6	56.1	50.3	48.5
CA	(18–24: 52.1)	(25–34: 65.5)	(35–49: 56.1)	(501: 59.1)	

GENDER

	M	F
West	53.1	50.5
CA	56.8	60.3

OCCUPATION

	White Collar	Blue Collar	Farm	Armed Forces
West	66.9	38.6	35.7	30.6
CA	76.4	38.0	(Service: 50.7)	

EDUCATION

	No Kinder-garten	Grade 1–11	Grade 12	Grade T12
West	48.1	29.9	39.3	81.0
CA		(t12: 37.0)	39.6	90.3

INCOME

	$3K	3–7.49K	7.5–9.9K	10–14.9K	15–24.9K	25K+
West	48.6	38.3	47.1	51.0	57.0	57.4
CA	(t7.49K: 51.9)		44.6	55.6	(15K1: 64.5)	

VICTIMIZATION EXPERIENCE

	Not Vict.	Vict.	Prop. Crime Only	Pers. Crime Only	Property & Personal
West	47.6	65.0	67.1	35.9	84.6
CA	55.7	66.7	71.5	38.4	67.3

Source: Data from Wolfgang, et al., 1985b.

where sample sizes raised questions about standard errors of scores, and the census regions. The federal regions provided the marginal advantage of 10 subdivisions compared to 9 census subregions. Geometric means from the ten regions were rank-ordered. Simple cluster analysis of the scores indicated three "natural" groups, and these were mapped (Figure 5.2). Regions I, VII, and V were statistically indistinguishable, separated by only 1.5 points. The lowest scores, indicating lower perceived severity, occurred in the South and East, with region VI (Texas, New Mexico,

TABLE 5.4. SAMPLE SIZES, GEOMETRIC MEANS, AND SEVERITY RATIOS, SELECTED STATES AND SMAs (INJURY RESULTING IN DEATH)

CALIFORNIA

Sample Size	Geometric Mean	Severity Ratio
1311	1140.7	58.4

MARYLAND

Sample Size	Geometric Mean	Severity Ratio
262	841.2	32.3

SACRAMENTO

Sample Size	Geometric Mean	Severity Ratio
63	845.5	49.4

WASHINGTON D.C./VA/MD

Sample Size	Geometric Mean	Severity Ratio
187	963.2	54.3

Source: Data from Wolfgang, et al., 1985b.

Oklahoma, Arkansas, and Louisiana) recording a geometric mean of 590.0 compared to 1,062.1 for region IX (California, Nevada, Arizona).

The low scores in the South were to be expected given the national relationship between socioeconomic status and perceived severity, and the consistently low per capita income of the South (census) region (US Bureau of the Census, 1986). The "core" low score regions were, in ascending order, VI, IV, II, and III. Why does the New York cluster resemble the Southern cluster? One possibility is that sampling error may have contributed to some apparent inconsistencies. Survey data suggested that sample sizes may have fallen below desirable levels (increasing standard errors) in some situations, and heterogeneity in subgroups (e.g., teenagers in the Northeast) may have contributed to anomalies at the subnational level. Furthermore, in parts of the New York cluster (e.g., New York City), serious violence is so commonplace that survey respondents may have been inured against it, thus tending to respond with lower severity scores.

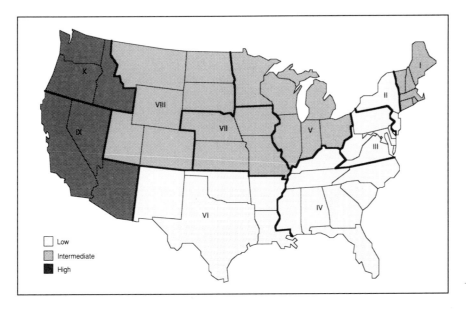

Figure 5.2. Upper, middle, and lower clusters of geometric means for the *NSCS* description "a person stabs a victim to death", by federal regions. *Source:* Data from Wolfgang, et al., 1985a, Appendix C, Table C-4, pp. 162–164.

MEDIATING FACTORS

Although various studies have minimized or denied the role of cultural or subcultural factors in southern violence (Chapter 4), the translation of perceptions of seriousness into the administration of justice in the South may be mediated by broadly accepted distinctive regional factors such as fundamentalist religious values, attitudes of whites toward blacks, and a complex of social and economic attributes. Even if the apparently cultural factors are actually expressions of underlying structural variables, the conditions are to some degree focused in the South and are identified with the South in popular perception. Homicides in the South, for example, tend to be disproportionately "primary" or "expressive", in which the objective is the injury of another person, compared to "secondary" (or "instrumental"), in which the homicide is committed in the course of another crime. In 1979, the rate of primary homicides per 100,000 persons in the South (9.1) was almost double that of the next ranking region, the West (5.5). For the Northeast region the comparable rate was 3.1 (Jason, Strauss, & Tyler, 1983). Also, firearm involvement is more likely than in the nonsouth (FBI, 1986).[2]

Religion

Analysis of religious interpretations of capital punishment shows the existence of substantial biblical justification as well as some contradiction. Evangelical denominations, such as the powerful Southern Baptist Convention, regard the Bible as having absolute authority (Marsden, 1987). A literal reading finds support in, for example, "He that smiteth a man so that he may die, shall surely be put to death" (Exodus 21:12) and "He who kills a man shall be put to death (Leviticus 24:17). On the other hand, "Thou shall not kill" (Exodus 20:13). The attitude of Southern Baptists may be epitomized by their historical acceptance of lynching, in spite of official opposition by the Convention. Miller, for example, cited an analysis of Southern Baptist association meetings in whose districts lynchings had occurred in the preceding 30 to 120 days. Of 117 such meetings, a local lynching was referred to in only one. By and large, drunkenness was regarded as a greater evil than lynching (Miller, 1958). In general, the Bible provides ample support for capital punishment. Clerics who oppose it on religious grounds are compelled to rely primarily on inferences based on Jesus' teaching of forgiveness of injustice, the imperative of reconciliation, and the idea that humans are created in the image of God (Bender & Leone, 1986). Given that evangelical denominations are regionally strongest in the South, it is to be expected that capital punishment would receive its strongest tacit acquiescence, if not overt support, there.

Racial Discrimination

Evidence that capital punishment has been applied in a racially discriminatory manner is overwhelming. The fact that 54.6 percent of the 3,959 executions between 1930 and 1972 were of African Americans does not in itself prove discrimination. However, research has shown that blacks have indeed been disproportionately sentenced to death (Radelet & Vandiver, 1986; Wolfgang & Reidel, 1975). In addition, homicides involving black offender and black victim have been less likely to attract

---

[2]See O'Connor and Lizotte (1979), Wright, Rossi, and Daly (1983) and related discussion in Chapter 4.

the death penalty, black offender-white victim more likely. Many executions have actually been administered as a penalty for rape rather than murder. In the period 1930–72, 89.5 percent of 455 rape executions were of African Americans, and all those executions were in southern or border states. In six jurisdictions—Louisiana, Mississippi, Oklahoma, Virginia, West Virginia, and the District of Columbia, there were no executions of whites for rape in the 42 years, compared to 66 blacks. In *Furman v Georgia,* Justices Douglas and Marshall explicitly drew attention to discrimination in the administration of the death penalty (Wolfgang & Reidel, 1975; Sellin, 1967). Evidence of discriminatory sentencing has continued to accumulate since *Furman v Georgia* (Anon., 1988).

CONCLUSION

Research has suggested that fear of crime victimization, and peoples' experience as crime victims, are better predictors of willingness to impose the death penalty compared to "abstract attitudes toward the criminal justice system" (Seltzer & McCormick, 1987). In this respect, the high rate of executions in the South is consistent, given that the probability of victimization is highest there. On the other hand, the relationship between perceived seriousness of crimes leading to death, and punishment meted out in the South, is paradoxical. Southerners, in their responses to the NSCS, said that serious violence is (relatively) less serious, and yet the most severe penalty has been administered frequently there.

An alternate, and perhaps more plausible explanation of the observed patterns is that lower perceived severity scores in the South are consistent with high rates of capital punishment because the severity of capital punishment is perceived to be less in the South compared to the nonsouth, given that execution is merely one of many ways in which human life can be taken. This interpretation finds support in Reed's view that southerners do not recognize the violence around them; it is an accepted part of life (Reed, 1982). Given the apparent link between perceived seriousness and SES, one may speculate that perceived seriousness will increase as per capita income rises in the South. The extent to which the overlay of fundamentalist religion and racial discrimination will inhibit up-leveling of southern severity scores as SES increases is open to speculation.

In the longer term, research on spatial variations in seriousness will occur at multiple scales of resolution. Regional analysis has a place, in terms of assessment of both aggregate levels of severity and related regional dynamics. At any scale, studies of crime should routinely apply severity weights when multiple crime categories are under consideration, in order to capture an image of crime more consonant with public perception.

LEGAL CASES CITED

Furman v. Georgia, 408 U.S. 238 1972.
Roe v. Wade, 410 U.S. 113 1973.

Chapter 6

HOMICIDE IN CITIES

In this chapter, we move from the very general regional scale to the sharper focus of comparisons between cities and a brief glimpse within one city: Washington, D.C. In the course of this discussion, we touch on the nature of the urban context of homicide, including fear of violence, and look more closely at the phenomenon of African American homicide. Homicide in ten large cities provides a comparative perspective to make the point that homicide differs quantitatively and qualitatively depending on the context and the way in which that context is measured.

When public attention is drawn to homicide and other serious forms of violence, the setting most often implicated is urban rather than suburban or rural. In public perception, the inner city is synonymous with fear and violence. The sheer volume of violence in American cities is overwhelming and frightening. New York City, for example, typically has more homicides in a year than Japan. The level of lifetime homicide risk for an urban resident in America has been calculated at 1 in 68 (Barnett & Schwartz, 1989). Comparable general levels of risk are (1 in) 153 for the U.S. as a whole, 100 for males (164 for whites and 28 for blacks) and 323 for females, broken down as 450 for whites and 117 for blacks (Langan & Innes, 1985). Although some rural areas, notably parts of the West, have high rates of violent death by various means including vehicle accidents, population-specific rates of violent crime as well as the absolute volume of violence in many cities are both extraordinarily high. If we examine certain age-sex cohorts in specific cities, the magnitude of the impact on, for example, young African American males, is put into even sharper focus.

Initially, however, attention should be drawn explicitly to an essentially mechanical question: the effects of boundaries on the way in which violence is perceived. In many situations, our statistical view of what is happening in a place is heavily influenced by the way that place or area is defined, that is, by its boundaries. This is an important issue in the

103

ecological perspective, given that boundaries around cities, census tracts, or even neighborhoods, may have been idiosyncratically conceived in the first place, or simply became functionally obsolete as the urban scene changed but the boundaries did not.

TABLE 6.1. SELECTED SOCIAL CONDITIONS IN BALTIMORE'S POLICE DISTRICT 4, COMPARED TO THE CITY AND METROPOLITAN STATISTICAL AREA

CONDITION	AREA		
	MSA	City	Area 4
Black (%)	25.5	54.8	98.1
Median household income	18,939	12,811	8,453
Median family income	21,794	15,721	9,819
Unemployed (%)	7.5	9.2	9.7
Old housing (t1940, %)	27.7	50.3	74.9
Persons per household	2.8	2.7	3.1
1.01 or more persons per room (%)	3.0	5.0	8.5
Persons below poverty level (%)	11.9	22.9	41.2

Data Sources: MSA, City data: U.S. Bureau of the Census, *State and Metropolitan Area Data Book, 1986.* Washington D.C., U.S.G.P.O., 1986. Area 4: U.S. Bureau of the Census, 1980, *Census of Population and Housing, Census Tracts, Baltimore, MD., SMSA.* PHC80-2-82. Washington D.C., U.S.G.P.O., 1983.

Notes to Tables in Chapter 6
1. Data refer only to the first identified victim or offender in each reported case. 2. Columns sum to approximately 100 in Tables 6.2–6.4 and 6.6–6.12. Differences from 100 are due to rounding. 3. Source of Tables 6.2–6.4 and 6.6–6.12 is analysis by author.

Source: Harries, 1987a.

GEOGRAPHY OF REPORTING AFFECTS RATES

Thus comparisons between places according to their crime rates, including rates of violence, may be misleading owing to the effects of geographic boundaries underlying the reporting process. When city boundaries happen to delimit an older core area with much substandard housing and a large proportion of poor minorities, crime rates are relatively high. Baltimore, St. Louis, and Washington, D.C. are examples. When city boundaries include a ring of newer, more affluent, suburbs, the effect is to "dilute" the higher crime rates of the "inner" city, giving a lower overall rate.[1] Los Angeles is an example of this type of boundary effect. This can be illustrated by data showing the social characteristics for a selected area of Baltimore (Table 6.1). Although Area 4 is part of the city and part of the metropolitan statistical area, the statistics describing it show it to be much more stressed than other areas. It is poorer, more crowded, has a lower level of employment, and older housing. Using the criterion of at least 20 percent below the poverty level as a definition of *underclass,* Area 4 is typical of underclass neighborhoods in inner cities across the country. It is also typical in that it experiences high levels of violence. Ideally, violence and other crimes should be studied at the largest possible geographic scale, i.e., in terms of the smallest areas. In practice, the city block is the smallest such unit feasible.

CONTEXT

The geography of violence is composed of several complexes of variables, some components of which, such as the elusive "culture," are controversial in that their contribution remains in doubt and may be more accepted in popular myth or folklore than in social science. Some have their roots at the national level in such phenomena as welfare policies, unemployment compensation, or supports for failing industries. National cultural traits might be implicated—a love of violence, a propensity to own firearms, media saturated with violent images, widespread abuse of drugs including alcohol, or ubiquitous racial and ethnic prejudice. Others are of a regional nature and may reflect elusive regional cultural phenomena alluded to in Chapter 4. Many would agree that the regional concept itself is ambiguous, with some arguing that census regions are acceptable as a basis for analysis, and others suggesting that even a state is much too large an area to be regarded as the possessor of a single culture. Intrastate cultural differences are often alluded to in the media and elsewhere—the difference between Northern and Southern California, between East Texas and West Texas, North Florida and South Florida, Oklahoma's "Little Dixie" and the rest of that state, Maryland's Eastern Shore compared to the Baltimore–Washington corridor, upstate Illinois compared to downstate, and so on. Whether perceived regional varia-

---

[1]For further discussion in the context of Stockholm, see Wickstrom (1985).

tions at this level have any independent meaning for rates of violence is unknown. As Chapter 4 indicated, essentially all the research on regions has operationalized them quite crudely, often with indicators for blocks of states. It is popularly believed that intrastate variations in culture (which may in reality be little more than intrastate variations in economic health, or perhaps more precisely—economic history) are responsible for differences in behavior.

Layered Interacting Stimuli

As the zoom lens moves in, metropolitan areas and finally cities and their subareas—communities, neighborhoods, city blocks—are seen as presenting conditions more or less conducive to violence. Each person exists in an extraordinarily complex environment of layered interacting stimuli, at the household, neighborhood, urban, metropolitan, regional, national, and even international levels. These stimuli may be positive or negative in the sense that they may contribute to a person's development and well-being, or may be destructive to the individual in some respects. In short, they may be more or less stressful. Stimuli depriving a person of livelihood or of family or other relationships of importance, or denying other customary aspects of lifestyle, such as food or religion, will tend to produce stress which may become manifested in antisocial behavior; some may be violent. Thus economic and/or social deprivation may translate into some form of violence.

The Geography of Stress

The critical question is: where is stress concentrated? Consistent with the polarization of American society, we find that the most deprived urban neighborhoods are usually limited in spatial extent, but are the repositories of a highly disproportionate amount of violence. The spatial coincidence between the geography of the underclass and the geography of serious violence is immediately apparent in the course of any field or map-based research. As Wilson, et al., (1988) have noted, poverty has become more *concentrated.* Between 1969 and 1985, the poverty population in central cities rose 77 percent and the percentage of inner city residents in poverty increased from 13 to 19 percent. In 1990, about 52 million Americans (about 20%) lived in a "poverty area"[2] (Bureau of the Census, 1995). Some suggest that such statistics exaggerate poverty by failing to take into account noncash income such as food stamps. However, the real value of AFDC (Aid to Families with Dependent Children) and food stamps declined 22 percent between 1972 and 1984 owing to the failure of the states to index such benefits to inflation. Urban poverty areas (census tracts with at least 20% below the poverty line) increased by 90 percent from 4.1 million to 7.8 million in the period 1974–85. *Extreme* poverty areas (where the rate of poverty exceeded 40%) doubled in population in the 1970–80 decade, and in 1990 about 4 percent of Americans lived in extreme poverty areas. In Chicago, for example, the total population of the city declined by about ten percent between 1970 and 1980, yet poverty expanded geographically and its incidence increased. This increased concentration has been due to the outmigration of the non-poor during a period of declining job opportunities, particularly in manufacturing where minorities tended to be employed. The ghetto in Chicago, noted Wilson et al. (1988) has gone from being *institutional* (i.e., a mirror of the larger society) to *physical*, lacking basic services and opportunities. The African American middle class has moved out, taking with it business for banks, retailers, physicians, and others. Those who are left:

> ... represent almost exclusively the most disadvantaged and oppressed segments of the urban black population—including those families that have experienced long-term spells of poverty and/or welfare receipt, individuals who lack minimal training and skills and have suffered periods of recurrent and persistent unemployment, adults who have dropped out of the labor force altogether, *and those who are routinely involved in the underground economy or resort to street crime as a means of survival.* (Wilson, et al., 1988:146; emphasis added.)

Fear, Violence and Stress

Fear of violence is a source of stress with major impact in urban settings. Research has shown that more dangerous environments do indeed inspire more fear (Smith, 1987). The idea that fear is heightened by higher levels of crime has been called the *victimization model* (Greenberg,

---

[2]Poverty areas are defined as census tracts or block numbering areas (BNAs) with at least 20 percent of the residents below the poverty line (in 1989 for the 1990 Census).

1986). Neighborhood disorder and deterioration tend to be linked to fear of crime, if only because declining neighborhoods are, by and large, high crime areas. However, the relationship between fear and victimization is not a simple one; there is evidence of the independence of fear from victimization, both in the U.S. and Britain (Greenberg, 1986; Smith, 1986). While fear is affected by victimization experience, and the rate of crime, the incidence of fear is greater than those factors would predict.

The *vulnerability* model incorporates the relationship between personal characteristics and fear. For example, the elderly, women, African Americans and the poor tend to have higher levels of fear, particularly in larger cities. Such groups are more vulnerable in terms of both the *social* and *physical* dimensions of vulnerability. They are physically vulnerable owing to lack of strength or agility. The elderly are particularly vulnerable socially owing to their isolation (Skogan and Maxfield, 1981). A report on crime in Washington, D.C. noted that fear of crime during an epidemic of drug-related killings in 1988 had turned some elderly into virtual hermits, although their risk of being victimized was actually quite low (Sinclair, 1988).

A third model, emphasizing *social control,* suggests that fear originates in the perception of breakdown of social control rather than in the crime rate itself (Greenberg, 1986). In this model, neighborhood discussion of crime and personal familiarity with victims tends to amplify fear of crime. Paradoxically, close-knit communities in which information is communicated rapidly and where levels of crime tend to be relatively low, tend to amplify fear most effectively. Some forms of the built environment have been linked to greater fear. Larger structures and high rise buildings appear to be associated with higher levels of fear than smaller buildings. Litter, vandalism, drunkenness and other incivilities have been shown to contribute to increased levels of fear. Racial and ethnic conflicts, too, have compounded the fear problem.

Research on fear in public housing has shown that all three models could be supported, but the social control model provided the strongest predictive power (Rohe & Burby, 1988). Fear has been shown to interact with other factors to accelerate neighborhood decline and reinforce both fear itself and conditions conducive to crime. Skogan (1986) has identified six such "feedback processes": the withdrawal of people from the life of the community, the breakdown of informal social control and neighborhood organization, business decline, the spread of delinquency, and population change. These changes culminate in "demographic collapse."

From a geographic perspective, an effect of fear is to reduce the role of territoriality or surveillance, the quasi-proprietorial feeling that people have about their neighborhood. As they feel more threatened, people "pull back" and concentrate on defending their immediate personal space—the home and its environs. Public spaces are, in effect, abandoned, conceded to vandals and others.

Smith (1986) concluded that fear expresses several characteristics of the inner city: low economic status, social disruption and isolation, and political marginality—a constellation of problems fundamentally associated with lack of power. Greenberg (1986) concluded that strengthening social networks, improving economic health and reducing victimization, are all necessary to achieve a reduction in fear.

Fear is a phenomenon that is in part a product of violence in the city. Given that fear has profound negative consequences such as stress, breakdown of neighborhood cohesiveness, and out-migration (Rohe & Burby, 1988), it must be recognized as part of the complex of conditions accompanying urban violence. Just as violence has its distinctive geography, so does fear. As the research suggests, the fear pattern may not correspond perfectly to the violence pattern, but they are likely to be similarly distributed, with peaks in the actual incidence of violence frequently, though not inevitably, matching peaks in the incidence of fear (see Smith and Patterson, 1980).

AFRICAN AMERICANS AND HOMICIDE

Mapping homicide clusters in major cities shows the spatial coincidence between the predominantly black underclass and violence (see Figures 3.1, 3.2, and 6.1). A regression analysis of homicide in Detroit for 1970, for example, showed that the levels of divorced females, female-headed households, and family income were the most important explanatory variables for homicide, emphasizing the roles of family instability and poverty. In St. Louis, too, homicide was linked to lower income environments including those containing large public housing units (Rose, 1977). McClain (1984) identified families below poverty level, migrant population, African American male population aged 15–24, African American male unemployment, vacant housing units, and household crowding as environmental factors most frequently incorporated in studies of African American homicide.

The overwhelming empirical evidence is that, in the United States, poverty and its associated conditions and processes are strongly implicated as the principal correlates of violence clusters. Even in the light of this often repeated pattern, care must be taken with assumptions about ultimate causes. Is poverty the ultimate cause of violence? Complete separation, not to say measurement, of competing causes of violence is difficult, but the disproportionate concentration of violence in poor African American communities strongly suggests the underlying role of racism in the production of the poverty linked to violence; this racism has its roots in the "unique history of slavery and oppression" of American blacks (Hawkins, 1986:119). However, the relationship is complex; the long history of denial of opportunity for African Americans contributed (and continues to contribute) to poverty, which constitutes the source of stresses thought to lead more directly to violence—what Harvey (1986) has called "the subculture of exasperation." Poverty is also self-reinforcing in that the poor are less able to grasp educational opportunities and therefore more likely to remain locked in the cycle of poverty. What is clear is that inner-city violence cannot be separated in the causal chain from conditions in the larger society. Analysis in Chicago, for example, has shown that the underclass phenomenon is becoming more conspicuous owing to the restructuring of the local economy. This transformation is rooted in changes in the form of capitalism in America resulting in substantial increases in unemployment among the less educated. The process of increasing spatial concentration of the very poor has been termed *hyperghettoization.* In marked contrast to conservative interpretations of the ghetto, focusing on moral issues, it is demonstrable that ghetto conditions are attributable to forces operating outside the ghetto domain (Wacquant & Wilson, 1989).

Data from the Supplementary Homicide Reports (SHR) (F.B.I., n.d.) aggregated for ten large cities for the period 1976–83 help illustrate some salient features of homicide and race. The cities are: Atlanta, Baltimore, Chicago, Cleveland, Detroit, Los Angeles, Miami, New York, Philadelphia, and Washington, D.C. They accounted for over 40,000 homicides in the eight years under review, out of a national total of 155,267 (26%). Cumulatively, the cities' populations were 34 percent African American, but black victims accounted for 61 percent of the total, and (known) black offenders 44 percent. Black victims were more likely to be attacked with a firearm compared to white victims, implying a general environment of greater dangerousness in some African American communities (Table 6.2). Among firearms, the handgun has become the main instrument and has grown in popularity in a short time (Rose and Deskins, 1986). In 53 percent of the 40,797 killings in the ten-city sample, a handgun was the weapon of choice.

TABLE 6.2. WEAPONS USED AGAINST VICTIMS, BY RACE, 1976–83 (%)

WEAPON	*RACE*			
	Black	*Other*	*Unknown*	*White*
Hand Gun	54.65	47.39	59.80	49.89
Other Gun	9.38	9.43	2.97	8.90
Knife	22.33	22.83	20.76	21.94
Personal	5.29	7.44	6.10	8.13
Blunt Object	4.09	6.70	2.47	5.24
Other	4.26	6.20	7.91	5.90
TOTAL N	24,793	403	607	14,994

African Americans were much more likely to be victimized by a family member or other person known to them, while whites were more likely to be victimized by strangers. However, these relationships are problematical owing to the large proportion of cases in which the relationship was unknown (Table 6.3). If those cases are a random sample of the other categories, then the tabulated distribution is representative. If the "unknowns" are biased, however, the table may be inaccurate. If reality is reflected in the table, the greater exposure of African Americans to known assailants may be attributable to heightened social interaction among intimates due to high levels of unemployment, compounded by the introduction of drugs and/or alcohol. High levels of teen pregnancy and the presence of many children increase costs and stresses. Further stress is introduced by the shortage of "family-sustaining" jobs or job prospects, preventing the formation of traditional, independent families (Anderson, 1989). Crowded and substandard housing, too, may contribute to social stresses, although density and crowding are probably over-implicated in the generation of violence (see: Baldassare, 1979; Freedman, 1975). Staples (1986) has pointed out that African American children are likely to be socialized into violence, with early exposure to robbery, rape, and other incidents. Furthermore, sexual aggression and spouse assault are overrepresented in poor African American communities.

The relatively high level of involvement of African Americans in

**TABLE 6.3. RELATIONSHIP OF VICTIM TO OFFENDER,
BY RACE, 1976–83 (%) (N 3 40,797)**

RELATIONSHIP	RACE		
	Black	Other	White
Family	11.84	4.55	7.44
Known	36.04	14.65	23.81
Stranger	15.96	21.78	21.54
Unknown	36.16	59.01	47.21
TOTAL N	24,793	1,010	14,994

violence among family and acquaintances is further reflected in the distinction between *felony* and *nonfelony* homicides. The felony type refers to homicides performed in the course of commission of other crimes, including rape, robbery, narcotics violations, arson, and gambling. Nonfelony murders cover arguments, fights due to the influence of drugs or narcotics, lover's triangles, gang killings, and other comparable events (Fox & Pierce, 1987). Blacks are significantly more involved in the nonfelony type as the data on relationships (Table 6.3) already suggested (Table 6.4).

TABLE 6.4. HOMICIDE CIRCUMSTANCES, BY RACE, 1976–83 (%) (N 3 41,404)

CIRCUMSTANCES	RACE			
	Black	Other	Unknown	White
Felony	16.44	38.21	21.42	24.20
Non-felony	52.95	31.27	26.69	41.26
Suspected felony	5.10	9.93	4.12	8.01
Justified homicide	5.79	2.73	3.46	3.92
Unknown	19.72	17.87	44.32	22.62
TOTAL N	24,793	1,010	607	14,994

Conspicuous differences on the basis of race also appear with respect to victim and offender ages and drug involvement. When the ages of victims and offenders were subdivided into three categories, 0–19, 20–29, and 30+, blacks were more heavily involved in the 20–29 category, compared to whites, illustrating the well-known fact that young blacks (particularly males) are at very high risk from homicide, a phenomenon attributed to "the persistent difficulty black males have in obtaining a viable masculine identity" (Humphrey & Palmer, 1986:65). O'Carroll and Mercy (1986) noted that the homicide rate for African American males aged 25–29 was 99.8/100,000 in 1983, the highest of any age or race cohort. The comparable rate for whites in the same category was 15.3 (see also Dennis, 1979). Detailed review of African American homicide victims by age revealed 25 as the modal year, with 2.6 percent of the incidents, followed by ages 26 and 27 (both 2.4%). The modal age of (known) offenders was 20 (2.1%) with age 21 accounting for 2 percent.

The drug epidemic beginning in the mid-to-late 1980s was not reflected in data for 1976–83; only 1.8 percent of the 40,000 incidents in the ten cities were identified as felony-type involving narcotics and drug laws. In those incidents, however, 70 percent of the victims were African American. Blacks were more likely than other racial groups to be involved in a homicidal brawl related to the influence of narcotics, while American indians and whites, respectively, were proportionately more involved in brawls attributable to alcohol.

Homicide in Washington, D.C.

The relationship between underclass conditions involving the African American community is illustrated clearly with respect to Washington, D.C. (Figure 6.1). Some 691 homicides were recorded in Washington between January, 1985 and June, 1988, a period of relatively *low* homicide rates, preceding the escalation of homicide with the spread of crack cocaine in 1988[3]. Fourteen census tracts experienced 10 or more homicides during this period. One tract (# 37) had 21 incidents among a (1980) population of 4,764, yielding a rate of 126/100,000 per year for the 3.5 year period, as follows:

$$(21/(4,764/100,000))/3.5 = 125.94$$

This compared to national rates averaging 8.3/100,000 for 1985–87. The 14 tracts were on average 94 percent black. Some 55 percent of the residents were at or below 200 percent below the poverty level,[4] and

---

[3]Through 1987, homicides in D.C. had not exceeded 250. After jumping to 369 in 1988, the total then exceeded 400 annually in the period 1989–93, dropping to 399 in 1994, then 360 in 1995 (Bowles, 1995; Castenada and Pan, 1996).

[4]Poverty level family income for a family of four in 1979 was $7,412. The 200 percent level was therefore $14,824.

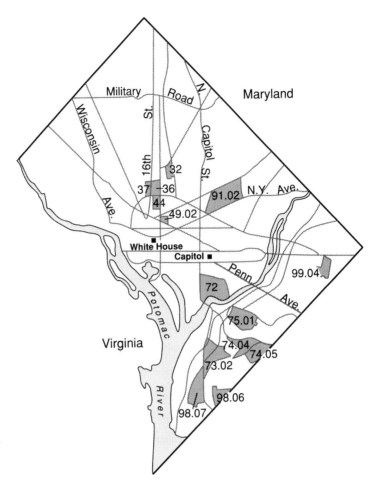

Figure 6.1. High homicide census tracts in Washington D.C., 1985–June, 1988. *Sources:* U.S. Department of Commerce, Bureau of the Census, 1980 Census of Population and Housing, Census Tracts, Washington D.C.-MD–VA SMSA PHC80-2-365, July, 1983; OCJP, 1988.

51 percent of the families were headed by females. In tract # 72, where 13 homicides occurred, 76 percent were at least 200 percent below the poverty level (Bureau of the Census, 1983; OCJPA, 1988). Part of tract # 99.04 achieved national notoriety as what *US News and World Report* called "the Drake Place combat zone," home to a housing project that saw 8 homicides, 92 (reported) assaults, 65 auto thefts, 154 drug arrests, and 27 robberies in calendar year 1988 (Moore, et al., 1989; see Chapter 8 for more detail). This staggering toll occurred in an area with a nominal 1980 base population of 4,056 of which 99 percent were African

American, and 50 percent at least 200 percent below the poverty level. Some 55 percent of the families were headed by females.

One of the tracts—# 49.02—where there were also 13 homicides, is a mile from the White House. Sixty-seven percent of the people were at least 200 percent below the poverty level. This may exemplify one of the sharpest gradients in quality of life anywhere in America. A similar contrast is seen at the other end of Pennsylvania Avenue where tract # 72 (14 homicides) is a mile from Capitol Hill. The inability of the Congress to enact effective anti-poverty legislation is some indication of the political and social—if not geographic—distance of African Americans from the seats of power.

HOMICIDE IN THE TEN CITIES

Having examined some aspect of the relationship between race on violence in aggregate terms for ten large cities, we turn now to a somewhat disaggregated view across a range of attributes having bearing on violence for the same set of cities. Initially, the demographic characteristics of victims are discussed—race, gender, and age. Then victim-offender relationships, weapons, homicide circumstances, and finally drug-related events are explored.

TABLE 6.5. BLACK POPULATION IN TEN CITIES, 1980

CITY	*TOTAL (000)*	*BLACK (000)*	*% BLACK*	*RANK*
Washington DC	638	448	70	1
Atlanta	425	283	67	2
Detroit	1,203	759	63	3
Baltimore	787	431	55	4
Cleveland	574	251	44	5
Chicago	3,005	1,197	40	6
Philadelphia	1,688	639	38	7
Miami	347	87	25	83
New York	7,072	1,784	25	83
Los Angeles	2,967	505	17	10

Source: 1980 Census of Population.

TABLE 6.6. RACE OF HOMICIDE VICTIMS AND OFFENDERS
IN TEN CITIES, 1976–83 (%).

(A) RACE OF VICTIM

RACE	CITY									
	ATL.	BALT.	CHI.	CLV.	DET.	L.A.	MI.	N.Y.	PHI.	DC
BLACK	79.82	76.23	68.40	70.23	81.23	43.31	46.50	47.66	75.46	87.51
OTHER	0.00	0.79	1.00	0.16	0.28	2.42	0.17	0.80	0.52	1.67
UNKNOWN	0.00	0.00	0.00	0.00	0.05	0.59	0.09	4.59	0.10	0.06
WHITE	20.18	22.98	30.61	29.61	18.45	53.69	53.24	46.95	23.92	10.75
TOTAL N	1,303	1,910	6,724	1,918	4,304	6,832	1,157	12,203	2,893	1,553

(B) RACE OF OFFENDER

RACE	CITY									
	ATL.	BALT.	CHI.	CLV.	DET.	L.A.	MI.	N.Y.	PHI.	DC
BLACK	60.40	52.41	55.61	53.86	57.37	35.16	38.29	28.89	61.56	48.36
OTHER	0.00	0.42	0.58	0.16	0.16	1.16	0.09	0.24	0.45	0.19
UNKNOWN	27.63	33.40	24.39	26.96	32.71	32.87	31.29	49.03	21.67	47.39
WHITE	11.97	13.77	19.42	19.03	9.76	30.81	30.34	21.84	16.32	4.06
TOTAL N	1,303	1,910	6,724	1,918	4,304	6,832	1,157	12,203	2,893	1,553

Race

Victim race, as one would expect, is strongly correlated with the racial composition of each city (Tables 6.5, 6.6). In Washington, D.C., for example, the population is about 70 percent African American and Washington recorded the highest percentage (88) of black victims. Atlanta and Detroit, other cities ranking high in terms of African American population, also had high proportions of black fatalities. On the other hand, Los Angeles, New York, and Miami, cities with much smaller African American percentages, recorded lower proportions of black victims, as anticipated. While a broad view of the relationship between a city's percent black and the percentage of black victims corresponds to expectations, one may ask why the percentages are not more or less identical.

Production Ratio

The ratio of the percentages of black homicide victims to black population (*"Production Ratio"*) can be calculated in order to provide a measure of the differential between expected and observed percentages. A value of 1.0 would indicate that the percent of victims is the same as the percent of the population that is African American, i.e., a theoretical expectation, other things being equal. A value >1.0 would indicate that the percent of homicide victims is higher than the African American population percent ("overproduction") and values <1.0 would express "underproduction."

No values are <1.0. The ratio actually varies from a high of 2.5 for Los Angeles to a low of 1.2 for Atlanta, indicating that, of the ten cities, Atlanta best approximates the theoretical expectation. The highest values of the ratio (Los Angeles, Philadelphia, New York, Miami) indicate an *excessively* disproportionate production of violence in the African American communities of those cities, given that in *all* the cities the percentage of black victims substantially exceeds the black proportion of the population. While detailed investigation of this excess production phenomenon is beyond the scope of this book, likely sources could lie in differences between the cities in terms of age/sex composition and in structural conditions such as proportion of the African American population below the poverty level, employment opportunities, and related factors. Income inequality, too, suggested by some as a source of intraurban stress, may be implicated, as may levels of gang activity and other distinctively local conditions embraced by the term "culture."

Offender data are consistently contaminated by the "unknown" category. However, if we adopt the reasonable assumption that the "unknown" approximate the known in their proportions, then the inference that African Americans also dominate the offender statistics in each city, at least on a *per capita* basis, is a plausible one. This notion is reinforced by the knowledge that most incidents are intraracial. If the Production Ratio is calculated for offender data, results predictably similar to those for victims are obtained, with the highest values for Los Angeles (2.07), Miami (1.53) and Philadelphia (1.62).

Gender

Table 6.7 reinforces the fact that males are disproportionately involved both as victims and offenders. For victims, the division between males and females was about 80-20 percent across the ten cities. For offenders, the picture is less clear owing to the fairly high and quite variable

TABLE 6.7. GENDER OF VICTIM AND OFFENDER IN TEN CITIES, 1976–83 (%).

(A) GENDER OF VICTIM

GENDER	CITY									
	ATL.	BALT.	CHI.	CLV.	DET.	L.A.	MI.	N.Y.	PHI.	DC
FEMALE	23.02	19.53	16.39	16.48	19.47	16.94	14.43	15.18	17.15	16.68
MALE	76.98	80.47	83.61	83.52	80.53	83.06	85.57	84.82	82.85	83.32
TOTAL N	1,303	1,910	6,724	1,918	4,304	6,831	1,157	12,194	2,892	1,553

(11 observations are missing.)

(B) GENDER OF OFFENDER

GENDER	CITY									
	ATL.	BALT.	CHI.	CLV.	DET.	L.A.	MI.	N.Y.	PHI.	DC
FEMALE	14.58	8.90	10.50	11.68	11.52	7.42	6.74	4.85	9.85	8.76
MALE	57.79	57.70	65.12	61.42	55.76	61.78	62.14	48.73	68.27	45.07
UNKNOWN	27.63	33.40	24.38	26.90	32.71	30.80	31.11	46.41	21.88	46.17
TOTAL N	1,303	1,910	6,724	1,918	4,304	6,832	1,157	12,203	2,893	1,553

**TABLE 6.8. AGES OF HOMICIDE VICTIMS AND OFFENDERS
IN TEN CITIES, 1976–83 (%).**

(A) VICTIM AGE

VICTIM	CITY									
	ATL.	BALT.	CHI.	CLV.	DET.	L.A.	MI.	N.Y.	PHI.	DC
0–19	9.44	13.14	15.85	9.96	12.31	14.71	8.12	13.13	14.41	9.47
20–29	31.39	37.23	38.36	34.78	34.83	36.67	30.86	33.39	34.74	32.45
301	58.71	49.32	45.55	55.21	52.76	47.61	60.07	51.47	50.78	57.50
UNKNOWN	0.46	0.31	0.24	0.05	0.09	1.01	0.95	2.01	0.07	0.58
TOTAL N	1,303	1,910	6,724	1,918	4,304	6,832	1,157	12,203	2,893	1,553

(B) OFFENDER AGE

AGE	CITY									
	ATL.	BALT.	CHI.	CLV.	DET.	L.A.	MI.	N.Y.	PHI.	DC
0–19	6.52	13.25	14.60	8.13	9.69	12.02	6.05	9.34	11.20	6.50
20–29	26.71	27.54	32.30	29.46	27.72	29.68	23.16	20.36	32.25	19.00
301	36.45	25.60	28.70	34.78	29.83	25.67	32.32	17.20	31.97	25.50
UNKNOWN	30.31	33.61	24.39	27.63	32.76	32.63	38.46	53.10	24.58	49.00
TOTAL N	1,303	1,910	6,724	1,918	4,304	6,832	1,157	12,203	2,893	1,553

proportion of offenders of unknown gender, although males dominate this population, too.

Age

Table 6.8 illustrates the consistent overinvolvement of the 20–29 age cohort, both as victims and offenders. In terms of specific ages, the general profile is similar, as would be expected, to the profile for blacks, with a clustering in the mid-twenties and a peak at age 25. Known offenders tended to be somewhat younger, with peaks at 20 and 25. As in the case of victim and offender gender, the "unknown" offender category appears to confound the data to some extent, although it is safe to assume that the proportion of unknown offenders that is in the 20–29 cohort is probably similar to that among the known offenders, again assuming that they are a representative sample of the known.

Since the 1976–83 period reviewed here, the "juvenilization" of homicide has escalated. Juvenile gang murders increased fourfold between 1980 and 1993, and the average age of persons arrested for murder declined. The rate of murder of 18–24 year-olds increased 14 percent between 1990 and 1993. In the 1990s, the 14–17-year-old cohort became a prominent component in the homicide picture (Thomas, 1995a).

**TABLE 6.9. RELATIONSHIP OF VICTIM TO OFFENDER
IN TEN CITIES, 1976–83 (%).**

RELATION-SHIP	CITY									
	ATL.	BALT.	CHI.	CLV.	DET.	L.A.	MI.	N.Y.	PHI.	DC
FAMILY	19.19	10.05	12.69	15.85	12.45	9.75	6.57	6.27	11.65	7.60
KNOWN	38.22	42.51	44.16	33.16	38.34	30.53	41.05	14.71	44.59	28.53
STRANGER	17.34	16.02	19.97	25.60	15.47	14.34	17.03	19.50	20.01	15.33
UNKNOWN	25.25	31.41	23.19	25.39	33.74	45.37	35.35	59.53	23.75	48.55
TOTAL N	1,303	1,910	6,724	1,918	4,304	6,832	1,157	12,203	2,893	1,553

Relationship of Victim to Offender

If conflicts between family members and other situations in which the victim and offender were known to each other (for example: neighbors, acquaintances, paramours, ex-spouses, employers or employees) are combined, it is clear that in all cities (with the possible exception of New York), the largest single category of relationships involved some degree of familiarity between victim and offender (Table 6.9). Variations between cities may be accounted for to a considerable extent by substantial differences in the "unknown" category. For example, New York was unable to account for relationship in 60 percent of its cases, compared to lows in this group of cities of 23 percent in Chicago and 24 percent in Philadelphia. Such large differences in SHR data have been attributed by Maxfield (1989) to organizational decision rules discouraging complete classification in New York. Overall, strangers accounted for only 18 percent of the incidents. Maxfield (1989) has argued that "stranger" percentages are probably *over*estimated in the SHR in that it is likely that the so-called strangers were in reality acquainted with each other.

TABLE 6.10. WEAPONS USED IN HOMICIDES IN TEN CITIES, 1976–83 (%).

WEAPON	*CITY*									
	ATL.	*BALT.*	*CHI.*	*CLV.*	*DET.*	*L.A.*	*MI.*	*N.Y.*	*PHI.*	*DC*
HAND GUN	57.41	50.37	56.04	63.56	50.63	42.80	62.14	54.97	51.23	56.34
OTHER GUN	8.52	7.85	7.54	11.37	17.33	18.59	9.77	3.02	6.19	3.41
KNIFE	18.34	27.59	22.04	11.57	16.80	22.85	12.79	24.78	26.65	22.28
PERSONAL	5.45	5.18	3.18	7.04	4.90	5.81	6.22	8.97	6.74	7.02
BLUNT OBJECT	4.37	4.19	6.14	3.60	5.55	5.12	3.72	3.13	4.53	5.09
OTHER	5.91	4.82	5.06	2.87	4.79	4.83	5.36	5.12	4.67	5.86
TOTAL N	1,303	1,910	6,724	1,918	4,304	6,832	1,157	12,203	2,893	1,553

Weapons

The clear preference for handguns as the instrument of homicide is reinforced by Table 6.10. Only in Los Angeles was the percentage of handguns below 50; in Miami it exceeded 60. When other firearms are included, the overwhelming dominance of guns is emphasized. This is to be expected for homicides compared to other forms of violence in that firearms are obviously more lethal. It is, of course, simply more difficult to kill with a blunt object, a knife, or a "personal" weapon (hands, fists, feet) than with a firearm. Over the ten cities, 62 percent of the incidents were due to firearms, a total of 25,300.

TABLE 6.11. HOMICIDE CIRCUMSTANCES IN TEN CITIES, 1976–83 (%).

CIRCUM-STANCES	CITY									
	ATL.	*BALT.*	*CHI.*	*CLV.*	*DET.*	*L.A.*	*MI.*	*N.Y.*	*PHI.*	*DC*
FELONY	18.73	27.49	19.05	14.86	19.68	22.97	18.76	18.21	13.93	25.37
NON-FELONY SUSPECTED	55.33	49.11	58.25	58.45	58.43	51.05	53.33	30.16	67.13	42.69
FELONY JUSTIFIED	0.38	3.25	10.53	1.62	3.95	20.37	7.17	0.34	0.38	1.80
HOMICIDE	4.45	3.46	8.72	4.80	4.55	5.52	4.93	3.43	4.94	3.99
UNKNOWN	21.11	16.70	3.45	20.28	13.38	0.09	15.82	47.87	13.62	26.14
TOTAL N	1,303	1,910	6,724	1,918	4,304	6,832	1,157	12,203	2,893	1,553

Circumstances

By and large, we would expect that the proportions of homicides in which victim and offender were known to each other should approximate the proportions of "nonfelony" homicides (Table 6.11) which are likely to involve assailants known to each other. Over the ten cities, differences in the nonfelony and known assailant percentages averaged 6.7 points, with the largest differences observed in Philadelphia and Los Angeles, the smallest in Chicago. Given that there are substantial "unknown" components, particularly in the relationship data, and that both felony and nonfelony homicides can "crossover" differences between "known" and "nonfelony" are to be expected. For example, the victim of a robbery resulting in a homicide may or may not be known to the offender, just as persons brawling due to the influence of narcotics or alcohol may or may not be known to each other. Furthermore, Maxfield (1989), has noted that the SHR are subject to distortion due to possibly premature local classification of "circumstance" and variations in decision rules used by police departments, referred to earlier.

TABLE 6.12. DRUG–RELATED HOMICIDES IN TEN CITIES, 1976–83 (%). (N = 40,797)

CITY	*ATL.*	*BALT.*	*CHI.*	*CLV.*	*DET.*	*L.A.*	*MI.*	*N.Y.*	*PHI.*	*DC*
FELONY DRUG	2.07	8.27	0.77	0.52	1.02	1.99	4.93	1.42	0.41	5.34

Drugs

In the time period under review, 1976–83, drugs were much less implicated in homicide than subsequently (Table 6.12). In no city were drug felonies (i.e., homicides committed in the course of violations of narcotics and drug laws) more than 8 percent of the total. Only two of the ten cities (Baltimore and Washington, D.C.) are prominent, with 8.27 and 5.34 percent respectively, although Baltimore data for a slightly different time period have been questioned by Maxfield (1989), who suggested that SHR coding errors may be responsible for the exceptionally high level of drug-related incidents and that robbery may be the better classification for many incidents labeled as drug-related (see also: Loftin, 1986). In the 1980s, the cocaine epidemic took hold, and it was symptomatic that by the late eighties, 26 percent of those tested who were arrested in homicide cases in Washington, D.C. tested positive for cocaine, 11 percent for PCP, and 7 percent for heroin or other opiates (OCJPA, 1988; see also Chapter 8).

In Philadelphia, less than one-half of 1 percent of homicides were attributed to drug felonies. While such statistics may seem so small as to be unbelievable in the context of the period 1985–95, they may be viewed as an indication of the extraordinary recent influence of drugs on patterns of violence.

CONCLUSION

Most homicides occur within cities, and the highest rates tend to occur in urban African American communities. Rate differences between cities may be due to substantive differences in local demographics, economic status, and perhaps cultural factors such as the prevalence of gangs, but may also be a reflection of boundary idiosyncracies or reporting and classification inconsistencies. In Los Angeles, for example, a substantial part of the African American community, including Watts, the source of the infamous so-called Watts Riot of 1965, is actually outside the city of Los Angeles. Thus, much of the violence erroneously attributed to the city is in fact a product of the County of Los Angeles or other subdivisions such as Compton. By the same token, a relatively low 35 percent of the homicide in Los Angeles is attributable to blacks for the simple reason that Los Angeles has a relatively small black population proportion (17%). However, the 35 percent indicated extreme over-production, given the size of the black population, as noted earlier in this chapter. New York and Miami are similar in this respect. Thus, the statistical picture of any city or neighborhood is in part a product of how boundary lines are drawn, and how people are arranged with respect to those lines.

Regardless of apparent variations in rates of violence between cities, a close-up view shows that the pathology of violence is usually focused in poor, often minority, areas. While fear is often exaggerated, the fact remains that such urban combat zones are extraordinarily violent by any comparative measure of cities in the more developed countries. A plausible theoretical position views *stress*, broadly interpreted, as the immediate, if not the ultimate source of violence. Conditions that have come to be associated with the underclass in America, encapsulated in the term *hyperghettoization*, are obviously stressful. Lacking mechanisms to alleviate the stress, its victims may resort to felonious remedies such as robbery, in the course of which violence may occur. Stress may also manifest itself in the form of interpersonal conflict generated, for example, by an argument between spouses over the allocation of scarce resources including money and space. Drug or alcohol abuse, too, may lead in turn to other complications, including violence.

Homicide among blacks is qualitatively different from that involving whites. This is not surprising given that the conditions under which African Americans find themselves are without parallel in the larger white community. The relationship between homicide and the underclass was illustrated with respect to Washington, D.C. where 14 census tracts— one a mile from the White House, another a mile from the U.S. Capitol— experienced 10 or more homicides in a 40-month period from January, 1985 through June, 1988.

Data for ten cities show that African American communities overproduce homicide in that the percentage of homicide incidents exceeds the black percentage of the population. Homicide in the cities, furthermore, is predominantly the province of younger males, both as victims and offenders. In at least 41 percent of incidents, victims and offenders were known to each other in some capacity. Firearms in general and handguns in particular are the overwhelming choices of homicide offenders. Prior to 1990, by far the single most important category of homicides in terms of circumstances was nonfelony, indicating the importance of conflicts between persons likely to be known to each other. However, this condition is changing, with a greater probability, in the mid-1990s, that homicide events are stranger-to-stranger, as noted in Chapter 3. The profile of homicides in ten cities also implied that drug involvement has rapidly escalated in recent years (see Chapter 8).

Chapter 7

ASSAULT ENVIRONMENTS

Chapter 3 made the point that homicide and assault are very similar in many respects and that numerous incidents of homicide would, in fact, have been classified as assaults had the victim survived as a result of a less lethal weapon or faster medical treatment. Homicide and assault can be regarded for many purposes as different locations on a continuum of violence; whether a given incident is one or the other is often a matter of chance. On the other hand, homicide and assault are not always identical in their attributes. As Dunn (1976) noted: "Although the intent of a small number of aggravated assaults may have been homicide, it is not warranted to assume the complete equivalency of aggravated assaults with homicide" (10). For example, assault is clearly seasonal, while homicide is not. (see Chapter 3).

Having focused most attention thus far on homicide, attention turns now to a closer look at aggravated assault, drawing in part on a relatively new body of environmentally-oriented research. In this context, "environment" is interpreted more narrowly than usual to mean part of the physical environment, specifically weather. This environmental research has dealt more or less exclusively with assault; the reason for this may not be immediately apparent. When serious violence is the subject of intraurban research, homicide has the distinct disadvantage from a statistical perspective that events are rare. This may seem like a peculiar remark, given that we are constantly assailed with information leading us to believe that homicides are actually very numerous. However, the probability of a homicide occurring in any given subarea of a city is quite small, particularly in a relatively short time period, such as one year.

In order to accumulate a large number of serious incidents of personal violence to represent urban patterns, analysts often turn to assault, for which many more cases are recorded. This provides a higher time-space density for statistical purposes and demands the accumulation of fewer years of data to achieve substantial incident counts which in turn imply sounder generalization. Assault is a more suitable research subject than rape or robbery. The former is too unreliably reported, and involves varying degrees of actual (as compared to threatened) violence so as to make it less satisfactory as a surrogate for serious violence. (This is not to imply that rape is not in itself violence, but it is a special kind of violence less representative of "generic" violence than assault.) Likewise, robbery is not as good a surrogate, principally owing to the highly variable degrees of violence actually occurring.

Intraurban detail for crime is often hard to obtain, necessitating as it does the cooperation of police departments and, in some cases, the funding necessary to pay for data acquisition. Given the strong resemblance between homicide and assault in many respects, including geography, assault is a reasonably acceptable analytical surrogate for serious violence in general. Furthermore, the US *National Survey of Crime Severity* (Wolfgang et al., 1985a) found that people assigned the highest seriousness scores to events involving physical violence or drugs (Bureau of Justice Statistics, 1983). Some 1,135,099 Americans were reportedly victims of aggravated assault in 1993 (a rate of 440/100,000), signifying vast aggregate medical costs, as well as untold psychological damages, and staggering losses of earnings (F.B.I., annual [1994]). This was also a substantial increase in rate from the 351/100,000 reported in 1987.

This chapter is organized around two themes. First, the "conventional" ecology of assault is outlined—place of occurrence, circumstances, and characteristics of victims and offenders. This perspective is illustrated with data from Baltimore. Second, discussion turns to the environmental perspective, drawing on recent contributions principally from geography and social psychology.

THE CONVENTIONAL ECOLOGY OF ASSAULT

Chapter 3 already established similarities between homicide and assault with respect to age, race, gender and locational patterns in a particular place. However, the comparisons done in Chapter 3 were limited to characteristics for which data were available for both homicide and assault in one city. When we look at data sources of broader scope, particularly the National Crime Survey (NCS), unfettered by the Chapter 3 need to match with homicide attributes, a more comprehensive view is possible. Since the NCS is a victimization survey, assault, unlike homicide, is included.

TABLE 7.1. PERCENT OF AGGRAVATED ASSAULTS REPORTED TO POLICE BY VICTIM CHARACTERISTICS, NCVS, 1992

VICTIM CHARACTERISTICS		AGGRAVATED ASSAULT REPORTED
Gender	Male	58
	Female	68
Race	White	63
	Black	59
Age	12–19	50
	20–34	64
	35–49	75
	50–64	64
	65 and above	69*

*Estimated

Source: Bureau of Justice Statistics, 1994, Tables 103, 104, 106.

The Reporting Issue

In contrast to homicide, which is better reported than any other crime, assault suffers considerable attrition between incidents and official reports. In 1993, for example, 53 percent of victimizations were reported to police. By and large, as incident seriousness increases, the probability of reporting increases. In 1993, an aggravated assault with injury was reported at the 58 percent level, compared to 31 percent for simple assaults without injury. The likelihood of reporting aggravated assaults varies with victim characteristics although relationships between attributes are not always consistent or clear-cut (Table 7.1). Females were more likely to report than males, blacks than whites, older than younger. Income and education relationships are more blurred. While one may expect that poorer, less educated respondents would be less likely to report, this is not necessarily the case; college graduates reported at about the same level as those with elementary education. However, this finding may be masked by qualitative differences in the assaults.

Less educated respondents may have been injured more seriously and may have been more likely to report for that reason. Education was more clearly positively correlated with reporting of incidents by the victim (compared to another household member or other person). The most important reasons for *not* reporting aggravated assaults were "private/personal matter or took care of it myself" (33%), and "did not think it important enough" (20%). By far the most important reason *for* reporting was "to keep it from happening again" (33%). As the value of economic loss increased, so economic justification for reporting assaults increased and the "obligation" justification diminished in importance (Harlow, 1985).

The fact that levels of reporting are not uniform across social and economic characteristics implies systematic geographic variations in the official (UCR) picture of assault and other crimes. However, one can make at once too little of this, and too much. While underreporting taints the UCR statistics for assault, the fact remains that the incidents reported are still so numerous as to be reasonably representative, particularly in view of the rather ambiguous relationships between reporting, income, and education. For example, of the 1,588,000 aggravated assault victimizations counted by the NCS in 1983, the 58 percent reported to police still represents over 921,000 incidents. It is by no means clear that the disaggregation of aggravated assault data to urban subareas presents any particular problem of distortion through reporting bias.

The Risk of Aggravated Assault

The Bureau of Justice Statistics has developed a modification of the standard victimization rate called the *Crime Risk Index* (CRI), applied to multiple year data from the NCS in order to provide a refined indication of the proportion of the U.S. population actually victimized each year. NCS estimates are based on semi-annual interviews with persons aged 12 and older in a rotating probability sample of some 60,000 households, or about 128,000 persons. Based on such a large sample, disaggregated estimates of various parameters are likely to be more accurate than similar disaggregations for single cities. A straightforward calculation of a percentage based on number of victimizations divided by population poses the possibility that persons victimized more than once in a given year counted multiple times, thus inflating the rate of victimization of individuals. By removing such double counts, the CRI provides a more

**TABLE 7.2. SELECTED VICTIM CHARACTERISTICS AND
THE CRIME RISK INDEX: AGGRAVATED ASSAULT, NCS, 1982**

CHARACTERISTIC	AGGRAVATED ASSAULT
Gender	
Male	1.30
Female	0.51
Race	
White	0.84
Black	1.31
Other	0.50
Age	
12–15	1.08
16–19	2.14
20–24	1.92
25–34	1.19
Marital Status	
Male	
Never Married	2.28
Married	0.72
Separated and Divorced	1.92
Female	
Never Married	0.80
Married	0.27
Separated and Divorced	1.37
Family income	
White, victims with:	
Less than $3,000	1.75
$25,000 and over	0.63
Black, victims with:	
Less than $3,000	1.59
$25,000 and over	0.91

Source: Langan and Innes, 1985, Table 1, p. 3.

accurate indication of individual victimization (Langan & Innes, 1985). Based on this adjustment, the 1982 CRI showed that 3.2 percent of the population were victimized by violent crime. Aggravated assault accounted for a CRI of 0.89 percent for the same year. Selected elements of the demographic breakdown of the CRI are shown in Table 7.2. Consistent with previous discussion, we see that young African American males are at high risk, as are *never married* and *separated and divorced* males and *separated and divorced* females. Assault victimization risk is also inversely related to family income.

Assault Relationships

Based on NCS data for 1982–84, aggravated assault victims were more likely to have been attacked by strangers (77 percent) compared to nonstrangers (39%). Among nonstrangers, acquaintances, rather than relatives, dominated (Timrots & Rand, 1987). Using NCS data for 1973–79, Rand (1982) found that most incidents were intraracial, with 71 percent of white victims reporting having been attacked by white assailants, 69 percent of black victims reporting black attackers. Conversely, 21 percent of white victims reported black offenders and 24 percent of black victims reported white. These data indicate that assaults are predominantly intra-community events.

TABLE 7.3. WEAPONS USED IN ASSAULTS, NCS AND UCR, 1973–82

(A) NCS (N = 51,358,000)

PERCENT OF VICTIMIZATIONS BY OFFENDERS WITH:

Gun	Knife	Other	Unknown	No weapon	Don't know
11.0	8.5	12.9	1.7	59.3	6.5

(B) UCR (N = 5,236,432)

PERCENT OF REPORTED CRIMES INVOLVING:

Any firearm	Knife or other cutting instrument	Other dangerous weapon	Personal weapon
23.2	23.0	27.2	26.6

Note: NCS (National Crime Survey) data include simple and aggravated assaults. UCR (Uniform Crime Reports) data are for aggravated assaults only.

Source: Rand, et al., 1986, Tables 3 and 10, pp. 2 and 4.

Weapons Used in Assault

About a third of all assaults (simple and aggravated) in the period 1973–82 involved armed assailants (Rand et al., 1986). Detailed categorizations show differences between methods of classification. The NCS data here combine simple and aggravated assaults while the UCR deal only with the aggravated assault subset. It would be expected, then, that the UCR data would emphasize guns, and this is the case (Table 7.3). Almost 60 percent of the NCS assaults—mostly simple assaults—involved "no weapon." Firearm involvement pushes a given incident along the violence continuum toward homicide so that whether an incident is destined to be a homicide or an assault becomes a function of marksmanship, weapon caliber, or other chance factors such as an object in the victim's pocket capable of deflecting a bullet. Some sense of the community ramifications of assault-related injuries is derived from data on the length of hospital stays connected with various types of weapons. The median number of days of hospitalization required for gunshot victims was 7.3, based on NCS data for 1973–82. Comparable values were: knife—5 days, "other"—4.1 days, and "unarmed"—3.5 days (Rand et al., 1986). Much of this medical care must be provided in the inner city, putting a great burden on the health care system, not only in terms of demand for bed space, but also insofar as many victims are unable to pay and become a charge on public health care resources.

Locational Aspects of Assault

Several studies have assessed the site characteristics of assaults, but their taxonomies of spaces generally fail to coincide, making comparisons difficult. Mulvihill et al., (1969), for example, found for a sample of 17 U.S. cities, that 27 percent of aggravated assault incidents occurred inside residences, 20 percent at other inside locations, and 53 percent outside. Dunn's (1976) study of assaults in Westchester County, New York, showed that 31 percent were in residences, 13 percent in restaurants or bars, and 56 percent in streets or parking lots. However, these proportions differed considerably depending on the geographic context; social areas with high assault rates were more likely to have street incidents and therefore less likely to experience assaults in residences. Victim age and location of victimization appear to be systematically related to some degree, consistent with a "routine activities" interpretation (Cohen and Felson, 1979; see also: Sherman, et al., 1989). Younger persons were more likely to be victimized in open spaces or at or near school, while older victims were about equally likely to be attacked at home or in public open space, according to NCS data for 1982–84 (Table 7.4). (For comparison of similar detail with the British Crime Survey, see: Davidson, 1989.)

ASSAULT UPDATE

NCS (or NCVS—National Crime Victimization Survey as it is now known) data for the period 1973–92 indicate that aggravated assault has

Serious Violence

TABLE 7.4. PLACE OF OCCURRENCE OF AGGRAVATED ASSAULTS, BY AGE OF VICTIM, 1982–84 (%)

AGE OF ASSAULT VICTIM	TOTAL	AT OR NEAR HOME	AT OR NEAR FRIEND'S OR NEIGH- BOR'S HOME	BUILD- ING	ON PUBLIC TRANS- POR- TION PARKING LOT	STREET OR PARK	IN OR OR AT SCHOOL	OTHER
12–15	100	13	9	2	5	41	26	(a)
16–19	100	14	12	7	13	38	9	7
201	100	29	9	11	11	30	2	9

Notes: (a) Too few cases to obtain statistically reliable data. Total may not sum to 100 due to rounding.

Source: Whitaker, 1986, Table 5, p. 7.

remained quite stable, varying only between 7.9 and 10.4 per 1,000 (Bureau of Justice Statistics, 1994). In 1992, the following generalizations applied to single offender aggravated assaults detected by the NCVS (Bureau of Justice Statistics, 1994):

- The perceived sex of the offender was male in 82.2 percent of the 1,098,860 incidents.
- Some 25 percent of offenders were perceived to fall in the 12–20 age range, 31 percent in the 21–29 category, and 37 percent were regarded as 30 and older. The rest were not known, not available, or under 12. The majority of offenders, then, were perceived to be under 30.
- Most offenders were perceived to be white (60%). Some 31 percent were black, and the rest "other" or "not known and not available."
- When whites were victims of aggravated assaults, the perceived race of the offender was white in 74 percent of the incidents, black in 16 percent. For black victims, 14 percent of offenders were white, 82 percent black, confirming that crimes of violence continued to be overwhelmingly intraracial.
- Of all aggravated assaults completed, with injury, 56 percent involved strangers. Of those attempted with a weapon, 71 percent involved strangers.
- Some 24 percent of incidents occurred at, in, or near the respondent's home, or on the street near home. Twelve percent took place at, in, or near a relative's or neighbor's home or on the street near that type of location. Twenty-eight percent were on streets not near their own or a friend's home.
- Handguns were used in 32 percent of aggravated assaults involving strangers, 21 percent of those involving nonstrangers.
- Households headed by females with their own children under 18 experience high assault rates (26/1,000 persons age 12 and over), compared to 16/1,000 for comparable male-headed households.
- Low family income (<$7,500) was associated with very high rates of aggravated assault—23/1,000. This compared to 6/1,000 for family incomes > =$50,000. Rates of assaults completed and attempted with a weapon were also exceptionally high at the <$7,500 income level—at least an order of magnitude higher than the next highest rate.

BALTIMORE AS A CASE STUDY IN ASSAULT

Data for Baltimore were acquired from the Baltimore Police Department for the years 1981–85. A geographic framework was developed using the Urban Pathology Index referred to Chapter 3 in connection with the discussion of Dallas. The Index was based on census tract data for substandard housing, African American population, and median household income. Index scores were much more ambiguous for Baltimore than for Dallas, where a clearcut taxonomy of areas into three groups was possible. In Baltimore, no clearly separated clusters of scores occurred; they were spread along a continuum from low to high. Police districts were assigned to four categories or areas, using police districts, or combinations of police districts, as the units of aggregation. Using this system, districts 4 and 5 became AREA 1; 2, 6, 8, and 9 became AREA 2; 1 and 3 became AREA 3, and district 7 became AREA 4 (Figure 7.1).

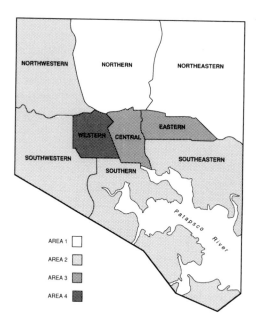

Figure 7.1. Baltimore City: area typology based on an Urban Pathology Index. *Source:* author.

Areas descend in order of socioeconomic status (SES) from highest (AREA 1) to lowest (AREA 4). Assault victims were divided approximately 25 percent white, 75 percent black, on the basis of about 20,000 cases over the three year period. By gender, victims were 69 percent

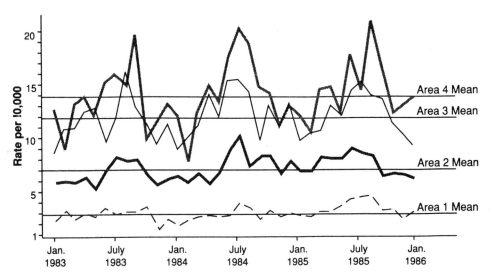

Figure 7.2. Baltimore City: aggravated assault rates by area according to socioeconomic status, 1981–85. *Source:* author.

male, 31 percent female. Although the so-called areas identified here are nothing more than a very gross typology, we see a remarkably consistent relationship between assault rates, expressed as the mean number of assaults per 10,000 persons over the three-year period, and the SES of the area as represented by data from the 1980 census (Figure 7.2). Rates varied from a low of 35.5 to a high of 167.5 per 10,000 persons (cf. Figure 3.1, lower panel). Area 4 is clearly in the greatest difficulty in terms of its assault rate (see Table 6.1 for related socioeconomic data). It is representative of an inner city underclass zone; as such it epitomizes similar areas in dozens of other cities.

Gender, Race, and Area

White assault victimization was more male-dominated than black. Of the 118 white victims in Area 4, 90 percent were male, suggesting something unusual about its social dynamics. In the same area, nearly 3,600 African Americans were victimized; indeed, the area is overwhelmingly black. The degree of preponderance of males among white victims may be due to their being visitors to the area, perhaps involved in drug traffic. Overall, male bias increased among whites as SES declined, from 75–25 percent in Area 1 to 90–10 in Area 4.

Age, Race, and Area

Proportions of victims falling into specific age cohorts were remarkably similar for both blacks and whites. Overall, about 42 percent of victims fell in the 10–24 age group, while 76 percent were included in the 10–34 bracket. No striking differences were observed across areas, with the possible exception that, in Area 4, white victims were more likely to fall in the 25–34 age group, less likely to be in the 10–24 range. Again, this would be consistent with a hypothesis to the effect that whites in the area were more likely to be adult visitors than residents.

Race and Relationships

In incidents involving African Americans, the assailant was more likely to be known to the victim as a relative or lover (16%), compared to incidents involving whites (11%), who were much more likely to be assaulted by strangers (31% versus 20%). Assault by acquaintances accounted for about half the incidents among both races (whites: 51%, blacks: 53%).

Race and Weapons

Overall, African American offenders were much more likely to use firearms, somewhat more likely to use cutting instruments, less likely to use other striking weapons, and much less likely to use personal weapons such as hands, fists, and feet. Theoretically, one might expect greater firearm use with lower SES on the grounds that more dangerous neighborhoods demand greater protection; however, no clear relationship emerged. The coarseness of the neighborhood classification may have prevented a clear view of such relationships.

Race and Setting

Study of assault settings suggested that black victimizations were disproportionately domestic, white cases nondomestic. Home-type settings (apartment, residence, inside a project) accounted for some 38 percent of the incidents involving blacks, but only about 25 percent of those involving whites, who were more likely to be assaulted in streets, taverns or nightclubs, parking lots, and yards.

A CLOSER LOOK AT VIOLENCE IN BALTIMORE

Follow-up research employing geographic information systems (GIS) methods in the 1990s examined relationships between social stress and violence in Baltimore City and Baltimore County in the period 1989–91 (Harries, 1995b), and juvenile gun crimes over the eleven-year period 1980–90 (Harries & Powell, 1994). Factor analysis of 24 social stressors at the small area (census block group) level permitted the visualization of a social stress (broadly synonymous with poverty) and violence (homicide and aggravated assault) "surface" spanning both Baltimore City and Baltimore County, in an attempt to develop a metropolitan view of violence, in contrast to the great majority of analyses which deal with single jurisdictions. Three zones, or clusters, of block groups with strong stress-violence linkages emerged, in East Baltimore, West Baltimore, and the Park Heights corridor (northwest Baltimore City). This pattern is illustrated in Figure 7.3.

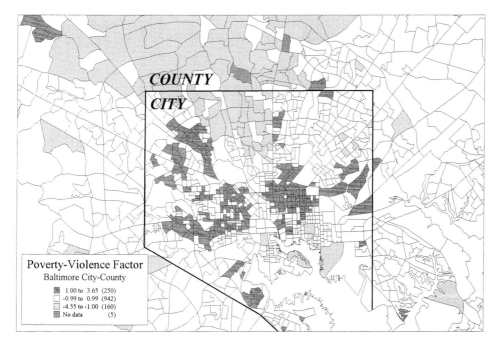

Figure 7.3. The poverty-violence pattern in Baltimore City and County (part). Areas are census block groups; scores are standard (Z) scores with mean = 0 and standard deviation = 1.0. *Source:* Harries, 1995b. Adapted by permission of the National Council for Crime Prevention, Stockholm, Sweden.

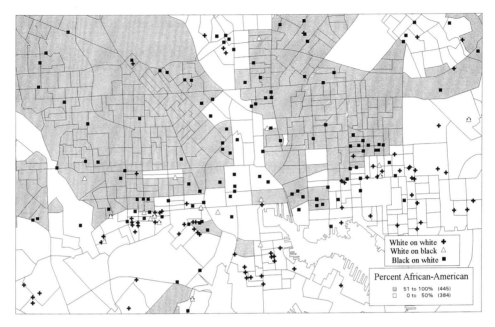

Figure 7.4. Juvenile shootings and race in Baltimore, 1980–90. Interracial incidents were most likely in racial transition zones. *Data sources:* Baltimore City Police Department and Census of Population and Housing.

Juvenile (under 18) shooting data provided insights relating to intra- and inter-racial incidents. While the overwhelming majority of juvenile shootings were intraracial, mapping of point data for individual incidents against a background map of the geography of race suggested that interracial incidents were most likely in racial transition zones (Fig. 7.4). From a pure "harm" perspective, any juvenile shooting is as abhorrent as any other. However, interracial shootings are particularly objectionable in that they raise the specter of race-based gangs out to avenge the shooting of a cohort, whether black or white. Thus it may be useful to focus anti-violence interventions on schools in the racial boundary zones.

BALTIMORE AND DALLAS

Comparisons between Baltimore and Dallas make several points. First, overall assault rates were markedly higher in Baltimore than Dallas, suggesting the possibility of differences in reporting protocols, as well as "real" differences attributable to the underlying milieux of demographic, cultural, and environmental factors. For example, it was noted in Chapter 6 that Supplementary Homicide Report (SHR) data indicated extraordinarily high levels of drug felony homicides in Baltimore, attributed by Maxfield (1989) to coding errors. However, it is possible that drug-related violence (taking coding errors into account) is indeed higher than in most inner cities owing to locational factors such as Baltimore's position closer to the midwest (compared to other east coast metropolitan areas) and its position on the New York–Philadelphia–Washington, D.C. corridor.

Inverse relationships between assault rates and SES implied sharp spatial gradients in violence apparently reflecting hyperghettoization (see Chapter 6). Differentials in age-cohort rates were quite similar. In both cities, too, weapon lethality increased with declining SES. Finally, the cities were similar in terms of their seasonal and shorter-term periodicities (see also: Harries, 1987b).

ASSAULT AND THE WEATHER[1]

Although the role of environmental factors has attracted more attention in recent years, a balanced view of all psychological, social, economic, and physical environmental variables has yet to be achieved, and may not be possible. This is due in part to the difficulty of reaching consensus on the nature of interactions in and between each subset. Arguments about the role of economic inequality in homicide exemplify this debate (see: Loftin & Parker, 1985). While consensus and balance are elusive, social ecology has tended to stress the importance of several clusters of variables in the search for explanation: family environment, peer environment, and situational factors (Gabor, 1986).

Family environment stresses the role of the family in the transmission of values, for example, and as the fundamental unit of social interaction, and hence of potential violent conflict. The peer environment is the context in which youths, in particular, learn and derive their inspiration for specific behaviors. Situational factors include the social, demographic, and economic characteristics of the area under analysis, the distribution of high-risk sites, and the level of interaction with those sites, the relationship between criminal opportunities and probabilities of detection, considerations of territoriality, and the substance abuse environment.

---

[1]This section is adapted in part from K.D. Harries and S.J. Stadler, Assault and heat stress: Dallas as a case study, in: D.J. Evans and D.T. Herbert (eds.) *The Geography of Crime* (London and New York: Routledge, 1989), pp. 38–58. Adapted by permission of Routledge.

These factors are set in a context of place, space, and location. Individuals are nominally able to control some aspects of their environment, such as who they choose to associate with and where they choose to be (at least for some activities). Other aspects of environment are not amenable to control (family, race, age).

Weather is a situational factor that had until recently received very little attention for a variety of reasons. First, as indicated more fully below, theoretical links between weather and criminal behavior have been speculative and have been associated with the excesses of Huntingtonian environmentalism (see below). Second, weather conditions vary on a regional basis, and are insufficiently extreme in many areas to warrant the suggestion that deviant behavior could be explained to any useful degree by atmospheric anomalies. Even in areas experiencing weather extremes, some years are much less extreme than others; all years are not equally suitable for the study of weather as a situational factor. Third, the concept of weather as "stress" has been neglected in the field of stress research, which has dwelt on poverty and illness as both sources and products of stress. As Linsky and Strauss (1986) have noted, stress research is rooted in psychosomatic medicine and mental health, rather than criminology. However, the stress perspective provides a useful bridge between conventional situational factors used in criminological studies, quality of life (QOL) analyses, and medical perspectives now coming into vogue. An example can be seen in Persinger (1980) where weather and human behavior are treated as parts of the same matrix.

As noted in Chapter 4, Linsky and Straus (1986) have suggested various ways in which stress may operate to encourage criminal activity. Whether stress theory and the more familiar QOL concept are significantly different as they relate to crime is moot (cf. Smith, 1973; Harries, 1976; Harries, 1995b). It would appear that high stress and low QOL are strongly correlated. Indeed, some of the same variables are typically used in the construction of both stress and QOL indexes. The proponents of stress theory emphasize the importance of cumulative effects. Again, it would seem that the concept of cumulation or additive effects is implicit in QOL. However, stress theory may have a more coherent theoretical base than QOL analyses in that stress may be more amenable to measurement and conceptualization than "quality."

In this vein, the focus here on heat stress is congruent with other aspects of stress theory. There is no question that the average person is physiologically stressed under certain combinations of heat, humidity, and air movement. Although the research reviewed here concerns heat stress, it has been suggested that comparable investigation should also be directed toward "cold stress", which involves not only the physiological effects of cold, but also the proverbial "cabin fever" suffered by those who are confined to dwellings or workplaces by prolonged periods of extreme cold. In the U.S. this phenomenon is most pervasive in the upper Midwest—Minnesota, Wisconsin, Michigan, for example—where winters are long and severe, with daily *maxima* at or below $-18°C$ ($0°F$) commonplace. From a criminological perspective, a derivative of cabin fever is increased actual or potential interpersonal interaction, and hence potential violence. Although weather-induced stresses with the potential to contribute to deviant behavior have been recognized in folklore for millennia, they have been almost totally ignored as components in the matrix of social science research.

Background

Two millennia ago the Greeks produced a substantial body of writings stemming from the idea that weather and climate affect human behavior; important contemporary works such as Landsberg (1969) & Tromp (1980) draw on this intellectual heritage. Hippocrates admonished physicians to first study the atmosphere when taking up residence in a new city; he believed that diseases varied by climate. At the time of the development of scientific instruments, both the physiologic and geographic species of environmental theory were alive. However, instrumentation tended to favor physiologic theory in that physiologic relationships could be readily demonstrated through direct observations of individuals.

The inherent difficulties in the production of plausible environmental theory notwithstanding, some writers fostered the notion of a link between temperatures and behavior. In the 1700s, the Abbe' du Bos attributed criminal behavior to abnormally high Roman summertime temperatures (Koller, 1937). Kant believed that too much heat dried out nerves and veins (Oliver and Siddiqi, 1987).

In the language of Social Darwinism, Ratzel's *Anthropogeographie* (1882) theorized that the direct and indirect effects of climate were powerful influences upon human behavior. His student, Ellen Churchill Semple, popularized his ideas in the fledgling graduate geography departments of the U.S.

Early academic geography in the United States was steeped in this climatic determinism, with Ellsworth Huntington as the most influential representative. In spite of Huntington's success, geographers increasingly opposed determinism in reaction to publications such as *Climate Makes the Man* (Mills, 1942) and the works of Griffith Taylor, who viewed human geography as being controlled by climate. Ironically, the downfall of the determinists lay in their attempts to integrate disparate threads of geography and history. The most common critique has been that they employed only the facts and impressions which supported their contentions and excluded equally viable, but contrary, evidence (see Oliver, 1973: Lee, 1954, Spate, 1952). The analytical inadequacies of the climatic determinists were due as much to the lack of reliable sources and computational capabilities as to the research paradigm under which they operated. Moreover, when the intellectual ties between geographic environmental theory and climatic determinism are examined, it is clear that they became one in the early twentieth century. Discrediting the climatic determinists served to halt geographic environmental theory in its tracks. In essence, threads of two millennia of environmental thought had been obliterated by the time climatic determinism had run its course. Geographers were understandably reluctant to pick up the debris of the environmental tradition. Rejection of determinism was reinforced by the emergence of socially-rooted topics important in their own right (Martin, 1973).

Although folklore, experience, and common observation demonstrate links between climate and behavior, such research in the social sciences became virtually moribund. In the 1960s and early seventies, a little research of a nominally environmental twist was done by geographers, but it was a cadre of psychologists who initiated studies at both the macro and clinical levels, looking specifically at crime weather relationships. These psychological studies have substantiated a link between abnormally high temperatures, irritability, and violent tendencies in laboratory subjects (Boyanowski, *et al.*, 1981; Baron & Bell, 1975; Sutherland & Cressey, 1978; Baron, 1972). Although psychology has harbored much controversy (Rotton, 1986), clinical studies support the notion that violence might be partially explained through high temperatures.[2]

---

[2] For a comprehensive review of the relationship between heat and violence from the psychological perspective, see: Anderson, 1989. See also: Rotton, 1993; Dubitsky, Weber, and Rotton, 1993; Cohn, 1990; Kenrick and MacFarlane, 1986.

Another theme identifiable in environmental research is the relationship between seasonality and crime. Most studies of temperature and violence have shown a warm season peak. Guerry recorded a summertime zenith in France in the 1830s (Anonymous, 1833). Dexter used an eight-year time series to connect temperatures and criminal assault in turn-of-the-century New York City (Dexter, 1904), and Cohen's examination of the *Uniform Crime Reports* of the 1930s showed the same phenomenon on a national scale (Cohen, 1941). Nineteen-eighty saw the publication of *Crime and Seasonality* which amply demonstrated warm season peaking in crime (Bureau of Justice Statistics, 1980). Yet the interpretation attributed the peaking entirely to nonthermal factors such as summer school vacations, holidays, and 31-day summer months. Geographers Lewis and Alford also took a seasonal perspective when they attempted to find climatic differences in the timing of the onset of higher warm season assault rates in the United States (Lewis & Alford, 1975). They theorized that the South should be the first region in the calendar year to experience higher assault rates and suggested that this might be associated with critical temperature thresholds. However, using national data, they found no tenable relationship.

The contemporary approach to environmentalism recognizes that environmental influences are complex and often marginal, but may be strong enough to warrant recognition and further exploration. Certainly, there is no question that the influence of the environment is still firmly embedded in the popular culture. This was epitomized by a quotation from Lt. Bobby Williams of the U.S. Park Police with reference to fights among juveniles on the Mall in Washington in the hot summer of 1988: "The temperature's making them restless. In one incident down there we had 10 or 12 arrests, and we just had officers respond to another one. It has to be the weather" (Duggan, 1988).

Recent Findings

Three studies are reviewed here, looking at the issue of thermal stress and violence in one city—Dallas—from somewhat different perspectives. The theoretical approach in this research rests on findings from a combination of folklore, clinical and social psychology, physiological climatology, and the sciences of indoor climate control and clothing. Expressed in the simplest terms, it is suggested that violence is a product of various complex environmental interactions, including the characteristics of the actors (such as age and gender), their social context, and the physical environment, of which the atmosphere is a part. Atmospheric influences are typically small, but their existence should be recognized and effects estimated insofar as possible.

The immediate theoretical precedent for the research came from clinical psychology, where evidence had accumulated to suggest that subjects stressed thermally became irritable and more prone to violence compared to a control group (Boyanowsky, et al., 1981; Calvert-Boyanowski et al., 1976). If thermal stress is indeed a universal phenomenon, then a relationship with officially measured violent behavior should be detectable in thermally stressful environments. For the purpose of investigating the hypothesized effect, the ideal environment would have to exhibit extreme conditions over a protracted time period. Furthermore, local levels of "normal" violence would have to be rather high in order to provide a sufficient number of incidents to allow some statistical insights and permit some degree of disaggregation of the data. Dallas, Texas, qualified according to these criteria.

The data base for all three studies consisted of aggravated assault data for the period March through October, 1980, and meteorological conditions for the same period. The study period was selected in order to permit the bracketing of the warmest months in order to ensure the inclusion of the most severe summer weather. Nineteen-eighty was selected for the extraordinary severity of its summer heat. The discomfort was particularly striking since it was conspicuous in an environment of climatic extremes. People in the southern Great Plains are accustomed to an annual temperature range on the order of at least 38°C (100°F), thunderstorms, drought, and tornadic winds. At the Dallas-Fort Worth airport, located at the fringe of the urban heat island, a temperature of 46°C (115°F) was recorded in 1980. It is likely that ambient shade temperatures in some parts of the inner city exceeded 49°C (120°F). Media attention focused on Dallas and other cities similarly affected in the Southwest, drawing attention to high rates of heat stroke and deaths attributable to heat stroke, particularly among the elderly. Media accounts tended to dwell on the various stresses caused by the heat, and their consequences. Emergency efforts attempted to distribute electric fans to those without air conditioning.

During the eight-month study period, some 4,309 aggravated assaults were reported to the police in the city of Dallas. Data on these incidents were acquired from the Dallas Police Department. The three studies dealt with: (1) the relationship between assaultive violence and a widely used discomfort index (DI) (Harries and Stadler, 1983), (2) differences in neighborhood responses to thermal stress (Harries, Stadler, & Zdorkowski, 1984), and (3) a hypothesized threshold effect, suggesting that violence will actually diminish above some temperature or comfort level, beyond which people become so uncomfortable that virtually all activities, including violence, are inhibited (Harries and Stadler, 1988).

1. *Assault and Discomfort*

Only a few studies in social psychology (e.g. Baron and Ransberger, 1978; Carlsmith & Anderson, 1979) and geography (Lewis and Alford, 1975) had considered the question of temperature effects as they related to violence. This research had either (a) not considered temperature directly, but had relied, rather, on a seasonal surrogate (Lewis & Alford), or (b) had used ambient temperature as the measure of thermal stress. Such approaches are either too coarse, in that they cannot hope to capture the possibly subtle relationships between thermal stress and the incidence of violence, or may be weak measures of discomfort, as in the use of ambient temperature.

It seemed appropriate, then, to test a DI taking into account not only temperature but also humidity, given the importance of the interaction between these conditions in the calculus of comfort. The three-dimensional patterns of urban thermal discomfort are quite complex and a complete description would have to account for the myriad combinations of temperature, radiant load, air movement, and humidity. A city-wide study must rely on some surrogate measures of thermal discomfort. In the case of Dallas, data came from the Dallas-Fort Worth regional airport located at the urban fringe. As suggested above, the level of discomfort was probably underestimated by both the ambient temperature and DI values. The 4,309 incidents were aggregated into 245 daily assault counts, and the DI was computed from nearly 6,000 hourly weather observations obtained from the National Climate Center. Daily maximum ambient temperature was also abstracted for comparative purposes.

Assault is by definition a human interaction. As such, it is likely to occur in informal social settings in homes or places of recreation, as noted in the discussion of conventional assault ecology. Such violence is apparently less likely in the workplace owing to the inhibiting effect of the public or quasi-public nature of most work settings, combined with the immediate threat of job loss. Assault, therefore, has a distinct weekly rhythm, with weekend peaks and weekday valleys. Given that opportunities for some types of recreation are increased in the summer owing to extended daylight hours and warm weather, a seasonal peak might be expected in the summer. However, a counter-argument can be developed to the effect that social interactions may be most intense in winter when people are confined in indoor settings for prolonged periods.

An analysis of variance model was developed, using day of the week, month (to capture possible seasonal effects), and DI as explanatory variables. The raw DI values were converted to a five-level classification reflecting generalized human reactions to the conditions represented by the index. The thresholds for these levels were DIs of 65, 75, 80, and 85.[3] The literature has established that virtually all people are comfortable at DIs below 65; above 85, most people experience severe distress. The three variables were quite successful in accounting for variations in assault frequencies ($F = 3.74$, $p < 0.0001$), with $R^2 = 0.71$. At the lowest discomfort level, some 15.7 assaults per day occurred; at the level of most discomfort the mean assault frequency was 20.3. The DI was still significant when it was forced last in the model ($p = 0.05$). The overwhelming effect of day of the week was illustrated by mean assault frequencies for Wednesdays (13.5) and Saturdays (27.0).

This analysis suggested that weather effects, almost entirely overlooked by criminologists and others in causal studies of violence, should be considered, particularly in environments prone to severe conditions.

2. Neighborhood Response

Having demonstrated a general thermal stress effect, attention turned to intraurban geography in order to examine the idea that neighborhoods classified on the basis of socioeconomic status (SES) could be expected to respond differentially to thermal stress. The rationale was that the affluent, through employment in indoor occupations, and air conditioning in cars and homes, would be able to ameliorate the effects of thermal stress. The poor, on the other hand, would be more likely to be employed in outdoor settings, and less likely to have access to functioning air conditioning.

Census data showed that about 90 percent of the dwellings in Dallas were air-conditioned in 1980. However, over 95 percent of the homes

---

[3]Note that the scale of the Discomfort Index is unique and is not in degrees Fahrenheit or Celsius.

occupied by whites were cooled, compared to 83 percent in black-occupied dwellings and 79 percent in homes occupied by Hispanics. The proportion of air conditioning systems that was central (one relatively efficient unit as opposed to smaller, less efficient units in one or more rooms) showed similar variation. Some 37,000 dwelling units in Dallas had no air conditioning in 1980. Based on the assumption that each dwelling was occupied by the average number of persons per household in Dallas in 1980 (2.51), it is estimated that some 93,000 persons were living without air conditioning. Based on the geography of low SES neighborhoods in the metropolitan area, it seemed that most of the people without air conditioning were likely to be subjected to the most uncomfortable temperatures of the urban heat island. According to the stress model, the lower SES people, poorly equipped to cope, could be expected to respond either behaviorally or in the form of mental or physical illness, or both.

Neighborhood status was measured by an Urban Pathology Index as indicated above and in Chapter 3. The index discriminated clearly between three groups of neighborhoods, designated as high, medium, and low status. Other factors, including the urban heat island, population density, substance abuse, and "calendar effects" should also be considered as potential contributors to violence, directly or indirectly.

The data did not permit intraurban analysis of thermal effects, and the heat island hypothesis was not tested. Population density could contribute to violence in that it is a surrogate for potential social interaction. Data relating to persons in multifamily dwellings provided a crude indication of density. Substance abuse could not be measured satisfactorily, but some indication of the role of alcohol was provided by counts of the number of incidents occurring in bars or in bar parking lots. "Calendar effects" refers to variations in activities caused by events with somewhat predictable schedules. These included weekends, school holidays and graduations, various public holidays, paydays, sporting events, and (some would argue) lunar cycles. The latter issue, apparently, can be dismissed (see Rotton & Kelly (1985); Harries (1986b)). The calendar effects hypothesis is akin to the "routine activities" interpretation of crime patterns (Cohen & Felson, 1979; Messner and Tardiff, 1985).

Neighborhood SES level was strongly and inversely related to assault incidence. The expected exaggerated response of low SES neighborhoods was confirmed; August exhibited a sharp peak, but for the low SES areas only (Figure 7.5), a phenomenon not clearly apparent in

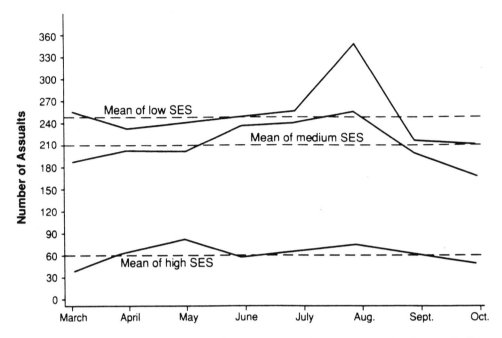

Figure 7.5. Relationship between assault frequencies, months, and neighborhood status, Dallas, 1980. *Source:* Harries and Stadler, 1984. (Copyright Association of American Geographers, 1984. Reproduced by permission.)

subsequent years (see Figure 3.1), perhaps due in part to the absence of comparable thermal severity in the later series. The density hypothesis was evaluated through analysis of rate differentials adjusted for different types of dwellings. Assault rates per 1,000 apartment units were exceptionally high in low status neighborhoods (20.0 in low SES, 2.3 in high SES). Apart from the pronounced weekend effect discussed above, other calendar effects and those hypothesized for substance abuse could not be substantiated unambiguously. Data inadequacies, particularly with respect to the latter issue, prevented adequate analysis.

3. *Threshold Effects*

Reviews of the literature of social psychology in the course of ongoing research led to a third line of questioning. The gist of the argument is found in Anderson and Anderson (1984). Two kinds of behavior are surmised in response to hot temperatures (as in response to stress in general): fight or flight. The tendency to fight is thought to occur at lower temperatures. Flight occurs above an "inflection point" beyond which aggression decreases as potential protagonists seek to escape the situation. The Andersons' test of the hypothesis detected a linear relationship between heat and violence, but not a curvilinear one (inverted U shape).

Using a data base extended to cover the period March 1, 1980 through October 31, 1981, with an N of some 10,000, some aspects of the Andersons' study were replicated (Harries & Stadler, 1988). Thermal stress was measured by the daily maximum DI and daily maximum ambient temperature. Two regression analyses were performed. In one, an "overall" model, *weekend* (operationalized as a dichotomy between weekend and nonweekend), *DI, DI squared, maximum temperature* and *maximum temperature squared* were the independent variables. Daily assault count was the dependent variable. DI and DI squared were both significant if entered alone after weekend. With linear DI and maximum temperature controlled, however, their quadratic counterparts were not significant. Disaggregation to the neighborhood level, also failed to show a curvilinear effect after linear variables were entered.

Scatter diagrams of the relationship between daily assault frequencies for the 610 days of the study period and the DI/temperature measures were inspected visually. They suggested a threshold at about 40°C (104°F), and at the corresponding DI, above which daily incidence levels declined. This threshold was independent of the weekend effect. In spite of this apparent threshold, so few days were found at the extreme levels of discomfort that little confidence could be put in this finding. Further study of 6°C (10°F) intervals using analysis of variance and difference-of-means tests also failed to suggest a threshold. Our findings supported those of the Andersons, insofar as weekend was the best predictor of assault frequencies, and thermal effects were linear.

Rigorous dissection of this issue, however, would demand neighborhood-level discomfort data. The failure to detect a curvilinear effect in Dallas using the available data does not prove the nonexistence of such a threshold, of course. Such a relationship may exist in other cities in other climatic regimes. Responses to thermal stress may be linked to the concept of normality in different environments. This issue of departures from normal as it relates to the Dallas context has been addressed by Stadler and Harries (1985); see also Kalkstein & Valimont, 1986, 1987; Stadler, Harries, & Kalkstein (1989).

Another approach to the concept of threshold is seen in Cheatwood's analysis employing *number of days in a row with a DI exceeding "the physiologically relevant" level of 79* as an explanatory variable. This study, specifically of homicide only, found that the *number of days* metric was significant, but explained relatively little variance. Aggression stimulated by physical discomfort appeared to be moderated by the inclination of people to adapt (Cheatwood, 1995; see also Cheatwood, 1988; Tennenbaum and Fink, 1994).

Synthesis

A finding of linear relationship between thermal stress and violence has become commonplace. What research initiatives are now appropriate? Comparative studies are necessary to permit the application of similar measures of violence and thermal discomfort to cities in distinctly different thermal regimes. Such comparisons would provide better understanding of several questions:

1. *Is relative stress important?* Put another way, are stress violence trend lines parallel in different thermal settings? If they are not parallel, is variation random or systematic? If the latter, what factors are at work?

2. *Do apparent linear effects show up in a variety of climatic regimes?* The corollary question is: Are linear effects only observed in severe summer regimes?

3. *Are there lag effects?* If so, what are they like, and do they differ across climatic regimes? A lag is understood to mean a short-term delay in the manifestation of stress, and it is socially conditioned. The individual is stressed, but waits until getting off work, for example, before "blowing up."

4. *Are there cumulative or additive effects of stress that cause people to "snap," but in quite different individual time frames?* Such cumulative effects are seen as longer term (days, weeks) than lags, and leading to overt reaction relatively late in the period of thermal stress.

Such questions should be examined in the context of a concern about violence that has spread across disciplines. Combination of the perspectives of criminology with those of "stress" sociologists, "quality of life" sociologists and geographers, social psychologists, and various public health approaches, yields a new synthesis of definition, theory, data, and method. When geographic space is superimposed on this synthesis, fresh insights will emerge.

Chapter 8

DRUGS AND VIOLENCE

The 1980s marked a new feature of serious physical violence in America: the heavy involvement of drugs, particularly cocaine, and, later, crack cocaine. Not until the mid-1990s were there emerging signs of a somewhat diminished level of drug-related violence as drug markets became (relatively) stabilized and cocaine use in the 18–25 age group diminished (Maguire & Pastore, 1995: Table 3.76). However, this somewhat positive information is tempered by the fact that drug "mentions" in emergency room episodes increased 1991–'92–'93 for marijuana, heroin, and cocaine (Maguire & Pastore, 1995, Table 3.81). The aggregate costs of drug abuse to American society were estimated at about $60 billion in 1983, with about one third of that crime-related (U.S. Department of Justice, 1988a). By 1989, a Gallup poll showed that 38 percent of Americans regarded drugs as the principal national problem, exceeding in significance crime and violence, homelessness, economic issues, and the budget deficit. However, by 1994, this percentage (38) had shrunk to 11, supplanted by crime and violence (37%) as the issue of the day (Maguire & Pastore, 1995, Table 2.1). Sixty percent of a sample of teenagers saw drug abuse as the most serious problem faced by their peers. Seventy-seven percent of Americans wanted stronger laws against drug users, 92 percent wanted stronger sanctions against drug sellers (Isikoff, 1989). The seriousness of the situation was indicated by the appointment of William J. Bennett as federal drug czar on March 13, 1989.

Links between the use of drugs and/or alcohol, and crime, have been clearly established. Violence, for example, is thought to be linked to alcohol use, given that alcohol reduces inhibitions and has been linked to aggressive behavior. Expensive addictions to heroin or cocaine are more likely to lead to economic crimes (U.S. Department of Justice, 1988a). A survey of prison inmates in 1986 showed that in the month before the crime for which they were convicted, some 43 percent used

151

drugs on a more or less daily basis and 19 percent were using heroin, methadone, cocaine, PCP, or LSD. Approximately 13 percent of inmates fit the profile of addicts involved in crime for financial reasons. The daily use of a major drug in the month preceding their crime was reported by 12.3 percent of inmates convicted of murder, and 11.2 percent of those convicted for assault (Innes, 1988). Among violent offenders, 28 percent of murderers reported that they were under the influence of a drug at the time of their offense, essentially identical to the level of involvement reported by those convicted of assault (Table 8.1).

**TABLE 8.1. DRUG USE BY STATE PRISON INMATES,
BY CONVICTION OFFENSE, 1986: VIOLENT OFFENSES**

	PERCENT OF INMATES CONVICTED OF EACH OFFENSE WHO:	
CONVICTION OFFENSE	*Were under the influence of a drug at the time of the offense*	*Had used a drug daily in the month before the offense*
All violent offenses	33.4	39.2
Murder	28.3	34.1
Manslaughter	20.0	23.4
Rape	32.0	34.3
Robbery	41.9	50.3
Assault	28.6	34.4
Kidnapping	37.2	44.3
Other violent offenses	31.8	31.0

Source: Innes, 1988, Table 3, page 3.

Major drug use history of state prison inmates, for violent offenders, is shown in Table 8.2. In general, those incarcerated for murder and assault were much less likely than robbers, but more likely than inmates convicted of other violent offenses, to report daily major drug use. About 50 percent of imprisoned violent offenders reported having been using alcohol immediately prior to their crime; among those convicted of assault, the percentage rose to about 60 (U.S. Department of Justice, 1988a). Arrest rates for drug abuse violations actually peaked in 1989 for persons 18 and older, white and black, but remained at relatively high levels through 1992, at more than twice the 1970 level. Arrest rates are not necessarily an accurate indication of the "real" level of drug abuse, however. As jails and prisons fill up, some jurisdictions may ignore lower

**TABLE 8.2. MAJOR DRUG USE HISTORY OF STATE PRISON INMATES,
BY VIOLENT OFFENSE CATEGORIES, 1986**

CONVICTION OFFENSE	*PERCENT OF ALL INMATES WHO USED A MAJOR DRUG:*				
	Never used a major drug	*Anytime in the past*	*Regularly in the past*	*In the month before the offense*	
				At all	*Daily*
Murder	13.5	10.0	9.9	10.7	7.4
Manslaughter	4.2	3.0	2.8	2.2	1.6
Rape	5.6	4.0	3.0	3.2	2.1
Sexual assault	6.6	3.7	3.5	1.5	1.5
Robbery	18.6	22.0	19.7	22.8	25.7
Assault	9.1	7.6	8.6	9.9	4.9
Kidnapping	1.6	1.8	1.9	1.5	1.9
Other violent offenses	1.0	0.7	0.7	0.3	0.7
Violent offenses	60.1	52.6	50.0	52.0	45.7

Note: Columns may not total "Violent offenses" value exactly due to rounding.

Source: Innes, 1988, Table 5, p. 4.

level drug abuse incidents in order to focus on gun-related crimes or higher level drug dealers.

Drug-related violence has become an integral part of gang activities. In the 1980s, Los Angeles became the gang capital of the U.S., with 70,000 members in Los Angeles County organized into about 700 gangs. In 1988, Los Angeles recorded 452 gang-related murders (NBC News, 1989). Gang activity is thought to be instrumental in spreading drug-related violence on a regional basis. The Untouchables, a Miami gang, broadened its range into other southeastern cities, including Atlanta, Savannah, and Montgomery. Los Angeles gangs are active in Denver, Vancouver, and on the East Coast. Chicago gangs have moved into Milwaukee, Minneapolis, and Racine, WI, and elsewhere. About 40 Jamaican gangs, or "posses," have become known for their exceptional violence and unique organization, employing local hired help but importing executives from Jamaica. Some posses are named for neighborhoods in Kingston, Jamaica, such as Riverton City, Maverly, and Waterhouse. Posses were linked to 350 murders in the period March 1987 to March 1988, alone, and Dallas had 35 posse-related homicides in 1987 (Morganthau et al., 1988). Posses have set up crack markets in Alaska and Hawaii, broadening their influence far beyond their East Coast base. Their arsenal of weapons has been expanded to include grenades, used to destroy the crack houses of rival posse members (Churchville, 1988a). Like other forms of violence, drug-related gang violence has a distinctive regional distribution (Figure 8.1).

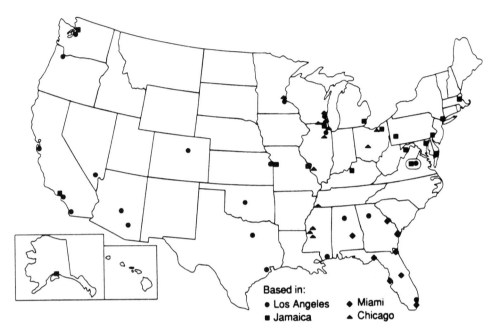

Figure 8.1. The spread of gang-related drugs and violence: home bases of gangs. *Source:* Morganthau, et al., 1988, p. 22. *Newsweek*, March 28. Christopher Blumrich. Adapted by permission of *Newsweek*.

The indirect effects of drug-related violence impact the very structure of neighborhoods causing people to stop seeing friends, avoid recreational activities, give up walking in their neighborhoods, and otherwise limit their geographical mobility. About a third of Washington, D.C. residents responding to a *Washington Post* poll (Morin, 1989a) indicated that drug-related concerns had prompted them to consider moving to the suburbs. The impact of drugs as assessed in the poll varied by age. Relatively more younger respondents had limited their mobility owing to drug-related fears. Parents of children aged 12–19 were asked whether they had told their child to avoid specific places because of drug-related concerns. Seventy percent of D.C. respondents said "Yes", compared to 45 percent of those in neighboring Prince George's County, Maryland.

DRUG–RELATED INCIDENTS IN
NATIONAL HOMICIDE DATA

Drug-related incidents were abstracted from the Supplementary Homicide Reports (SHR) for 1976–1983. Of the overall total of 155,267 incidents contained in the file, by far the most numerous among those events explicitly identified as having drug involvement were "felony-type: narcotics and drug laws." Records for some 2,524 such incidents were examined. The modal victim was aged 24–26, and male, with about equal probability of being white (48.3%) or black (50.1%), indicating a much higher *per capita* rate of occurrence among blacks than whites. Firearms were used in 80.4 percent of cases, with the handgun as weapon of choice (62.5%). Most relationships between victim and offender were indeterminate (40.6%). Of those in which relationship could be attributed, acquaintances accounted for 38.9 percent, strangers 10.7 percent.

Nonfelony type drug-related homicides, described as "brawl due to influence of narcotics," were less numerous (N = 445), but similar in general characteristics to the felony-type. The typical victim was male (85.6%) and a little more likely than felony-type victims to be white (51.2%). Firearms were less likely to be used (72.8%), perhaps due to the lesser degree of premeditation and planning in a "brawl." However, the handgun was still the clear favorite (57.8%). Knives and other cutting instruments were more likely to be used in the nonfelony drug-related homicide, compared to the felony type (17.1% versus 11.7%). Relationships were also somewhat different between the homicide types. Acquaintances were the principal category in the nonfelony (53%), followed by "indeterminate" (19.6%) and "stranger" (10.6%). "Stranger" proportions were essentially identical between felonies and nonfelonies.

LACK OF SPATIAL RESEARCH

A spatial analytical view of drugs and drug-related problems is virtually nonexistent, apart from a handful of ecological studies such as those by Nurco and co-workers relating to Baltimore (Nurco et al., 1979; Nurco et al., 1984). A spatial perspective of drug-related violence has not been attempted to date. At present, knowledge of spatial patterns and interactions is largely intuitive and informal. Everyone knows that some inner city communities are drug- and violence-ridden. However, this information is gleaned from the media—particularly newspapers—and only to a lesser degree from scholarly literature. Given the dearth of scholarly data on the rapidly changing drug scene, this chapter relies to a considerable degree on detailed coverage of events in the Washington, D.C. metropolitan area provided by the *Washington Post* and various news magazine.

Understanding of spatial relationships surrounding violence-related drug and crime issues is extremely crude. Territorial, displacement, boundary, and diffusion effects have not been documented, except in vernacular or anecdotal frameworks. Spatial variables tend to be taken for granted as constant. They are not. The influence of propinquity, the friction of distance, laws hemmed in by political boundaries, the decay of custom over distance—all are essentially *spatial* phenomena with impacts on drug use and related patterns of behavior, including violence.

For example, a comprehensive literature review of the field of drugs and crime (Gandossy et al., 1980) examined methodological questions, patterns of drug use and criminal behavior, life cycles, economic issues, and drug treatment. The only references of a spatial nature were, specifically, "Where are addicts likely to reside?" (p. 24) and "Where are women addicts likely to reside?" (p. 57). Discussion then focused on the regional and social milieus in which addicts live, drawing on Chien et al., 1964, Nurco and Lerner, 1972, Brown et al., 1973, Kozel et al., 1972, Ball, 1965, Ellinwood et al., 1966, Chambers et al., 1970, and Cuskey et al., 1972. However, spatial dynamics were not even alluded to, indicating the magnitude of the gap in the literature.

SPACE AND PLACE

The concepts of space and place have been neglected in research on drug-related violence. Ley (1975) noted in the context of gangs that

> place is not a constant, and studies of the street gang should show sensitivity to its variabilities. Moreover, once local conditions exist propitious to the emergence of the gang, there is a feedback mechanism whereby the gang adds its own distinctive contribution to the meaning of its environment. Thus, there is a spatial ecology which leads to the formation of the gang, and then an ongoing social ecology which lends meaning to space.

One might extend this argument from study of the gang to study of drug culture, drug-related violence, and the patterns of behavior giving them expression.

THE WASHINGTON, D.C. AREA AS A CASE STUDY

On the day of his appointment in 1989, drug czar William Bennett was quoted as saying that violence related to drugs in Washington, D.C. was "as bad as it can get" and he would name the district a "high intensity drug trafficking area" as permitted by the Anti-Drug Abuse Act of 1988. By mid-March, the district had experienced 107 homicides, about twice as many as at the same date in 1988, an indication of the escalation reportedly associated with drugs (Isikoff & Pianin, 1989). Toxicology reports for 724 homicide victims in the period 1985–June, 1988 showed that 67 percent were positive for substances including alcohol (28%), cocaine (28%), and PCP (24%) (OCJPA, 1988). Similar problems have surfaced in other metropolitan areas.

Neighborhood Vignettes

The sketches that follow are based on extensive coverage of drug-related crime in the *Washington Post* spanning much of 1988 and 1989. News stories or special features have been drawn on to provide characterizations of drug-related phenomena at the neighborhood level. The accounts all relate to Washington D.C. or its suburbs in Maryland and Virginia, yet the scenarios are repeated in many other places around the U.S.

Langley Park Apartments, Prince George's County, Maryland

In two feature articles, Harriston (1988a, 1988b) described the Langley Park complex in the Maryland suburbs of Washington, D.C. as composed of 16,000 persons in 2,607 apartments in a one square mile development. Built about 1950, the development was racially all white until about 1965. Then, a rift developed between renters and owners and ethnicity became more diverse. The nonwhite population increased from one percent in 1960 to five percent in 1970 and 75 percent in 1988. As ethnicity and race diversified, cultural links such as language and religion broke down and interethnic squabbling broke out. Design features of the complex intended to attract residents forty years ago (courtyards, good highway access, parking, breezeways, and laundry rooms) now serve to make a perfect drug market.

In spite of a large Hispanic population, few of those arrested as either buyers or sellers of drugs are Hispanic. Consequences of the large proportion of immigrants include: fear of police owing to illegal status, and fear due to parallels drawn to police death squads in the immigrants native countries. Another consequence, according to residents, is that police have, until recently, tended to ignore the area. One resident was quoted as saying that "the county does not recognize any of your problems unless you're white Anglo-Saxon."

In the first five months of 1988, some 68 drug arrests were recorded, including 45 "major" crimes. One bizarre form of crime noted at the apartments consists of ordering pizza, then robbing the delivery people. In a *Washington Post* poll cited by Harriston, one third of the residents had heard gunfire in the last year and one third said they thought someone had been attacked nearby. Public telephones have been removed to prevent their use by drug dealers; apartments have been taken over by dealers. Residents do not become involved in community affairs, conforming to the model outlined in the discussion of Drake Place (see below).

Potomac Gardens, Washington D.C.

The Potomac Gardens public housing project, just off Pennsylvania Avenue, is 12 blocks southeast of the U.S. Capitol. It opened in 1967 and contains 144 units for seniors, 208 for families. Like Langley Park, it is also an ideal drug market, and has been a drug market almost since it opened. It has three- and six-story buildings around open courtyards. Dealers, numbering as many as 100, use the central part of the area known as "the strip"; when police arrive, dealers and buyers retreat into the maze of hallways or simply out to the surrounding streets. According to an account by Duke and Price (1989), only 10 households were headed by a male and female in 1989; 60 percent of the residents were under 25 and mostly male. Physical conditions are poor, with some 46 vacant units in March, 1989. Conditions are typical of the 60 public housing projects in D.C., most of which host drug markets. In Potomac Gardens, drug traffic is split about evenly between crack and heroin. Five homicides, all drug-related, were recorded in the Gardens in the first four months of 1989.

Paradise Manor

According to Horwitz (1988b), this public housing development in northeast Washington, D.C. fits the now-familiar pattern: many boarded-up units, broken doors and windows, graffiti. Like other exemplary drug markets, such as Langley Park and Potomac Gardens, the area consists of blocks of three-story apartments around a central yard. Some 1,175 people live in 666 apartments. As in the other projects, the yard is the focus of the drug market. Residents help crack dealers by preparing or "cooking" cocaine into crack in their apartments. The volume of drug business was such that at least one gang of dealers employed two electronic money counters. In April 1988, residents sought the help of the Nation of Islam to rid the area of dealers.

Gangs and Neighborhoods

An overview of individual housing projects and various other neighborhoods shows endemic problems with on-going drug-related violence. Implanted among the known drug markets, however, is gang activity that can be related to a component of the violence in the District of Columbia. According to a report by Horwitz and Lewis (1988), gang-related violence accounted for at least 20 homicides between mid-June and mid-November, 1988. Two principal gangs (or "crews" as they call themselves) have a total of about 150 members and are geographically clustered in neighborhoods in the vicinity of Gallaudet University in N.E. Washington, a few blocks from Union Station. Given the large number of homicides accounted for by the gangs, it is surprising that they appear to be quite localized. The most notorious of the incidents involving the gangs was the very brutal murder of Catherine Fuller by some members of the "Eighth and H Crew" in 1984.

Violence escalated in June, 1988, when the leader of one of the gangs, the Trinidad, was killed. Reportedly, the gangs are using the Los Angeles Crips as a model and it is thought the Crips have supplied the Washington gangs with drugs, particularly cocaine. The incentive for expansion of Los Angeles gang influence is the price difference, for cocaine and crack, of approximately 100 percent between Los Angeles and other cities (NBC News, 1989). However, whether gang members function primarily as an extension of the gang or as individuals, is unclear. Much of the gang violence appears to be a product of internecine conflict among the gangs over drugs and gang organization, or some combination of such factors. Interestingly, the gang phenomenon in Washington is not randomly distributed, even within or between neighborhoods, and is not, at least as far as public data can document, a dominant social phenomenon, even within poverty areas. This implies the key role of a few strong personalities in a few locations, possibly influenced by out-siders such as the Crips or Jamaican posses.

The Micro-Environment of a Drug Market: Drake Place

Drake Place, S.E., in Washington, D.C., is nominally about 660 yds (610m) in length, and is located 4.2 miles (6.8km) east of the U.S. Capitol. The *Washington Post* described it as "one of the city's bloodiest patches of land" (Sanchez & Wheeler, 1989), and it was dubbed "the meanest street in Washington" by *U.S. News and World Report* (Cary, 1989). In the local census tract in 1980, median household income was $13,820 and 21 percent of families were below the poverty level. Of the 893 families, 55 percent were single parent. In 1988, 8 homicides, 92 assaults, 65 auto thefts, 154 drug arrests, 27 robberies and 25 burglaries were reported in the immediate vicinity (Figure 8.2).

Although the street was first developed in the 1930s, the problems of Drake Place are linked to a public housing project called East Gate Gardens, added in 1966. Marijuana dealing began in the late 1970s at the intersection of Drake Place and 51st St. (Figure 8.2). PCP was added in 1985, crack cocaine in 1987. Dealers moved off the street and into East Gate Gardens where transactions could be hidden more easily. Apartments were taken over as crack houses, then out-of-town dealers became involved, at which time violence rapidly escalated (Cary, 1989).

Debris, bullet holes, and graffiti mark the area, which residents describe as most unsafe after 11 PM. The behavior of residents has been affected, with a reduction in social trips and a clear increase in commu-nity fear complicated by the use of local children in the drug business and the concomitant anxiety experienced by their parents (Sanchez & Wheeler, 1989). Drake Place reportedly experienced increased drug activity as a result of the displacement of dealing from the Paradise Manor area in 1988. There, drug selling was curtailed by police and the Nation of Islam (see above for a description of Paradise Manor). This tendency of drug markets to pop up in new locations after suppression prompted a police official to refer to the markets as "Silly Putty" (Horwitz & Wheeler, 1989). (Other apparent displacement effects have been seen. Wheeler (1988) noted the effect on drug markets at 9th and U, NW, and the Sursum Corda apartments at 1st and M, NW, when Hanover Place, NW, reportedly the top ranking cocaine market in D.C., was occupied by police in 1986.)

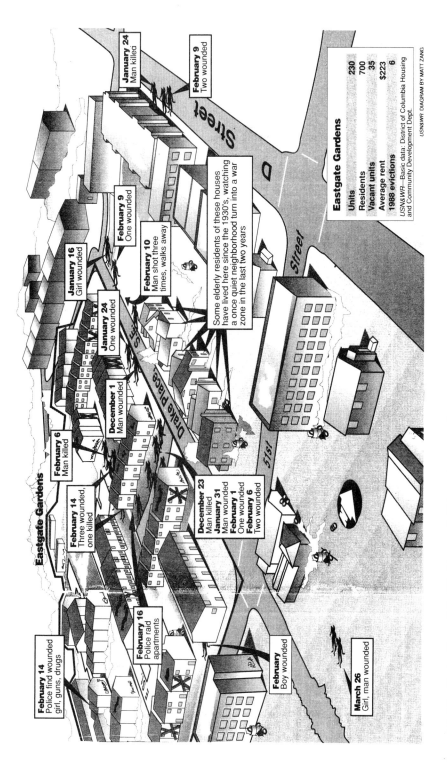

Figure 8.2. The Drake Place, S.E. (Washington D.C.) combat zone. *Source: U.S. News and World Report,* April 10, 1989, pages 30–31. Copyright, 1989, *U.S. News and World Report,* April 10, 1989. Reproduced by permission.

East Gate fits with a general Washington, D.C. pattern in which organizers of Neighborhood Watch programs and property managers who try to evict drug users or dealers are intimidated and have received death threats. Many residents work to *keep* drug dealers in the area; dealers pay for favors with "money, groceries and romance" (Brown, 1989a). Dealers are often perceived by residents as Robin Hood types who need community support. That support is bought in much the same way that politicians buy support with pork barrel legislation, or special interest groups buy politicians with political contributions. Community efforts against drugs are also undermined by slow police response, or no response at all (Brown, 1989b).

(Not all attempts at removal of drug activity fail. Accounts indicate that the greatest success is achieved if the community acts in concert before the area is completely dominated by drug activity. Such "removal," however, fails to account for displacement and impact on new host locations. Net social cost may actually increase. For additional reports, see: Duke, 1988; Wheeler, 1989.)

The physical geography of East Gate is favorable for a drug market. A hill above the complex allows sellers to look out for both customers and police, creating what the *Washington Post* referred to as a "king-of-the-hill" environment—"an almost perfect setting for an open air drug market"—with quick exit routes, "labyrinthine" buildings, and darkness, in combination with vacant lots and dilapidated apartments. New York crack dealers established themselves at Drake Place by renting space from female tenants and supplying them with free crack. The high quality of the crack offered by the New York dealers has given Drake Place a reputation drawing buyers from Maryland and West Virginia, turning it into a kind of regional center (Horwitz & Wheeler, 1989).

Drake Place appears to have achieved its notoriety for several reasons. The physical setting, including topography and the layout of buildings, in addition to other aspects of the microenvironment, are suited to the needs of a drug market. Local demographics suggest a poor population easily taken advantage of by dealers with money and drugs to offer in return for space. Neighborhood Watch is neutralized by threats against organizers and informers. A displacement effect may have accentuated an already intractable problem. Also, management problems at East Gate and the inability of police to provide effective surveillance or response, may have also contributed to the breakdown of social control.

Social Pathology, Drugs, and Violence

These vignettes emphasize the relationship between social pathology and drug-related violence. Studies of Baltimore by Nurco and co-workers (1972, 1984) showed a connection between narcotic addiction and deprivation; research based on a factor analysis of census tract data concluded that one underlying factor called *generalized social pathology* provided a substantial level of statistical explanation of addiction. Variables strongly linked to this factor included the illegitimate birth rate, venereal disease, and percent of population unmarried. Nurco et al. concluded that indications were that traditional values with respect to family had broken down, although whether this breakdown was a cause or an effect was unknown. The anecdotal data outlined above suggest that the ramifications of drug trading and use in poverty areas are becoming more entrenched and complex.

DRUG MARKETS

Spatially Focused Activities

A striking feature of drug-related violence is that it appears to be an exaggerated version of the day-to-day patterns of serious violence that existed before the drug invasion. Many neighborhoods that were known for high levels of violence in the 1970s are now known for high levels of drug-related violence. The distribution of such violence is distinctly nonrandom. Washington, D.C. provides a striking example of this focused violence, with tourists wandering the Mall area of museums and monuments with seeming impunity, while poor residential neighborhoods off the more beaten track suffer through the experience of a war zone (Figure 8.3). The drug and nondrug conflict zones are sharply demarcated; if we think in terms of gradients of violence as we move among these worlds, those gradients are extraordinarily steep, more akin to the edge of a cliff than to a gradual transition. Given that drug markets are just that—markets—the geography of marketing provides analogs to assist understanding.

Street or walk-in-type markets typically have a focal point, a center or strip where the businesses are physically located. They have a market area from which customers are attracted. They generate traffic and varying degrees of competition between sellers, depending on product

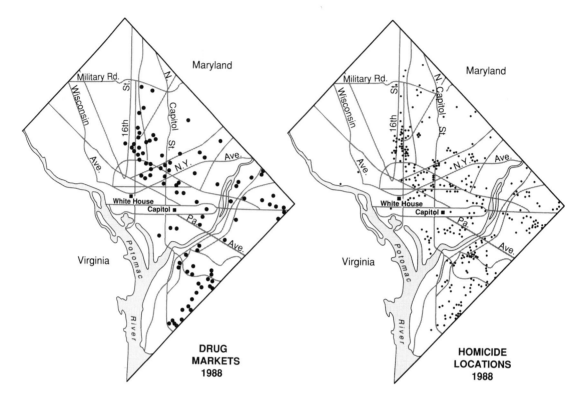

Figure 8.3. Drug market and homicide locations in Washington D.C. *Source: Washington Post,* January 13, 1989, p. E1. Adapted by permission of the *Washington Post.*

differentiation. For example, if all drug dealers are selling the same product, competition will be more intense than if each is selling a product clearly differentiated from the rest, in which case each dealer has a local monopoly. Thus drug markets may vary qualitatively in that their physical form, economic, and social organization are all variable, just as they are in any other market. Nevertheless, spatial focus is a constant. A particular dwelling, for example, is either a crack house, or it is not. A street corner or apartment yard is either known as a market or it is not. It is this spatial focus of drug markets that makes them a conspicuous element in the picture of serious violence. Reuter (1983) has noted several reasons that explain the localization of illegal markets in general: difficulties associated with monitoring the performance of distant agents, problems related to communication and the transportation of illegal substances over long distances, and the increased number of law enforcement agencies, both local and federal, who can potentially become involved in the transaction. However, the extension of Los Angeles gangs to about 50 other cities by late 1989 would appear to contradict the assertion that markets will remain local. The diffusion of Crip and Blood influence appears to have been spurred by a massive price difference between Los Angeles and the hinterland, providing sufficient incentive to overcome the difficulties cited by Reuter.

In a detailed analysis of the characteristics of street drug markets in Washington, D.C., Garreau (1988) pointed out that open air drug markets have developed rapidly: in 1976, there were reportedly 7, 81 in 1987, 91 in late 1988. Open settings are preferred, noted Garreau, primarily because they allow quick getaways. Heavily littered locations (so that drugs thrown down have no clear owner), are favored, as are commercial strips providing hiding places and shelter. Alleys with lots of trash are also popular; the trash prevents the intrusion of police vehicles. An important difference between conventional markets and drug markets is the lack of comparison shopping, owing to the urgency of transactions. In the interests of rapid dealing, prices are extremely uniform, with real price variation concealed in product differentiation by quality or quantity. Another difference between conventional and drug markets is that conventional markets, such as supermarkets, offer many product lines. Drug markets, however, tend to be set up in the form of what Garreau calls "drug boutiques" specializing in particular drugs, again in the interests of rapid service.

The demographic differentiation of drug markets is shared with conventional markets: older users tend to prefer heroin, younger PCP and crack. Dilaudid is preferred by whites. Cocaine is a higher status drug than heroin. More experienced users look for stronger versions of drugs, sometimes known by brand names. Thus users sort themselves to some degree by boutique, and by drug preferences. A reality-based drug market research would, in theory, reveal markets oriented to the demographics prevalent in each market area.

In drug markets, like "normal" markets, rent is used as a means of sorting retailers. However, in drug markets, "rent" is paid in the form of violence, with the greatest "price" paid for the best locations. In theory, a rent curve could be constructed, with degree of seriousness of violence on the Y axis and distance from the most desirable drug market location on the X axis, in a manner analogous to the bid rent model prevalent in urban economics and urban geography. (For further discussion of related issues, see Reuter, 1983, chapter 6.) Violence is also used as a tool in personnel management, to keep workers in line.

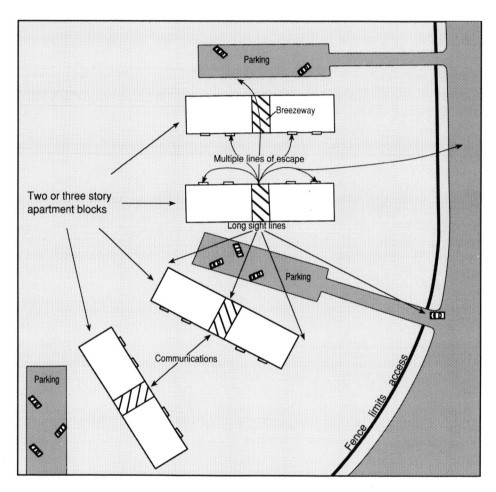

Figure 8.4. Drug market design. *Source:* Garreau, 1988, p. A14. Adapted by permission of the *Washington Post.*

Garreau (1988) also identified three desirable attributes of drug markets: *easy on-off, wide-openness* (Figure 8.4), and the presence of *barricades.* The easy on-off concept involves maximum traffic control in the form of a one-way street made narrow by cars parked on one side. Dealers can see who is coming and going. However, police can also control such streets by blocking the street or storming it against the traffic flow. A good example is the loop from 14th Street N.W. in Washington, D.C., around

Fairmont Street and University Place. Wide-openness implies long lines of sight for spotting approaching police, sheltered breezeways, and numerous escape routes to apartments, other breezeways, and adjoining woods (Figure 8.4). The Paradise apartments in Washington are a good example of wide-openness. The fencing of courtyards in the complex had the effect of keeping cars out, as intended, but that exclusion also kept out police cars and reduced the ability of police to apprehend drug dealers.

Barricades include any obstructions easily negotiated by drug runners while blocking police access. Garreau cited the example of Montana Terrace, N.E., in Washington, D.C. There, slopes are steep and stairs, fences, and curbs make the area virtually impenetrable for a police officer either in his or her vehicle, or on foot weighted down with gear. Teenage, male, unencumbered runners have the edge.

Thus different drug markets have unique geographies, both in terms of topography and their built environments, each offering a particular set of advantages. When economic organization favoring rapid service to specialized clienteles is combined with ruthlessly efficient social organization and specialized geographical advantages, one is better able to understand (a) how drug markets have been able to proliferate, and (b) why social control in the form of both policing and community involvement, has been relatively ineffectual.

The broader society generally views drug markets as morally repugnant, a threat to the entire social fabric. This impression is reinforced by media accounts of violence and child neglect of staggering proportions. However, the fact that authorities have difficulty co-opting residents in drug-affected areas indicates that the Robin Hood phenomenon may be stronger than has been generally appreciated. Drug dealers are apparently able to ameliorate to some degree the stresses and tensions of various communities by offering employment at high wages, and additional types of financial and other assistance. Robin Hoods need community support to survive; whether that support grows entirely out of physical fear of retribution or a more complex mix of variables, is unclear. Anecdotal information suggests that heavily drug-impacted communities are polarized into "acceptors" and "rejecters." Acceptance occurs through the dependency created by addiction, economic, and social benefits. Rejection is based on moral grounds or moral arguments on combination with fear of consequences to self or dependents.

Complicating the economic analog is the underlying pattern of poverty and related stresses forming a background over which drug transactions take place. Clearly, the patterns interact. The promise of high stakes in drug dealing lures young men who realize that they have no other opportunities—certainly none with comparable income potential. Naturally, it is the home turf of such young men that becomes the scene of their drug-related activities. Local contacts, including gang members, are part of their business assets, their "goodwill," but also part of their liabilities in that most incidents of violence occur between nonstrangers. Drug markets, then, become focal points of violence in the context of a larger neighborhood or community in which levels of violence are already higher than in the city at large. Drug-related violence, of course, is not confined to drug markets, but may occur in any setting involving drugs. Duke (1987) has identified three types of drug-related homicide: those concerning battles over turf, "drug deals gone sour," and murders committed by people under the influence of drugs. However, drug markets tend to constitute "hot spots" owing to the clustering of drugs, cash, weapons, and people. Where gangs are active, "turf" is no longer fought over for its own sake; it is actually sales territory.

SUBURBANITES AND DRUGS

Aside from police "interference," it would seem that drug markets are quite efficient in an economic sense. One important exception is that suburban buyers are constrained from substantial participation in central city drug markets by two factors: fear, and the growing availability of sources of supply in the suburbs. This is counter to the popular perception that white suburban drug users sustain central city drug problems. For example, in Operation Clean Sweep, a major drug crackdown conducted in the District of Columbia over a period between 1986 and 1989, 80 percent of the 47,896 arrests were district residents.

Interactions between the district and its suburbs in terms of drug dealing are quite complex. Goldberg (1989) has identified three main groups of suburban drug buyers: African Americans from neighboring Prince George's County buying from district drug markets just across the district line, blacks and whites who work in D.C. buying as they commute to or from work, and mostly white residents of more distant suburbs who keep returning to the district owing to established relationships with dealers. While fear is thought to inhibit transactions between suburbanites and urban dealers, some authorities indicate that the fear has been exaggerated; drug dealers are not usually so foolish as to kill their customers. Furthermore, most disputes resulting in violence are between dealers rather than between dealers and customers. Another factor overlying the "market demographics" of drugs is the degree of crowding in local jails. D.C. facilities are severely overcrowded (so much so that inmates are exported to other states, including Texas) with the result that penalties in the district are much less severe than in adjacent suburbs. This is common knowledge, and counteracts the fear factor noted earlier.

DISPLACEMENT AND LAW ENFORCEMENT ISSUES

What happens to patterns of violent crime when an area is purged of drug dealers? Is there a significant displacement effect in terms of drug dealing and the associated patterns of violence? Does displacement occur more with some types of crime than others? How do political and social boundaries impact such displacement? Can a purge of drug activities in one area lead to conflicts which actually increase the net amount of violence in society at large? These issues have important policy implications and are sources of considerable concern for many citizens and policy makers. In 1988, for example, Virginia Morris, the Chair of the Washington, D.C. 6th Police District Citizen's Advisory Council expressed alarm because police in the adjacent Prince George's County, Maryland, were "adding new muscle" and would be pushing drug dealers back across the district line into her area (Wheeler and Horwitz, 1988).

Questions about displacement and related issues have never been answered in a definitive way. As a result, little is known about the effectiveness of law enforcement efforts or the impacts of enforcement on communities and other entities directly or indirectly affected.

Crime Displacement

Displacement is an important policy question in at least two substantive areas, owing to the substantial resources allocated to area-specific, anti-drug crackdowns and "sweeps." The substantive areas may be categorized as related to *law enforcement* and to *community social structure and organization.*

Law Enforcement Implications

With respect to law enforcement, the fundamental question is whether such activities actually suppress drug crimes and drug-related violence, or merely displace the activities to another area or jurisdiction. The jurisdictional point is important; if crime is displaced within a jurisdiction, the net impact on that area in terms of law enforcement resources is theoretically unchanged. If, however, crime is displaced across a jurisdictional boundary, the problem then creates new net demands on the impacted agency.

Community Social Structure and Organization

Apart from the issue of the effect of displacement on police agencies, there is the broader social issue of the impact on community social structure and organization. If police activity has the effect of moving violence and other crimes to an area in which crime had not been prevalent previously, then police action is, from a community perspective, criminogenic. This is an extremely serious issue, with implications for community relations, police policy and morale, and the entire social and economic structure of the affected community. That this topic has drawn little research attention, however, is understandable. Cause and effect are hard to pin down; affected communities may not have the collective will or energy to recognize the process or to articulate concerns.

Theory

Displacement is a concept rooted in several issues with theoretical significance: territoriality and its subset, guardianship; fear psychology, spatial behavior theory, threat theory, and the complex of interrelationships incorporated in environmental criminology. The threat concept provides an attractive and concise framework within which to abstract the displacement phenomenon. At the intuitive level, one can appreciate that crime will not be displaced unless criminals perceive themselves to be effectively threatened by police activity. For displacement to occur, criminals' perceived threats of arrest or other sanctions must be greater in the "sending" area than in the "receiving" area. Churchville (1988b) presented an anecdotal example of the geography of threats in southeast Washington. An apartment manager acts as a kind of vigilante:

> An invisible line cuts through horseshoe-shaped Park Chester Apartments, separating the drug dealers and users from the decent, hard-working families. Three

people were shot to death within four blocks and 10 hours of one another this month [October, 1988] on the wrong side of that line... at... Park Chester II, young mothers herded children out of cars and into apartments... around the curb less than a block away at Park Chester I, bleary-eyed men smoked nervously in apartment entrances. Thin young women sat on building steps, some listless, others agitated as if they'd drunk too much coffee... between January and August, police have answered 553 calls for police help on that block, 62 of them involving drugs... they have made 47 drug-related arrests and have investigated reports of at least five shootings or stabbings... [1]

The vigilante, Annette Richardson, apparently exerts effective guardianship through the use of social sanctions (her presence and reproving remarks) which have effectively prevented crime displacement (or—a different phenomenon—diffusion) from Park Chester I to Park Chester II. Churchville's report presents the paradox of a 52-year-old matron exerting a more effective threat than the Washington, D.C. police department. This example serves to illustrate the guardianship power of phenomena other than formal law enforcement, and to emphasize the complexity of the displacement issue.

Another significant guardianship phenomenon is seen in the form of the activities of Black Muslims providing residential patrols in New York, Washington, D.C., and elsewhere (e.g., Gaines-Carter and Mintz, 1988; Hackett, et al., 1988). Territorial "reclamation" by police can be enormously expensive. For example, the Hanover Place case in Washington, D.C. resulted in 1,176 arrests in 1986 at a cost of $2 million in police overtime pay. Such experiences make it necessary to consider whether police action alone, police action in concert with community action, or community action alone are viable prevention strategies. If so, what permutations, if any, work under what conditions? The Hanover Place case, although apparently nominally effective, resulted in reported displacement to other established drug markets as noted earlier. (See also: Carter & Hill (1979) for additional insights.) New research is needed to clarify these issues.

GROWING UP IN THE INNER CITY

The attitudes of young male dealers were exemplified in a report in the *Washington Post* by Dash (1989). Wayne B. Bennett, known as "Jamaican Wayne," age 20, had carried a pistol since he was 17. Now in

---

[1] Reproduced by permission of the *Washington Post*.

prison on a shooting conviction, his code of conduct was the same as it had been on the streets: never back down, die or kill if necessary to defend your honor, and protect your reputation and manhood "at all costs." A review of his formative years showed that he became involved in progressively more serious violence, much of the time in order to develop a reputation as a street fighter. This involvement in violence occurred in a context in which violent acts have become progressively more likely to involve firearms. In the sixties and seventies, cheated dealers or suppliers would break a limb, or whip a victim with a coat hanger. Today, violence is on a higher level, and dealers must be willing to shoot those who cheat them in order to avoid being exploited.

Children's Play

Other accounts have noted how childrens' play has come to mimic the behavior of drug dealers, providing a kind of acculturation to the role of dealer's runner. Unlike most other children's game roles which remain fantasies for their participants, players of drug games can aspire to graduate to the roles they are playing within a few years. Players in Washington, D.C. are typically age 6 to 10 and play "Hustlers." Children mimic all the paraphernalia used by drug dealer: fake cocaine or crack, sandwich bags, foil for fake PCP cigarettes, Monopoly money, toy Uzi machine guns, and fake pagers. Roles are also copied, with "good guys" (hustlers) and "bad guys" (police). Division of labor is faithfully replicated: runners, lookouts, users, and police "jump-out" squads[2] (Sanchez, 1988).

Such data indicate the depth of the penetration of drug influence in poverty areas. While it has become unfashionable to refer to a "culture of crime" and sharp debate surrounds the issue of whether fundamental values differ between urban communities, the penetration of drug-related roles and terminology into play in the inner city suggests a juvenile environment differing sharply from that seen in the suburbs. The seeds of value inversion seem to be present in that police are seen as villains in the inner city and as helpers in the suburbs. The co-option of children into drug marketing is hastened by the fact that they are not subject to the adult criminal justice system, permitting them to perform criminal acts without the threat of adult criminal penalties. Furthermore,

---

[2]For a detailed explanation of "jump-outs," see Lait (1989).

the experience of many inner city children runs counter to anti-drug campaigns in that they have brothers or sisters who, however ephemerally, appear to be successful in their drug businesses, making lots of money and avoiding addiction, arrest, or violence (Sanchez, 1988). Ambivalence on the part of both children and their families is reinforced by the large flow of income children can provide to parents or other family members through their drug-related activities.

CONCLUSION

Significant issues surrounding the geography of drug-related violence remain to be explored. The almost complete lack of research means that discussion is presently limited to speculation and review of anecdotal information. Yet significant commitments of resources are made without informed debate on the consequences of various types of anti-drug enforcement efforts. Data available at the time of writing relating to the 1989 federal anti-drug initiative showed that drug czar William Bennett was requesting $200 million of additional support for state and local law enforcement and $295 million in aid for Peru, Bolivia, and Colombia. Drug treatment was to increase from $621 to $925 million, prevention and education from $941 m. to $1.2 billion. Prison construction would grow from $715 m. to $1.3 billion. The overall federal budget for drug countermeasures would increase 34 percent from $5.4 to $7.5 billion.

The debate over methods tends to dwell on the dichotomy between prevention, treatment and education, favored by the political left, and increased law enforcement, the strategy of the right. Even the cursory review outlined here suggests that a debate in these terms misses two points. First, allocating resources substantially to one of these policy directions is likely to predict failure, given that the streets must be made safer than they are, but that those children who have not yet become ensnared in the drug culture must have resources directed toward them in the hope of preventing their capture.

Second, policy horizons appear to be much too narrow, and short, in keeping with the proclivity of American culture to maximize results in annual cycles, mimicking the corporate demand for maximization of annual dividends. This inherently (impossibly?) short time frame is combined with an apparent misunderstanding of the degree to which drug-related violence is tied to the economic health of inner cities in general and of African American communities in particular. As a result, it is difficult to be optimistic about the chances of success of federal anti-drug programs. The so-called Watts Riots of 1965 provides an unfortunate example of an area (actually South-Central Los Angeles rather than Watts) targeted with various federal programs and yet today, by all accounts, a more dangerous and difficult environment in which to live than it was a quarter of a century ago.

At root, it seems that an expensive commitment to fundamental change in the mainly African American inner cities is politically unpalatable; defense, space, and agricultural programs are more likely to garner congressional support. Former drug czar Bennett clearly favored the law enforcement strategy, apparently discounting the prevention side of the equation (NBC News, 1989). In the following chapter, the discussion is extended by consideration of some policy questions relating to violence.

Chapter 9

PUBLIC POLICY IN SPATIAL CONTEXT

In 1993, violent crimes as defined by the FBI decreased by 2 percent, while homicide *increased* some 3 percent to a total of 24,526 incidents. The national homicide rate was 9.5/100,000, but for inner cities >250,000 the picture was much bleaker; New Orleans recorded 80.3/100,000 for the highest rate among cities, followed by Washington, D.C. (78.5/100,000), and St. Louis with a rate of 69.0/100,000 (FBI, annual, and Maguire and Pastore, 1995). The precise order of the cities is unimportant; what is significant is that the leading cities for violence have profound poverty, homelessness, drug-related predation, and the constellation of associated social ills, such as child abandonment, abuse, and neglect; blighted educational systems; elevated fear levels; continued outmigration of those able to move; employment losses; housing abandonment; arson, and an array of public health problems.

For example, infant mortality (widely regarded as an indicator of poverty and lately of drug use) in the District of Columbia increased from 19.3 per 1,000 live births in 1983 to 19.6 in 1987, 23.2 in 1988 and 32.3 for the first six months of 1989 (Abramowitz, 1989), and it remained stubbornly high in the 1990s. Comparable rates elsewhere were: about 17 in Cuba, 32 in North Korea, 38 in China, and 110 for all of Africa. This increase was attributed to drug use by women of child-bearing age and comes in the face of declining infant mortality in the South, from 13/1,000 in 1983 to 12 in 1987. Other poor, African American, inner cities such as Detroit and Baltimore also have exceptionally high rates (Rich, 1989a).

Violence is one facet of a series of interrelated and mutually reinforcing problems. They cannot be effectively confronted in isolation from one another. Violence is a symptom of other serious pathologies, and attempting to reduce it through the criminal justice system alone is bound to fail. Underlying causes will not have been addressed. In this chapter, some policy issues related to violence are discussed.[1] Primary consideration is given to the relationship between poverty and violence, but particularly that subset of the poor that has come to be known as the *underclass,* where, according to the most informed analyses, the breakdown of social norms is most complete and hopes for remediation in the foreseeable future are slight.

Other issues are really secondary to deep poverty. One that has attracted considerable attention is *gun control,* an approach much more complex than contemporary rhetoric would suggest. Given the upsurge in *drug-related violence* from Washington, D.C. to Medellin and Bogota, policies directed toward reduction of demand for, and supply of, drugs are of particular interest. Appointment of a federal drug czar in the late 1980s and the unveiling of a national policy by president Bush in 1989 attracted considerable attention and raised hopes that a solution had been found. The 1980s and 1990s also saw the emergence of interest in violence reduction in the *public health* field. The realization that injuries—including those due to interpersonal violence—made substantial claims on health care resources prompted the public health profession to investigate ways in which the paradigms of surveillance, epidemiology, and health education could assist in violence reduction. Also in the 1980s and 1990s, a wind of change blew through another profession—*policing*—with the emergence of the community- or problem-oriented model, in contrast to incident-based enforcement. Problem-oriented policing acknowledged the need to recognize that crime occurs in a finite sociophysical environment—a community. At least some conditions or events triggering crime are local and may be amenable to local manipulation.

POVERTY, VIOLENCE, AND POLICY

Even a casual observer of the urban scene will conclude that poverty and crime, including violence, tend to occur together, a view confirmed by more formal analysis, showing that "poverty is apparently causally related to crime at the individual level" (Berk, et al., 1980:766).[2] Violence is a phenomenon found wherever humans congregate, but poor

---

[1]For more comprehensive discussions of policy issues, see, for example: Rosenbaum (1986) and Wilson (1983).

[2]For discussion of the relationship between crime and unemployment, see, for example: Kohfield and Sprague, 1988; Devine et al., 1988; Cantor and Land, 1985.

communities seem more vulnerable that the affluent, where other forms of deviance, particularly the white collar variety, are more likely. However, a simplistic poverty-violence assumption is unacceptable; not all poor persons or poor areas are strongly prone to serious violence.

It has been shown that young African American males[3] are particularly at risk for violence; by and large, older persons are less likely to be involved, either as offenders or victims. Thus we observe an interaction between poverty, race, maleness, and youthfulness. It is those areas possessing all these components in relatively high concentrations that are most subject to what might be termed "background" violence, i.e., a continuing high level of violence as opposed to isolated incidents attracting attention as exceptions rather than as the rule.

At least two perspectives are available from which to view poverty. The *cultural* view, generally identified with conservative interpretations, regards the poor as having different values from the rest of society, and behaving differently as a result. This view has come under increasing attack in recent years. In a study undertaken by the National Academy of Sciences (Jaynes & Williams, 1989), it was pointed out that the validity of a culture of poverty is called into question by at least three conditions: (1) Many people move in and out of poverty, whereas the culture of poverty thesis predicts that poverty is a more or less permanent condition, (2) The poor fail to consistently show stereotypical characteristics of poverty, and (3) Various studies comparing poor and nonpoor have failed to find significant differences between the groups in terms of goals and values. DiIulio (1989), too, has argued that the cultural interpretation is both false and misleading. He concedes that culture of poverty notions do apply, but only to "the underside of the underclass," the criminal element among the poorest of the poor, who, for the most part, share the values of the larger society.

The *situationalist*, or *structuralist*, on the other hand, sees the behavior of the poor as a product of their position in society; they do not have different values, but they are unable to exercise the values of the larger society owing to circumstances (Waxman, 1983). In the United States, dominant values include material success, consumerism, and conspicuous consumption. Unable to compete in this arena, the poor turn to alternatives, including crime, which in turn may include violence. From

---

[3]For anecdotal insights on the plight of African American male youth, see: Welsh (1989) and, on the specific issue of African American youth becoming inured to the violence around them, see Goldberg (1989).

the structuralist viewpoint, the condition of the national economy may force more people into the stresses of poverty, increasing the probability of deviant behavior. Analysis by Brenner (1984) and Brenner and Swank (1986), for example, has suggested that the relationship between homicide and recession is "substantial."[4] The impact of economic stresses is far from geographically uniform; a salient fact relating to poverty and its relationship to the geography of violence is that poverty is becoming more concentrated in inner cities (Knox, 1988; Sawhill, 1988).

The Underclass[5]

In the 1980s, concern began to mount for the so-called *underclass,* a term used to describe the poorest African American ghetto populations, repeatedly described by such terms as "extremely destructive," and "bereft of hope" (Patterson, 1986). The underclass, however, is to be distinguished from the poverty population at large on the basis of its being characterized by exceptionally high levels of welfare mothers, ex-criminals (or unapprehended criminals), drug users, and school dropouts. Sawhill (1989) has noted that of the 32 million poor in 1987 (those below the 1987 poverty level of $11,611 for a family of four), about a third were elderly, a third were in temporary poverty due to job loss or other transient circumstances, and a third were "chronically poor"; it is from the latter group that the underclass comes. Research done by the Urban Institute (Sawhill, 1989) used 1980 census data to identify underclass neighborhoods (census tracts) on the basis of high[6] levels on all four of the following measures: dropout rates, families with children headed by females, welfare dependency, and unemployment or irregular employment among adult males. On this basis, 880 underclass neighborhoods were identified for 1980, containing 2.5 million people of whom 1.1 million were poor. Salient characteristics in underclass tracts were *lack of education* and *lack of males.* The lack of males can be attributed to their premature death, their incarceration, recruitment by

---

[4]See Cook and Zarkin (1986) for a critical review of Brenner (1984).

[5]For an historical perspective on the development of the underclass, see Lemann, 1986a,b.

[6]"High" in this context meant at least one standard deviation above the mean for the U.S. It should be pointed out that the census tracts so identified were almost all urban as tract data are not available outside Metropolitan Statistical Areas (MSAs—made up of urban counties). A resource available for many rural areas—Census County Divisions, analogous to census tracts—has apparently not been used to identify pockets of rural underclass.

the armed forces, and simple census undercount. The effect of the "missing men" is to exacerbate breakdown of the family (Jargowsky, 1989).

What makes the underclass different, according to DiIulio (1989), is not obvious traits such as welfare dependency, but also extraordinarily high levels of criminal victimization, both direct (in the form of homicides, assaults, rapes, and robberies) and indirect (in the form of lost economic development, males lost to violence or incarceration, child neglect and abuse, infant mortality, and so forth). Urban violence deters development in that bankers are reluctant to lend money for development in violence-prone neighborhoods and business tenants are unwilling to locate in areas seen as unstable or dangerous (Knight & Sherwood, 1989).

The underclass is *small* (1.1 million of 29 million in poverty in 1980) and *heavily minority.* Those better-off leave underclass-leaning neighborhoods if they can, so such areas "tip" toward containing essentially all underclass persons (Sawhill, 1989). We have no idea how much violent crime is accounted for by the underclass tracts nationally, or even in specific cities, indicating the degree of failure, in spite of available technology, in implementing integrated information systems that would permit monitoring of entire classes of social environments across American cities.

The two major concerns surrounding the underclass in the 1980s came to be *violent crime* and the deterioration of *family life,* the latter epitomized by the dramatic decline in the percentage of African American husband-wife households, from about 80 percent in the 1960s to 45 percent headed by women by the mid-1980s. Well over half of all births to African American women were outside marriage by 1982. This trend, in turn, meant growing numbers of predominantly black poor women and children. Patterson (1986) noted that earlier efforts to contain poverty had come from threats to the welfare of the middle class in the 1930s or "the optimism of affluence" in the 1960s, and he suggested that such considerations were likely to govern approaches to poverty in America in the foreseeable future.

The decline of manufacturing in American cities hastened consolidation of the underclass as higher-paying jobs were replaced by lower-paying, or not replaced at all, and union influence declined. Poverty became more prevalent in inner cities, where poverty rates increased from 13 percent to 19 percent between 1969 and 1985. Furthermore, the percentage with incomes more than 25 percent below the poverty level increased substantially between 1970 and 1982 (Harris & Wilkins, 1988).

Overall, poverty intensified in the 1980s and advances achieved in the social "safety net" unraveled (Burghardt & Fabricant, 1987). While the actual number of poor has diminished (from 35.8 million in 1983 to 32.5 million in 1987), those below the poverty threshold have not moved closer to it. Welfare benefits, including food and housing aid have not kept up with inflation, the minimum wage has not increased, eligibility has been cut in some programs, and unemployment has remained high in the 1980s (Rich, 1989b). In this context, research has shown that the economic progress made by African Americans since the 1940s has slowed or stopped in the last two decades. In the words of a report by the National Academy of Sciences (Jaynes & Williams, 1989, p. 4): "many black Americans remain separated from the mainstream of national life under conditions of great inequality," an observation attributed in part to continued discrimination. Based on his research on homicide patterns in Philadelphia in the nineteenth century, Lane (1980), too, urged that the separate economic development forced on urban African Americans must be ended.

Young males, regardless of race, are at risk with respect to serious violence, either as victims or offenders, or both, and ethnographic data from Brooklyn, New York, has tied lack of access to employment among young males to "more sustained and prevalent involvement in intensive criminal activities and to periods of probation and incarceration" (Sullivan, 1989: 52). This problem tends to be at its most serious in the African American community owing to lack of access to jobs and lack of training to equip young people for steady employment at a wage permitting independent living. As Hughes (1989) has noted: "A renewed war on poverty should seek to reconnect the ghetto to opportunity. Employers, governments and neighborhood organizations can work together to reconnect the ghetto to the social and economic life of our diverse and fragmented metropolitan regions."

A dimension of the discrimination issue is that the underclass, by virtue of its perceived and actual characteristics, becomes entirely isolated from the larger society. Its members come to be seen as addicted, crime prone, generally unreliable, and therefore unemployable. They are employees of last resort and, in any case, their labor surplus cannot connect with the labor shortage in the suburbs owing to the inadequacies of transportation networks. Furthermore, the minimum wage jobs available to those with a high school education cannot sustain a family. Jobs with wages capable of sustaining independent existence demand at least "some college."

Thus the isolation of the underclass is complete, and self- and other-directed acts of destruction become normative; underclass neighborhoods become "no man's lands" visited only by residents and emergency and other service providers compelled to enter.

Strategies for Reducing the Underclass

Sawhill (1989) has argued that several strategies could help ameliorate the underclass, including investing in children, providing support for those families that want to move out of the ghetto, replacing the welfare system with some form of income support related to employment, and providing incentives for young people to defer childbearing and complete educations.

DiIulio's approach (1989) involved a three-pronged attack on the problem of crime and the underclass: (1) *More intensive community-style policing* would be aimed at improving protection in underclass neighborhoods. (But it is unclear that manpower is available for such an effort; it would have to be integrated with neighborhood watch type activities and they tend not to work in such areas. See Herbert & Harries, 1986; Connelly, Harries, & Herbert, 1987; see also: Walinsky, 1995.) (2) *More intensive community-based correctional supervision programs.* Offenders are in practice just put back on the streets and left to their own devices. DiIulio argues that intensive supervision programs (ISPs) are needed on a much wider basis. ISPs are cheaper than incarceration, saving about $6,500/year/offender. "Shock incarceration" also needs to be evaluated carefully (the so-called "boot camp" approach). (3) *More programs aimed at diverting ghetto youngsters from drugs and criminal pursuits.* Crisis intervention programs are needed to bring gang leaders in contact with community leaders.

Bottom-Up Solutions

A degree of geographic flexibility in the form of implicit recognition that places are different should be retained in any theoretical or programmatic solution to underclass pathologies. While it is unfashionable to put undue emphasis on the uniqueness of places, since such uniqueness undermines the generality of theory, places *are* unique and the specific nature of the underclass in each place should be acknowledged and accommodated in the development of solutions. Residents must contribute to solutions—they live the stresses on a day-to-day basis. Some underclass characteristics, such as subjection to discrimination, are undoubtedly universal, but others may be more subtle, such as the way in which social networks are used to facilitate drug dealing and the nature of the local drug economy and the ways in which that economy is exploited, developed, and defended. The role of violence in underclass communities should be better understood, particularly in a comparative qualitative sense. How does violence in South Los Angeles differ from that in Washington, D.C. in terms of the purposes served, patterns of victimization and offending, and degree of gang involvement? If all conditions and attributes surrounding violent incidents could be placed in a multidimensional matrix of objective and subjective measures, would there be clusters in the multidimensional space? What would such clusters mean? Would underclass violence appear separately from "other poverty" violence, distinguished by more lethal weaponry, greater frequency, and greater drug involvement?

GUN CONTROL

Assumptions about gun control tend to be overly simplistic. Advocates pursue the concept as though it promises to end violence in America, while opponents emphasize that "guns don't kill people, people kill people." To a considerable extent, gun control in the U.S. is a case of shutting the barn door after the proverbial horse has bolted. By the time serious attempts at gun control began, such a massive number of firearms was in the hands of citizens (200 million, more or less) that *ex post facto* attempts at control were probably doomed to failure.[7] Comparisons with other more developed countries in Northwest Europe, for example, are odious; private gun ownership never achieved levels in those countries comparable to that in the U.S. Furthermore, the cultural climate has been, and is, different.

In Europe, there was no need for the frontier notion of the firearm as a viable form of personal security. Guns were for hunters, of whom there

---

[7] Also of considerable concern is the upward drift of numbers of stolen guns (about 300,000 per year) and the recent very large increase in U.S. pistol production, on the order of some two million units per year in the mid-1990s. (*Source:* Author's analysis of raw data underlying Zawitz, 1995. Data kindly provided by the Bureau of Justice Statistics.)

were few owing to high population densities, lack of spaces to hunt in and lack of creatures to hunt for. Handguns were quite pointless; criminals did not have guns, and in some countries, e.g., the U.K., neither did police. For a while, a criminal ethic operated to the effect that "we won't use guns if you don't" in the context that guns were, in any event, difficult to get.

In the U.S., on the other hand, gun ownership has been a constitutional right, guaranteed by the second amendment, a fact that has provided a kind of cultural endorsement for the notion of universal gun ownership. *Not* owning a gun bordered on the unpatriotic. Perfect hindsight suggests that if it had been possible to enforce strict gun control early in the nation's history, a basis might now exist for effective control.

Consistent with its record of weak gun control, the U.S. has historically been an essentially free market for guns, leading to more guns, in greater variety, than in any other more developed country. It is estimated that anywhere from 35 to 70 million handguns are in circulation, and licensing will not change that number. Thousands of gun laws at the municipal, state, and federal levels appear to have been ineffectual in controlling guns, particularly handguns, responsible for the largest fraction of gun crimes. After all, criminals, by definition law breakers, are unlikely to obey gun control laws.

Furthermore, it is quite unclear exactly what "gun control" means (Lizotte, 1986). Is it laws to punish criminals committing crimes with guns? Is it licensing of owners? Is it restrictions on certain types of guns, such as "Saturday Night Specials?" Handgun control has attracted considerable support, but Lizotte (1986) has argued that a handgun ban would result in a shift to shotguns, sawed-off shotguns, or rifles. The established relationship between gun caliber, death, and injury suggests that a shift of this sort by only 20 percent of handgun criminals would result in a doubling of the crime-related death rate. This displacement effect, however, has been disputed by Sproule & Kennett (1989) on the basis of evidence from Canada. In any case, a total ban on handguns in the U.S. is probably unenforceable owing to fourth amendment provisions preventing illegal search and seizure (quite apart from costs).[8]

---

[8]For a detailed analysis of the gun control issue, see Kleck, 1991, 1995, and Alba and Messner, 1995a,b.

Comparisons between the United States and Canada

Some research has provided a geographical perspective on the issue. The role of cultural differences with respect to guns was demonstrated in a study by Sloan et al. (1988), comparing the firearm environments of Seattle, Washington, and Vancouver, British Columbia for the period 1980 through 1986. These cities were selected for their proximity, similarity, and shared cultural values (shared, that is, except with respect to gun control). Robberies, burglaries, assaults and homicides were compared between the cities. The rate of assaults involving firearms was seven times higher in Seattle than Vancouver and the age- and sex-adjusted relative risk of homicide death was significantly higher in Seattle than Vancouver. This "excess" hazard lay in the much higher risk of handgun murder in Seattle, compared to Vancouver and was attributed to a much higher level of firearm ownership in Seattle. Sloan et al., (1988: 1261) felt able to conclude that "restricting access to handguns may reduce the rate of homicide in a community."

The effect of differences in gun control laws has been illustrated, also in the context of a U.S.-Canada comparison, by Sproule and Kennett (1989), who noted that the effectiveness of gun control has not been clearly demonstrated in the U.S., in contrast to a "significant decrease" in shooting homicide rates in Canada following the enactment of "stringent" gun control in 1976. They suggested that "discrepant findings regarding the benefits of gun control between Canada and the U.S.A. are likely the result of differences in the rigour [sic] and pervasiveness of gun control. In comparison to Canada, gun control in the United States, particularly pertaining to handguns, is remarkably lax" (pp. 245–246).

What makes Canadian law stronger than its American counterpart is that it is federal (Criminal Code of Canada) and quite restrictive in terms of the criteria for handgun ownership. By contrast, U.S. law, as noted elsewhere, is fundamentally state or local and may be circumvented by crossing to another jurisdiction. Analysis showed that firearms were less involved in Canadian killing and that American murder rates were higher for *handguns alone* than the *total* Canadian rate. In light of this finding in combination with the earlier research showing that Canadian shooting homicide declined after the introduction of gun control in Canada (Sproule & Kennett, 1988), it was concluded that "Canadian gun control, especially the provisions pertaining to handguns, does have the beneficial effect of saving lives" (Sproule and Kennett, 1989:249).

U.S. Examples

In another comparative study, Jung and Jason (1988) evaluated gun control laws in East St. Louis, Illinois and Evanston, Illinois against a background that included mixed findings for Boston, MA, Washington, D.C., and Michigan. In Boston, gun assaults and armed robberies declined after a gun control law, but nongun assaults and nongun robberies increased, suggesting the displacement effect noted by Lizotte. Homicides fell overall. In Washington, the sale and transfer of handguns was prohibited (1977), and this appeared to result in a decrease in handgun deaths in domestic altercations, although, overall, the effect of the law was unclear. Homicides, as noted below, remained flat, then increased dramatically in the late 1980s. In Michigan, homicides, robberies, and assaults did not change significantly.

Jung and Jason suggested that certain types of gun control legislation seem to be more effective than others. For example, where the penalty for gun control violation is small, there is no deterrent effect, since the robber or offender in other cases of serious violence is likely to draw a much more severe penalty for the crime itself than for the weapons violation incorporated in it, so the incentive is to simply ignore the gun law.

The Illinois laws were enacted in 1981 (East St. Louis) and 1982 (Evanston). In East St. Louis, residents were prohibited from carrying firearms in the street. In Evanston, handguns were banned. In both cities, *firearm assaults* decreased[9] prior to the law. In East St. Louis, firearm assaults increased after the law, in Evanston, there was no change in the post-law period. For *firearm robberies,* East St. Louis decreased pre-law and increased post-law, the same pattern as firearm assaults. In Evanston, no change was observed before or after. Jung and Jason suggested that penalties need to be sufficiently harsh to ensure a deterrent effect. They also noted that the media may have had a role in the pre-law reductions in both cities; about 80 newspaper stories were run on the pending legislation in both places. This possibility reinforces the idea that gun control is an extraordinarily complex issue. Local social context, previously existing levels of gun ownership, media involvement, levels of penalties embedded in the laws, gang culture, and other issues, may all be influential.

---

[9]The terms "increase" or "decrease" here are used in the technical sense to mean statistically significant change.

Approaches to Gun Control

Zimring (1986) cited six different approaches to gun control, none of which has been particularly effective for a variety of reasons: "place and manner" restrictions, harsher penalties for firearm violence (see McDowall et al., 1992), preventing high-risk groups from owning guns, permissive licensing, registration, and reducing numbers of handguns. Compounding the inherent difficulty of attempting to impose control when the problem is already of unmanageable proportions is that authority for gun control is found at both the state and federal levels. Inevitably, guns drift from less to more restrictive environments, such as from Virginia and Maryland into Washington, D.C., and lack of boundary controls makes such drift both inevitable and uncontrollable. A spatial view of guns and gun control would reveal a complex patchwork of laws and peaks and valleys of gun crime.

The geographies of gun law and gun behavior, in theory, should show some degree of congruence, at least if the laws are working. In practice, the distributions are probably unrelated for a variety of reasons, including the difficulty of enforcement. The most draconian of gun laws means little if it cannot be enforced. Even if it is assumed that the *de facto* (legal and illegal) gun ownership "surface" is essentially uniform among small geographic areas, this says little about the spatial surface of illegal use, which is coincident with the geography of homicide and assault and peaks primarily in inner city poverty areas.

What gun control policy, if any, could effectively address this localized peaking in illegal ownership and use, the phenomenon accounting for much of the concern about gun control? Gun control advocates would argue that there should be more controls; the National Rifle Association, the most outspoken advocate of firearm permissiveness, would oppose controls as an abridgement of second amendment rights. It is not clear that either more controls or continued permissiveness will have a significant effect on outcomes. Marginally, if controls prevent weapons from falling into the hands of some persons prone to violence, then some violent incidents may be prevented or reduced in severity given that the weapon used will be less effective.

Well-publicized multiple killings in the late 1980s using semiautomatic weapons such as the AK-47 rifle led to calls for a ban on these assault weapons on the grounds that they have no legitimate use in private hands. If such a ban were enacted and effectively enforced, the displacement effect to other firearms would be beneficial in that other weapons are less lethal. President Bush would not support a ban, however, in spite of poll data showing a clear majority of the population in favor (Abramson, 1989). Piecemeal state or local efforts are unlikely to have much effect. As the debate continues, the number of assault weapons in private hands continues to grow. Although imports of such weapons have been banned, domestic production continues, rendering the ban on imports essentially pointless. Also, even though assault rifles have received a great deal of publicity, the fact remains that the weapon of choice in most gun crimes is the handgun (Zawitz, 1995).

Even a marginal reduction may not be achieved in practice and if there were such a reduction it might be offset by displacement to other weapons if specific guns are banned or restricted. The reverse of the desired effect may occur in that a ban on handguns, for example, could trigger a black market in weapons circumventing *all* licensing or registration requirements and resulting in a higher level of gun ownership than would have occurred without a ban. Furthermore, the illicit gun trade itself may act as a crime generator and thus contribute further to the overall toll of violence.

This scenario may be playing in Washington, D.C., where handguns were banned in 1977. In the years following, handgun homicides remained stable at around 100 per year and then took off in 1987 and reached about 240 in 1988. This happened in the face of firearm seizures of 2,065 in 1987 and 2,478 in 1988. Detailed analysis of violence in Washington, D.C. for the (longer) period 1968–87 showed that "the adoption of the gun licensing law coincided with an abrupt decline in homicides by firearms (a reduction of 3.3 per month, or 25%) and suicides by firearms (reduction 0.6 per month, or 23%)" (Loftin et al., 1991:1615; see also Goldstein, 1991). However, this decrease was eventually rendered moot by the massive outburst of violence related to the introduction of crack cocaine in the late 1980s.

It was estimated that some 55 to 60 percent of the guns seized in Washington, D.C. were from Maryland and Virginia. In the 1980s, it was estimated that about twice as many guns came from Virginia as Maryland (Lewis, 1988). In 1995, however, Maryland exceeded Virginia for the first time in terms of supplying handguns used in violent crimes in Washington, D.C., suggesting that Virginia's law limiting handgun purchases to one per month, enacted in 1993, may have been somewhat effective. Maryland introduced legislative proposals in 1996 mimicking

Virginia's law in the hope of preventing "straw purchases" in which persons without (known) criminal records would buy large numbers of guns for resale (Jeter, 1996).

Regardless of the intrinsic value of gun control, opinion about it is clearly a creature of geographic context. In a 1988 vote on a weak gun control measure to limit "Saturday Night Specials" in Maryland, for example, rural areas typically voted heavily against the measure. In Garrett County, in rural western Maryland, the vote was overwhelmingly anti-control. In precinct 13, 83.5 percent of the votes were against, 3.7 percent for (the balance of the 100% did not vote on this issue). In contrast, precinct 17 in the predominantly African American inner city of Baltimore voted 74.1 percent for and 15.9 percent against. Precincts in suburban counties tended to be polarized according to degree of development, with those more developed voting for, the more rural against. However, degree of development is not necessarily well correlated with degree of risk; it appeared in the Maryland case that low-risk suburbs had essentially the same voting pattern as the high-risk inner city, but presumably for different reasons. The suburbs vote for control as a matter or principle, the inner city in the hope of getting guns off their streets.[10]

Research on gun ownership in the inner city has shown that young urban African American women (who are least likely to be protected by the criminal justice system and most likely to be victimized) are more likely to own guns than any other group, presumably for protection. Whether this strategy actually works for them is unknown, although it has been shown that criminals prefer to victimize unarmed citizens. Handgun control, then, could increase the rates of injury and death for poor African American women (Lizotte, 1986). Such scenarios serve to further demonstrate the complexity of the gun control issue and demonstrate that a constellation of unintended consequences may follow from well-meaning gun control policies.

Cook (1983) concluded that firearm availability has a "profound influence" on patterns of violent crime, and that gun availability is "directly related to the homicide rate." Unfortunately, however, concern for these problems cannot be readily translated into effective control through law. At the theoretical level, it is clear that levels of gun

---

[10]I am indebted to my colleague Dr. Robert Earickson for providing access to Maryland gun control vote data.

availability are associated with violent crime. If there were no firearms, no gun-related crimes would be possible. While the relationship may not be linear, the probability of any given conflict or crime involving a firearm at some stage is in part a function of the availability of a weapon. A result that policy seems unable to elicit is to deprive the "bad guys" of guns while permitting the "good guys" to keep them.

Is there any point whatsoever in legislating gun control? This question should be answered on at least two levels. *Objectively,* the results of gun control are varied and ambiguous; to say that gun control in the U.S. appears not to work at all may be too strong, but it certainly appears not to work, or not to work well, in a number of contexts in which it has been tried. Nevertheless, in the *subjective* sociopolitical arena it may be argued that people need the reassurance, however misguided, that comes from indications that lawmakers are *trying* to solve "the gun problem." If efforts are to continue, as they surely will, policy makers should, in a perfect world, strive to inject a degree of rationality into the legislative process by avoiding the futility and possible counterproductivity in such exercises as banning handguns in one jurisdiction but not in adjoining ones, or even of banning one type of weapon and not others, given the possible adverse displacement effects alluded to above. Penalties, too, should be carefully crafted to avoid those so light that deterrence fails.

Again, even constructive suggestions are likely to fall prey to historical inertia—municipalities and states will only reluctantly surrender any of their authority to write gun control legislation, thereby ensuring continuation of the ineffectual crazy quilt of control laws. Neither the context of present levels of gun ownership nor the culture of lawmaking are likely in the foreseeable future to facilitate effective gun control.

DRUGS AND VIOLENCE

The late 1980s were marked by a scramble by politicians to make political hay out of the drug issue. This had the effect of subverting what could have been a relatively objective debate and turning it instead into an exercise in shrill claims, self-righteous denunciations, and simplistic "good guy, bad guy" scenarios. This degeneration was exemplified by the revelation that a bag of crack cocaine, used by President Bush as a prop in a drug speech in September, 1989, had been confiscated from a teenage drug dealer who was lured to Lafayette Park, in front of the White House, by a drug enforcement administration agent. This was done so that the facts would fit a line written into the President's speech. Lafayette Park is not known as a drug dealing location, and the dealer, when told where the buy was to be made, is reported to have replied "Where the [expletive] is the White House?" (Isikoff, 1989).

A major issue in the context of drug-related violence is that young people, particularly young African American males, are heavily involved. In this connection, Brounstein et al., (1989) surveyed 387 minority male adolescents in the District of Columbia in order to find out how adolescents involved with drugs or criminal activities of other kinds differed from those not involved. They found that users differed from nonusers in several respects: users' heads of household were less educated, other household members were more likely to be drug/alcohol users, users saw themselves as less similar to parents in terms of values and attitudes, they perceived less support in the home and a lower quality home environment, and they were less likely to be in school or to perceive school as a positive environment. Peer, school, home, and personality factors were good predictors of drug use, including: lack of interest in school and a perception of lack of support at school, degree of difference in attitude compared to parents, and level of substance abuse by friends.

Findings implied that interventions must be customized to the behavior of specific target groups. For example, those who use, but do not sell drugs should be treated differently from those who sell but do not use. It was recommended that prevention should be in schools, home, media, and community. *Schools* should reach youth more effectively, experiment with substance abuse programs, employ special teacher training, make more use of volunteers to identify kids with problems, have clear rules and enforce them fairly, target those who have or will drop out, and improve record-keeping. In the *home,* the principal need is for better parenting. In the realm of *media,* TV and radio could be very influential given that kids watch a lot and listen a lot. *Community organizations* should provide activities, parent support groups, and related activities or services designed to enhance community cohesion. *Local government* should develop alternatives to incarceration. Better screening is needed, weeding out minor and first-time offenders. The report concluded that "the problems of drug use, sales, and juvenile crime are based to a large extent on major societal problems, such as past discrimination, low income, poor housing, and poverty . . . these issues need to be addressed. Nevertheless, the drug problem is too great not to face it directly" (Brounstein et al., 1989:ES 11).

The National Commission on the Causes and Prevention of Violence (1969) advocated "improvement of the response to narcotic and drug use." In the course of its discussion, the Commission noted that "severe criminal sentences seem to have little deterrent effect," and further, that

> despite these prohibitions, the illegal use of narcotics and dangerous drugs appears to be increasing, with a commensurate increase in the number of addicts who may be forced into illegal activities to sustain their habits. By the same logic, the involvement of organized crime in this lucrative trade is almost sure to increase commensurately. We recommend . . . initiation of a massive effort on all aspects of drug abuse, amendments to existing federal and state laws governing the manufacture, sale, and distribution of narcotics and dangerous drugs, and new approaches for the treatment of offenders (National Commission, 1969:746).

Of course, no such "massive effort" has been forthcoming on "all aspects of drug abuse." Rather, the major initiative launched by President Bush in 1989 put overwhelming evidence on law enforcement approaches. Experts saw little hope in such an approach; they regard the key to the problem as reducing self-destructive behavior through education. Also, the President's equating of the drug problem to crack is unrealistic; eventually some other substance will replace crack as the drug of choice. The view from the streets, too, was that the plan was "too limited" and "too simplistic" (Schmalz, 1989). Public perception of the plan was that it was not far-reaching enough. Poll respondents favored long prison terms for those convicted of selling cocaine, and some 13 percent favored the death penalty for this offense. Only a small minority (10%) favored some form of legalization (Morin, 1989b).

Overall, the law enforcement oriented program announced by President Bush is unlikely to have much impact either on the crime rate or the drug problem. According to Gottfredson and Hirschi (1989b), the typical crime is spur-of-the-moment, involving little time or skill. They noted two facts reducing the effectiveness of law enforcement. First, *offenders are highly versatile and thus unpredictable,* suggesting that the common denominator is not type of crime, but "low self-control." If drug use and other crimes are found together, they argued, it is not because drug use is causing the other type of crime, but that various types of crime produce immediate gratification. Serious violence of the type discussed here may be an exception to this assertion, however, in that drug dealing has clearly generated violence over turf, nonpayment, and other drug-related issues.

Second, *drug use and crime diminish with age.* This makes long sen-

tences quite pointless and extremely expensive; offenders will be imprisoned long after their criminal behavior has gone away, at an average cost
of $25,000 per person per year. At this price, cynics have noted, offenders
could be sent to Harvard. Childhood behavior is a good predictor of
future delinquency. Therefore, according to Gottfredson and Hirschi,
prevention must be directed toward children. In this scenario, parenting,
not policing, is the key. (See also Chapter 2.)

Is Legalization a Solution?

As the costs of drug control escalate and the effectiveness of such
efforts becomes increasingly doubtful, debate inevitably turns toward
the legalization option. That debate has been muted, however, as public
opinion is so opposed to legalization, and politicians are thus constrained
from embracing it, regardless of its possible advantages. Baltimore mayor
Kurt Schmoke (1988) and Ethan Nadelmann (1989), among others,
have argued persuasively in favor of legalization. In testimony before the
U.S. House of Representatives Select Committee on Narcotics Abuse
and Control, Schmoke described the U.S. policy of zero use of all illicit
drugs as " . . . both unambiguous and unimaginative . . . [and] unattainable
. . . zero tolerance . . . is not a policy at all—it's a fantasy." Schmoke
described the case for decriminalization as "overwhelming," and argued
that drug abuse is a health problem that should be handled by the public
health system, not by the criminal justice establishment. After all,
addicts tend to return to addiction after incarceration, indicating that
confinement achieves no useful purpose, apart from separating the addict
from the community. But the model for other diseases is confinement in
a medical facility, not a prison. The consequences of the present approach
are that: (1) Addicts commit crimes to permit the purchase of drugs; if
drugs were cheaper, as they would be if legalized, the incentive to
commit crimes would diminish. (2) The criminal justice system is
chronically overloaded, and it is essentially impossible to build enough
prisons to hold all the drug offenders. (3) Attempts to shut down
supplies have failed. (4) Children are victimized in a variety of ways. (5)
The spread of AIDS is assisted. (6) Our laws tend to foster the importation of more concentrated forms of drugs, in order to reduce volume,
and (6) To control access to drugs but not to tobacco and alcohol is
highly inconsistent. More than 350,000 people per year die prematurely
of tobacco-related diseases, yet tobacco is cheap, readily available, and

heavily advertised. Schmoke recommended that the role of public health in drug treatment and prevention should be expanded, and that the role of the criminal justice system should be redefined, including exploration of the likely impacts of decriminalization.

Nadelmann, similarly, argued that prohibition of drugs now is as much of a failure as prohibition of alcohol was in the 1920s. Federal, state, and local expenditures on drug enforcement amount to at least $11 billion, with minimal impact. The dollar value of the drug black market is between $10 and $50 billion per year, a sum that could yield rich tax revenues. No drug, noted Nadelmann, is as liable to produce violent behavior as alcohol. The unregulated drug supply is often contaminated or of unknown strength. Like Schmoke, Nadelmann argued that AIDS is promoted by the present laws, and also drew attention to the problem that law enforcement resources are directed toward the harassment of drug consumers who are not harming others. He predicts a tax yield of "at least $10 billion per year and possibly much more," funds that could be applied to treatment, education, and other programs. Nadelmann estimated alcohol-related deaths at 50,000 to 200,000 per year, and tobacco-related deaths at 320,000 per year, compared to only 3,562 victims of illegal drugs in 1985. He did acknowledge that legalization is risky; compared to the failure of current approaches, however, he argued that the risk is worth taking. While there is little public support for decriminalization, indications are that some heads are being turned (see, for example, Raspberry, 1989) as the utter failure and staggering expense of present policies become more obvious. However, others have noted that the legalization of drugs poses the risk of enormously increased levels of use, as was the case following removal of the prohibition of alcohol (See, for example, Inciardi and McBride, 1990; and Inciardi et al., 1995).

VIOLENCE AND PUBLIC HEALTH

Over the last decade or so, violence has increasingly become a topic of interest to the public health community, both in the United States and abroad (see, for example, Delamothe, 1988). As Foege (1985) noted, premature death has historically had two leading causes: *infectious diseases* and *violence*. The former have substantially come under control through the use of vaccines and antibiotics. Violence, however, has not proven amenable to solutions offered in various realms, including health, politics, religion, and law enforcement.

Injury, intentional and unintentional, is the most significant issue not yet under effective attack by public health professionals. Injury accounts for 4.1 million years of life lost before age 65 per year, while heart disease and cancer account for 3.8 million. The budget for injury, however, is only a fraction of that for heart disease and stroke. Foege (1985, 1988) pointed to the need for better surveillance, or measurement, and also the need for better understanding of violence in its broad context. He noted that effective leadership in combatting violence would most likely come from the local level and be followed by federal action, citing the example of the adoption of the first child restraint law in Tennessee, followed by adoptions in other states (Foege, 1985).

Education

One expression of a public health approach to the violence issue is represented by the work of Prothrow-Stith (1985, 1989) in Boston. The Boston Youth Program curriculum on anger and violence has been established in four high schools and one community agency. The intent of the curriculum is to raise the students' threshold for violence "by creating a nonviolent ethos within the classroom and by extending [the student's] repertoire of responses to anger." Pre- and post-tests demonstrated the effectiveness of the curriculum, although change in knowledge accounted for more of the difference than did change in attitude. Prothrow-Stith advocated a national health education initiative using a standardized version of her curriculum (Prothrow-Stith, 1985). However, whether the curriculum actually works to reduce violence is unclear; a rigorous evaluation of it is under way, based on data from Compton, CA; Detroit; Gary, IN; Houston, New York; and Philadelphia. Prothrow-Stith has noted that: "The public health model of disease as applied to violence makes it glaringly obvious that the fundamental causes of violence in our society lie in our environment, our social environment" (Zylke, 1988).

Other physicians have suggested incorporating violence counseling into medical practices seeing adolescents in higher risk areas (Stringham & Weitzman, 1988).

Injury Measurement

Apart from epidemiological and educational models, public health can also contribute in the realm of measurement of severity of physical injury. Allen (1986) advocated an advance over methods developed thus far by criminologists relying on such criteria as whether or not the victim requires hospitalization, the number and location of wounds to the victim, and firearm caliber in combination with the number and location of wounds. Such methods are generally unacceptable; the Abbreviated Injury Scale (AIS) overcomes the problems of the measures developed by criminologists by using an ordinal code system to confer severity values on more than 500 specific injuries. Subsequently, the AIS was modified to assess multiple injuries based on the AIS scale for individual injuries, in a scale known as the Injury Severity Score (ISS), described by Allen as "a valid measure of injury severity." The underlying problem with the operationalization of the AIS/ISS system is that criminal justice data do not embrace the elements necessary for inclusion in the scale. Such data are best obtained from hospital records, not accessible to criminologists. Applications of the AIS/ISS system could be found in criminal victimization studies, the impact of career violent criminals in terms of injuries caused, and in victim compensation.

Is the Public Health Model Applicable?

The tools of public health—epidemiology, surveillance, risk group identification, and risk factor definition and exploration, followed by the development and evaluation of intervention programs (Rosenberg, Mercy, & Smith, 1984; Mercy and O'Carroll, 1988)—have traditionally been directed toward the detection and amelioration of infectious diseases (see also Jason, 1984.) Whether they are adaptable to dealing with a problem with fundamentally social causes is unclear. Some types of violence or injury may be more amenable to the public health model than others. Injury in auto accidents, for example, has been reduced through the use of seat belts and lower speed limits. But such strategies have no clearly practicable analog with respect to homicide.

The discussion here has shown that violence is primarily a creature of the inner city African American community, where the array of social problems is complex and overwhelming. It would appear that a solution independent of amelioration of the chronic stress experienced in the inner city is likely to fail, regardless of the tenacity of any particular interest group. Public health, as an institution, has neither the resources nor the personnel, at the present time, to make a profound impression on the problem. Political experience in the 1980s and 1990s showed that the public and their political representatives are amenable to law enforcement types of "solutions" at the expense of other kinds of initiatives, including public health. The inertia linking public health to disease as traditionally perceived may take a generation to overcome. While this education of the public is in progress, massively larger resources will need to be allocated to public health initiatives if public health is to make progress on violence reduction. Most troubling, however, is that the public health community has not produced a model clearly demonstrating how public health methods will reduce homicide and assault. The conventional tools listed above are powerful, indeed, but the missing link is just how they will be operationalized in the reduction of homicide.

What will the intervention programs be and how will they work? Can they be expected to have a significant effect in reducing serious violence? Given that no one discipline has been able to impact the violence issue, it should be assumed that future efforts must be interdisciplinary. How will public health incorporate perspectives from other disciplines? How will other disciplines accommodate the public health view? No clear answer seems to be emerging, as of the mid-1990s.

Whitman (1988), while approaching the issue of violence from a public health standpoint, argued that the public health approach should embrace broader issues. He identified four categories of violence prevention: *"doing nothing"*, *education, legislation, environmental modification,* and *restructuring society* in order to reduce racism and poverty, conditions contributing to violence. "If violence is a health issue," wrote Whitman, "then its prevention will be pursued honestly when major medical journals begin to publish articles that cite capitalism, racism, and sexism as causes." Whitman advocated several principles to guide violence prevention, including: fight racism, sexism and poverty; provide communities with the tools they need for violence prevention; do things *with* people to prevent violence, rather than *to* them; and avoid blaming victims.

Straus (1986) has noted that family violence, in particular, should involve caution in the involvement of medical agencies and professionals in primary prevention. First, public health expectations may be exceeded owing to the fact that some of the causes of family violence are not recognized as health-related but are seen, rather, as religious or moral issues, such as male dominance in the family. Straus suggested that for this reason, only a selection of risk factors should be put on the public health agenda. Second, problems are associated with the medicalization of various issues, including stigmatizing labeling and the intrusion of a profession into a realm for which its practitioners are not trained. Furthermore, attention may be drawn away from the social issues underlying the violent behavior. Straus ultimately advocates "the sociological-ization of a medical problem, not the medicalization of a social problem."

A search of the *Current Contents* data base indicated that a substantial stream of research on the issue is not forthcoming, as yet. The search revealed 188 entries containing the key words *public health*. None of the titles contained the terms *crime, homicide, injury, murder,* or *violence.* Titles suggested that AIDS and other issues have moved attention away from violence as a public health concern. While this search was far from all-inclusive, it is indicative of the dearth of new statements on the issue.

COMMUNITY POLICING AND VIOLENCE

A new approach to policing involves apprising police officers of the ecology of their areas and involving them in local problem solving. The underlying assumption is that crime is not an isolated phenomenon "treatable" only through law enforcement. It is seen as a "product" of the community in the sense that local conditions, such as presence of the underclass and the constellation of connected problems are local and may be relieved at the local level. This approach, variously known as *community policing* or *problem-oriented policing* (Goldstein, 1979; Eck & Spelman, 1987) contrasts with *incident-oriented policing* dealing with events in isolation from their context, without follow-up or understanding of antecedents. In problem-oriented policing, police officers become part social workers, part community organizers. In one model tried in Newport News, Virginia, a four-stage problem-solving process was developed: scanning, analysis, response, and assessment. At the *scanning* stage, an issue is studied in order to determine whether it is a significant problem. During *analysis,* data are collected from various sources with the objective of understanding the problem, including its causes. The *response* stage attempts to develop solutions and *assessment* involves an evaluation of the effectiveness of responses to the problem (Eck & Spelman, 1987).

Can problem-oriented policing have a significant impact on serious violence? The idea that all forms of violence could be reduced through this approach is far-fetched, but certain types of violence may be at least partially ameliorated by informed police action. Wilson and Kelling (1989) noted that some 60 percent of police calls come from only 10 percent of addresses. Many incidents are domestic and have the potential for escalation into serious violence. Evidence from Minneapolis showed that arrest of wife-battering husbands was more effective than other strategies in preventing more violent incidents; domestic violence also was one of the problems tackled in the course of development of the concept of problem-oriented policing in Newport News. Data are not available, however, to indicate whether strategies for reduction in domestic violence were actually successful.

Problem-oriented policing is not intended as a panacea for all the inevitable inadequacies of police services; it is an alternative model of policing with a more integrated and community-rooted approach compared to traditional incident-based methods. Whether problem-oriented policing has the potential to significantly reduce serious violence is doubtful. An analogy between policing and public health may be helpful. Neither institution alone has the resources nor the operational model to reduce violence significantly. As noted elsewhere, violence, particularly that rooted in the underclass, is clearly not amenable to any form of amelioration that is incapable of addressing such deeply-rooted issues as racism and poverty. Neither policing nor public health can effect that sort of structural change in society, either separately or together.

PREVENTING VIOLENT CRIME

Some twenty years ago, the National Commission on the Causes and Prevention of Violence (also known as the Eisenhower Commission), a body provoked into existence by civil disturbances in African American communities in the 1960s (National Commission, 1969) profiled violent crime, outlined its causes, and made recommendations for its prevention. Daniel Patrick Moynihan, in an introduction entitled "Toward a National Urban Policy", outlined ten points of a proposed urban policy including an attack on the poverty and social isolation of minorities in central cities, an effort yet to be brought to fruition, more than twenty years after the report was published.

How can violent crime be prevented? Suggestions are plentiful. The

National Commission on the Causes and Prevention of Violence (National Commission, 1969), for example, argued for:

1. Doubling the national expenditure on the criminal justice system
2. Restructuring urban life (the details were not specified)
3. The ten point program for a new urban policy outlined by Daniel Patrick Moynihan, including attacking the problem of the poverty and social isolation of minority groups in central cities.

Indeed, the final statement of the report was recycled from an earlier government commission (President's Commission on Law Enforcement and Administration of Justice, 1967) which said:

Warring on poverty, inadequate housing and unemployment, is warring on crime. A civil rights law is a law against crime. Money for schools is money against crime. Medical, psychiatric, and family counseling services are services against crime. More broadly and most importantly every effort to improve life in America's "inner cities" is an effort against crime.

Under "Guidelines for Action and Research," the National Commission referred to "prevention of crime and violence through elimination of basic causes" involving six recommendations or "themes of social reconstruction": (1) reduce economic deprivation through jobs, income supplements, homes; (2) greater community participation to reduce alienation; (3) increase educational and family services programs; (4) provide equal, quality education; (5) create "new roles for youth" to demonstrate that change can be effected through democratic institutions; (6) reduce prejudice and discrimination. Another six recommendations related to crime and the criminal justice system: (1) better response to violence among inmates, (2) reduced violence by law enforcement personnel, (3) better drug prevention, (4) better response to the role of alcohol in violence, (5) suicide prevention, (6) more and better coordinated research (National Commission, 1969).

However, a cursory observation of the urban environment indicates that the steps suggested by the Commission, even had they been appropriate, have not, in fact, been tested with a level of consistency and commitment of resources sufficient to effect change. This explains why both the problem and the suggested solutions are essentially unchanged after nearly a generation.

While old solutions have never received a fair test, there is also room for new ideas. For example, given that young African American males are at such great risk in terms of violence as victims and offenders, alternate strategies for their education should be considered. One possibility is that African American, male, middle school and high school students could be gender-segregated so that education and counseling specific to boys could be practiced. Another concept that deserves consideration is that of locating field hospitals in underclass areas in order to provide the fastest possible medical care. Whether care would be faster with such field units than it is with the regular emergency services is unclear, but the concept could be examined.

CONCLUSION

A common measure of the magnitude of a war is the number of deaths and injuries. By this measure, domestic violence shows that the U.S. is involved in a major conflict, with some 100,000 lives lost every five years or so, and many more serious injuries—the equivalent of roughly two Viet Nams. In the course of the twentieth century, approximately a million lives will have been lost to violence at the hands of our fellow citizens. Yet this carnage seems to fall in a national blind spot. If this many people had been killed in military action, the citizenry would be outraged. Yet the view persists that the greatest threat to U.S. security is the military of the Soviet Union, which no longer exists. The need for massive military forces, including the continued occupation of Germany, is clearly less today than at any time since World War II, and massive cuts in defense spending have occurred in the 1990s.

Given the actual breach of national security presented by violence in the cities, massive resources should be diverted from military applications and used to target the small underclass, with a view to eliminating the underclass phenomenon within a generation, by allocating resources to the various solutions outlined earlier. It is a tired refrain; yet again, however, the real war should be a war on poverty.

Included among the solutions to which funds must be allocated over and above tract- or neighborhood-level funding is a powerful program of public indoctrination aimed at reducing racial discrimination. This illustrates the point that some solutions are essentially local and lend themselves to local solutions. Housing, schools, drug treatment and education, and health fall into this category. Other issues are part of a broader fabric, including discrimination, employment, and transportation. Complicating the formulation of effective policy is the linkage and interdependence between neighborhood level, city/metropolitan level, and state/national level issues. The challenge is to coordinate and manage a cluster of serious, seemingly intractable problems simultaneously. Resources without management and coordination would be wasted, as they have been in the past. Only a radical political and administrative model will have a hope of even partial success. Strategies must be *problem-driven*, rather than imposed from above by existing structures. Revelations of the influence-peddling and other indiscretions at the Department of Housing and Urban Development during the Reagan presidency illustrate the latent or actual weaknesses of the present administrative arrangements. Whether the political will and consensus necessary to accomplish radical change are present, however, is doubtful. The underclass is an essentially inarticulate, fragmented constituency, but a small fraction of the U.S. population. One would prefer to conclude a book on a dismal subject with a note of optimism for the future. But the facts fail to justify a hopeful position.

BIBLIOGRAPHY

Abramowitz, M. (1989). Infant mortality soars here: Mothers' crack use blamed in increase of nearly 50 percent. *Washington Post,* September 30, pp. A1, A13.

Abramson, J.E. (1989). Ban those assault weapons. *Washington Post,* October 2, p. A15.

Alba, R.D., and S.F. Messner (1995a). Point Blank against itself: Evidence and inference about guns, crime, and gun control. *Journal of Quantitative Criminology,* 11:391-410.

Allen, R.B. (1986). Measuring the severity of physical injury among assault and homicide victims. *Journal of Quantitative Criminology,* 2:139-156.

Allison, J.A. (1993). *Rape: The misunderstood crime.* Newbury Park, CA: Sage.

Amir, M. (1971). *Patterns of forcible rape.* Chicago: University of Chicago Press.

Anderberg, M.R. (1973). *Cluster Analysis for Applications.* New York: Academic Press.

Anderson, C.A. (1989). Temperature and aggression: The ubiquitous effects of heat on the occurrence of human violence. *Psychological Bulletin,* 106:74-96.

Anderson, C.A., and D.C. Anderson (1984). Ambient temperature and violent crime: Tests of the linear and curvilinear hypotheses, *Journal of Personality and Social Psychology,* 46:91-97.

Anderson, E. (1989). Sex codes and family life among poor inner-city youths. In: W.J. Wilson (ed.), The ghetto underclass: Social science perspectives, *The Annals of the American Academy of Political and Social Science,* 501:59-78. Newbury Park: Sage.

Aneshensel, C.S. (1992). Social stress: Theory and research. *Annual Review of Sociology,* 18:15-38.

Anonymous (1833). *Westminster Review,* 18:353-356.

Anonymous (1988). The death penalty in Maryland. *Washington Post,* February 16. [editorial].

AP [Associated Press] (1995a). Homicides drop for third straight year. *Washington Post,* October 24, p. A6.

AP [Associated Press] (1995b). FBI data show 12 percent decline in murder, biggest drop in decades. *Washington Post,* December 18, p. A4.

Archer, D., and Gartner, R. (1976). Violent acts and violent times: a comparative approach to postwar homicide rates. *American Sociological Review,* 41:937-963.

Archer, D., and Gartner, R. (1986). *Violence and crime in cross-national perspective.* New Haven, CT: Yale University Press.

Bailey, W.C. (1984). Poverty, inequality, and city homicide rates: Some not so unexpected findings, *Criminology* 22:531-550.

Bailey, W.C. (1976). Some further evidence on homicide and a regional culture of violence. *Omega,* 2, 145-170.

Baker, J.N. and B. Cohn (1988). Crack wars in D.C., *Newsweek,* February 22, pp. 24, 27.

Baldassare, M. (1979). *Residential crowding in urban America.* Berkeley, CA: University of California Press.

Baldwin, J. (1979). Ecological and areal studies in Great Britain and the United States, in: N. Morris and M. Tonry (eds.) *Crime and Justice: An annual review of research.* Chicago: University of Chicago Press, pp. 29-86.

Ball, J.C. (1965). Two patterns of narcotic addiction in the United States. *Journal of Criminal Law, Criminology, and Police Science,* 52:203–211.

Ball-Rokeach, S.J. (1973). Values and violence: A test of the subculture of violence thesis. *American Sociological Review,* 38:736–749.

Barnett, A., and E. Schwartz (1989). Urban homicide: Still the same. *Journal of Quantitative Criminology,* 5:83–100.

Baron, R.A. (1972). Aggression as a function of ambient temperature and prior anger arousal. *Journal of Personality and Social Psychology,* 21:183–189.

Baron, R.A. and P.E. Bell (1975). Aggression and heat: Mediating effect of prior provocation and exposure to an aggressive model. *Journal of Personality and Social Psychology,* 31:825–832.

Baron, R.A., and V.M. Ransberger (1978). Ambient temperature and the occurrence of collective violence: The "Long, Hot, Summer" revisited. *Journal of Personality and Social Psychology,* 36:351–360.

Baron, L., and M.A. Straus (1988). Cultural and economic sources of homicide in the United States. *The Sociological Quarterly,* 29:371–390.

Bender, D.L., and B. Leone (eds.) (1986). *The death penalty: Opposing viewpoints.* St. Paul, MN: Greenhaven Press.

Berk, R.A., Lenihan, K.J., and P.H. Rossi (1980). Crime and poverty: Some experimental evidence from ex-offenders. *American Sociological Review,* 45:766–786.

Blau, J.R. and P.M. Blau (1982). The cost of inequality: Metropolitan structure and violent crime. *American Sociological Review,* 47:114–129.

Block, R. (1979). Community, environment, and violent crime. *Criminology,* 17:46–57.

Block, C.R. (1985). *Lethal violence in Chicago over seventeen years: Homicides known to the police, 1965–81.* Chicago: Criminal Justice Information Authority.

Block, C.R. (1984). *How to handle seasonality.* Chicago: Criminal Justice Information Authority.

Block, R. (1977). *Violent crime.* Lexington, MA: Lexington Books.

Block, C.R. (1987). *Homicide in Chicago.* Chicago: Center for Urban Policy, Loyola University of Chicago.

Booth, C. (1902–03). *Life and labor of the people in London,* 17 vols. London: Macmillan.

Bowles, S. (1995). Number of D.C. homicides drops to 399, a 6-year low. *Washington Post,* February 6, p. B3.

Boyanowski, E.O., J. Calvert, J. Young, and L. Brideau (1981). Towards a thermoregulatory model of violence. *Journal of Environmental Systems,* 1:81–87.

Brantingham, P.J., P.L. Brantingham, and D. Butcher (1986). Perceived and actual crime risks. In: R.M. Figlio, et al. (eds.), *Metropolitan Crime Patterns,* Monsey, NY: Criminal Justice Press, pp. 139–160.

Brantingham, P.J., and P.L. Brantingham. (1984). *Patterns in crime.* New York: Macmillan.

Brantingham, P.J., and P.L. Brantingham (1981). *Environmental criminology.* Beverly Hills and London: Sage.

Brearly, H.C. (1932). *Homicide in the United States.* Publication No. 36, Patterson Smith Reprint Series in Crime, Law Enforcement and Social Problems. Montclair, N.J.: Patterson Smith, 1969 ed.

Brenner, M.H. (1984). *Estimating the effects of economic change on national health and social well-being.* Washington D.C.: Joint Economic Commission, U.S. Congress.

Brenner, M.H., and R.T. Swank (1986). Homicide and economic change: Recent analyses of the Joint Economic Committee Report of 1984. *Journal of Quantitative Criminology,* 2:81–103.

Brounstein, P.J., Hatry, H.P., Altschuler, D.M., and L.H. Blair (1989). *Patterns of substance use and delinquency among inner city adolescents.* Washington D.C.: The Urban Institute.

Brown, DeN.L. (1989a). Some residents being won over by the enemy in D.C. drug war: Dealers often buy loyalty with cash, threats. *Washington Post,* August 13, pp. A1, A18.

Brown, DeN.L. (1989b). Crime-fighting groups find it's not as simple as dialing 911. *Washington Post,* August 13, p. A18.

Brown, B.S., R.L. DuPont, and N.J. Kezel (1973). Heroin addiction in the city of Washington. *Drug Forum,* 2:187–190.

Brownmiller, S. (1976). *Against our will: Men, women, and rape.* New York: Bantam.

Bulletin of the New York Academy of Medicine (1986). *Homicide: The public health perspective,* 62.

Bureau of Justice Statistics (Annual, [a]). *National crime survey.* Washington D.C.: U.S. Department of Justice.

Bureau of Justice Statistics (Annual, [b]). *National prisoner statistics.* Washington D.C.: U.S. Department of Justice.

Bureau of Justice Statistics (1980). *Crime and seasonality.* Washington D.C.: U.S. Government Printing Office.

Bureau of Justice Statistics (1983). *Report to the nation on crime and justice.* Washington D.C.: U.S. Government Printing Office.

Bureau of Justice Statistics (1984). *Sentencing practices in 13 states.* Washington D.C.: U.S. Department of Justice.

Bureau of Justice Statistics (1987a). *Capital punishment, 1986.* Washington D.C.: U.S. Department of Justice.

Bureau of Justice Statistics (1987b). *State felony courts and felony laws.* Washington D.C.: U.S. Department of Justice.

Bureau of Justice Statistics (1994). *Criminal victimization in the United States, 1992.* Washington D.C.: U.S. Department of Justice.

Bureau of the Census (1983). *1980 census of population and housing, census tracts, Washington D.C.-MD-VA SMSA, PHC80-2-365.* Washington D.C.: U.S. Department of Commerce.

Bureau of the Census (1995). *Statistical brief: Poverty areas.* Washington D.C.: U.S. Department of Commerce.

Burghardt, S., and M. Fabricant (1987). *Working under the safety net.* Newbury Park, CA: Sage.

Byrne, J.M., and R.J. Sampson (1986). *The social ecology of crime.* New York: Springer-Verlag.

Calvert-Boyanowski, J., E.O. Boyanowski, M. Atkinson, D. Goduto, and J. Reeves (1976). Patterns of passion: Temperature and human emotions. In: Krebs, D. (Ed.), *Readings in social psychology: Contemporary perspectives.* New York: Harper and Row, pp. 96–98.

Cantor, D. and K.C. Land (1985). Unemployment and crime rates in the post–World War II United States: A theoretical and empirical analysis. *American Sociological Review,* 50:317–332.

Carlsmith, J.M., and C.A. Anderson (1979). Ambient temperature and the occurrence of collective violence: A new analysis. *Journal of Personality and Social Psychology,* 37:337–344.

Carter, R.L., and K.Q. Hill (1979). *The criminal's image of the city.* New York: Pergamon Press.

Cary, P. (1989). A tale of the American dream that shattered: The meanest street in Washington. *U.S. News and World Report,* April 10, pp. 30–31.

Castenada, R., and P.P. Pan (1996). Homicides fell 10% last year. *Washington Post,* January 16, pp. B1, B4.

Centers for Disease Control (1983). *Homicide surveillance report, 1970–78.* Atlanta.

Centers for Disease Control (1986). *Homicide surveillance: High-risk racial and ethnic groups — Blacks and Hispanics, 1970 to 1983.* Atlanta.

Chambers, C.D., R.K. Hinesley, and M. Moldestad (1970). Narcotic addiction in females: A race comparison. *The International Journal of the Addictions*, 5:257–278.

Cheatwood, D. (1988). Is there a season for homicide? *Criminology*, 26:287–306.

Cheatwood, D. (1995). The effects of weather on homicide. *Journal of Quantitative Criminology*, 11:51–70.

Chien, I., D.L. Gerard, R.S. Lee, and E. Rosenfeld (1964). *The road to "H": Narcotics, delinquency, and social policy.* New York: Basic Books.

Churchville, V. (1988a). Jamaican gangs spread drug war. *Washington Post*, June 29, p. A13.

Churchville, V. (1988b). Woman keeps vigil against SE drug traffic. *Washington Post*, October 22, pp. B1, B4.

Clarke, R.V. (1983). Situational crime prevention: Its theoretical basis and practical scope. In: M. Tonry and N. Morris (eds.) *Crime and Justice: An Annual Review of Research*, Vol. 4. Chicago: University of Chicago Press, pp. 225–256.

Cloward, R.A., and Ohlin, L.E. (1960). *Delinquency and opportunity: A theory of delinquent gangs.* Glencoe, IL: Free Press.

Cohen, S. (1980). *Folk devils and moral panics.* London: MacGibbon and Kee.

Cohen, L.E., and M. Felson (1979). Social change and crime rate trends: A routine activities approach. *American Sociological Review*, 44:588–607.

Cohen, J. (1941). The geography of crime. *The Annals of the American Academy of Political and Social Science*, 217:29–37.

Cohn, E.G. (1990). Weather and violent crime. A reply to Perry and Simpson, 1987. *Environment and Behavior*, 22:280–294.

Connelly, N.M., K.D. Harries, and D.T. Herbert (1987). Dysfunction in the urban system: An evaluation of neighborhood crime prevention in Tulsa, Oklahoma. *Journal of Environmental Systems*, 17:115–130.

Cook, P.J. (1983). *Robbery in the U.S.: An analysis of recent trends and patterns.* Washington D.C.: U.S. Department of Justice.

Cook, P.J., and G.A. Zarkin (1986). Homicide and economic conditions: A replication and critique of M. Harvey Brenner's new report to the U.S. Congress. *Journal of Quantitative Criminology*, 2:69–80.

Cook, P.J. (1983). The influence of gun availability on violent crime patterns. In: M. Tonry and N. Morris (eds.) *Crime and justice: An annual review of research.* Chicago: University of Chicago Press, pp. 49–89.

Cooper, C.S., D. Kelley, and S. Larson (1982). *Judicial and executive discretion in the sentencing process: Analysis of state felony code provisions.* Washington D.C.: Washington College of Law, The American University.

Curtis, L.A. (1975). *Violence, race, and culture.* Lexington, MA: Lexington Books.

Cuskey, W.R., T. Premkumar, and L. Sigel (1972). Survey of opiate addiction among females in the United States between 1850 and 1970. *Public Health Review*, 1:6–39.

Dash, L. (1989). A dealer's creed: Be willing to die. *Washington Post*, April 3, pp. A1, A8.

Davidson, R.N. (1981). *Crime and Environment.* London: Croom Helm.

Delamothe, T. (1988). Violence: Next on the public health agenda? *British Medical Journal*, 297:6644, pp. 314–315.

Dennis, R.E. (1979). The role of homicide in decreasing life expectancy, in: H.M. Rose (ed.), *Lethal aspects of urban violence*, Chapter 2, pp. 17–30. Lexington, MA: Lexington Books.

Denton, H.H. (1989). Tension grows between police, Toronto blacks. *Washington Post*, January 22, p. A31.

Devine, J.A., Sheley, J.F. and M.D. Smith (1988). Macroeconomic and social-control policy influences on crime rate changes, 1948–1985. *American Sociological Review*, 53:407–420.

Dexter, E.G. (1904). *Weather influences: An empirical study of the mental and physiological effects of definite meteorological conditions.* New York: Macmillan.

DiIulio, J.J. (1989). The impact of inner city crime. *The Public Interest,* 96:28–46.

Dixon, J., and A.J. Lizotte (1987). Gun ownership and the "Southern Culture of Violence." *American Journal of Sociology,* 93:383–405.

Doerner, W.G. (1975). A regional analysis of homicide rates in the United States. *Criminology,* 13:90–101.

Doerner, W.G. (1978a). The index of Southernness revisited. *Criminology* 16:47–59.

Doerner, W.G. (1978b). The deadly world of Johnny Reb: Fact, foible, for fantasy? In: J.A. Inciardi and A.E. Potteiger (eds.) *Violent crime: Historical and contemporary issues.* Beverly Hills, CA: Sage, 1978, pp. 91–97.

Dubitsky, S., R. Weber, and J. Rotton (1993). Heat, hostility, and immune function: The moderating effects of gender and demand characteristics. *Bulletin of the Psychonomic Society,* 31:534–536.

Duggan, P. (1988). Repair workers toil, pupils broil in 92-degree heat. *Washington Post,* June 1, p. D1.

Duke, L., and D.M. Price (1989). A microcosm of despair in D.C.: Housing project's drug market born of poverty, neglect. *Washington Post,* April 2, pp. A1, A28–30.

Duke, L. (1987). Clues, witnesses are scarce in SE boy's death. *Washington Post,* December 19, pp. F1, F6.

Duke, L. (1988). NW neighbors seek help in standing up to dealers. *Washington Post,* December 18, pp. B1, B12.

Dunn, C.S. (1976). *The patterns and distribution of assault incident characteristics among social areas.* Albany, NY: Criminal Justice Research Center.

Eck, J.E., and W. Spelman (1987). *Problem-solving: Problem-oriented policing in Newport News.* Washington D.C.: U.S. Department of Justice, National Institute of Justice.

Elazar, D.J. (1972). *American federalism: A view from the states,* 2 ed. New York: Thomas Crowell.

Ellinwood, E.H., W.G. Smith, and G.E. Vaillant (1966). Narcotic addiction in males and females: A comparison. *The International Journal of the Addictions,* 1:33–45.

Ellis, L. (1989). *Theories of rape: Inquiries into the causes of sexual aggression.* New York: Hemisphere.

Evans, D.J. and D.T. Herbert (eds.) (1989). *The geography of crime.* London: Routledge.

Farley, R. (1980). Homicide trends in the United States. *Demography,* 17:177–188.

FBI [Federal Bureau of Investigation] (Annual). *Uniform crime reports.* Washington D.C.: U.S. Government Printing Office.

FBI [Federal Bureau of Investigation] (n.d.). *Uniform crime reports: Supplementary homicide reports, 1976–1983.* Washington D.C.: U.S. Department of Justice.

Felson, M. (1989). The metropolis and crime in the twenty-first century. Lecture delivered to the Departments of Geography and Sociology, University of Maryland Baltimore County, Baltimore, MD. April 3.

Fingerhut, L. (1994). The impact of homicide on life chances: International, intranational, and demographic comparisons. In: C.R. Block and R.L. Block (eds.) *Questions and answers in lethal and non-lethal violence, 1993.* Washington D.C.: National Institute of Justice, pp. 7–21.

Foege, W.H. (1985). Violence and public health. In: *Report of the Surgeon General's workshop on violence and public health.* Washington D.C.: U.S. Department of Health and Human Services and the U.S. Department of Justice, pages 19–23.

Foege, W.H. (1988). Injury as an issue in violence. *Bulletin of the New York Academy of Medicine,* 64:780–787.

Fox, J.A., and G.L. Pierce (1987). *Uniform crime reports [United States]: Supplementary homicide reports, 1976–83 (ICPSR 8657)*. Ann Arbor, MI: Inter-University Consortium for Political and Social Research.

Freedman, J.L. (1975). *Crowding and behavior*. San Francisco: W.H. Freeman & Co.

Gabor, T. (1986). *The prediction of criminal behavior: Statistical approaches*. Toronto: University of Toronto Press.

Gabor, T., et al. (1987). *Armed robbery: Cops, robbers, and victims*. Springfield, IL: Charles C Thomas.

Gaines-Carter, P., and J. Mintz (1988). Muslims nurture legacy of power. *Washington Post*, April 20, A16.

Galliher, J.F. and H.E. Pepinsky (1978). A meta-study of social origins of substantive criminal laws. In: Krohn, M.D. and R.L. Akers (eds.), *Crime, law, and sanctions: Theoretical perspectives*. Beverly Hills, CA: Sage, pp. 27–38.

Gandossy, R.P., J.R. Williams, J. Cohen, and H.J. Harwood (1980). *Drugs and crime: A survey and analysis of the literature*. Washington D.C.: USGPO.

Garofalo, J. (1987). Reassessing the lifestyle model of criminal victimization. In: Gottfredson, M.R. and T. Hirschi (eds.) *Positive criminology*. Newbury Park, CA: Sage, Chapter 2, pages 23–42.

Garreau, J. (1988). The invisible hand guides D.C.'s visible menace: Street-corner drug trade provides a model of capitalism, say economists, police. *Washington Post*, December 12, pp. A1, A14–15.

Gastil, R.D. (1971). Homicide and a regional culture of violence. *American Sociological Review*, 36:412–427.

Gastil, R.D. (1975). *Cultural regions of the United States*. Seattle: University of Washington Press.

Georges-Abeyie, D., and K.D. Harries (1980). *Crime: A spatial perspective*. New York: Columbia University Press.

Gibbs, J.J. (1979). *Crime against persons in urban, suburban, and rural areas: A comparative analysis of victimization rates*. Washington D.C.: U.S. Department of Justice.

Glaser, D. (1979). A review of crime-causation theory and its application. In: N. Morris and M. Tonry (eds.) *Crime and justice: An annual review of research*, Vol. 1. Chicago: University of Chicago Press, pp. 203–237.

Goldberg, J. (1989a). Fear of drug violence in D.C. slows some suburban buyers. *Washington Post*, July 27, pp. A1, A17.

Goldberg, J. (1989b). Death losing meaning for youths left calloused by violence. *Washington Post*, September 18, pp. E1, E5.

Goldstein, A. (1991). D.C. gun law works, or so a new study says: Bloody years after 1987 aren't covered. *Washington Post*, December 5, pp. D1, D6.

Goldstein, H. (1979). Improving policing: A problem-oriented approach. *Crime and Delinquency*, 25:236–258.

Gottfredson, M.R., and T. Hirschi (1987). The positive tradition. In: Gottfredson, M.R. and T. Hirschi (eds.) *Positive criminology*. Newbury Park, CA: Sage, Chapter 1, pp. 9–22.

Gottfredson, M.R. and T. Hirschi (1989a). A propensity-event theory of crime. In: W.S. Laufer and F. Adler (eds.), *Advances in criminological theory*, Vol. 1. New Brunswick, NJ: Transaction Publishers, pp. 57–68.

Gottfredson, M.R., and T. Hirschi (1989b). Why we're losing the war on crime. *Washington Post*, September 10, p. C3.

Greenberg, M.R., G.W. Carey, and F.J. Popper (1987). Violent death, violent states, and American youth. *The Public Interest*, 87:38–48.

Greenberg, S.W. (1986). Fear and its relationship to crime, neighborhood deterioration, and informal social control. In: James M. Byrne and Robert J. Sampson, *The social ecology of crime.* New York: Springer-Verlag, pp. 47–62.

Gurr, T.R. (1981). Historical trends in violent crimes: A critical review of the evidence. In: M. Tonry and N. Morris (eds.) *Crime and justice: An annual review of research.* Chicago: University of Chicago Press.

Habermas, J. (1968). *Knowledge and Human Interests* (Translated by J.J. Shapiro.) Boston: Beacon Press.

Hackett, G., et al. (1988). Saying "no" to crack gangs. Angry citizens fight back against the drug trade. *Newsweek,* March 28, p. 29.

Hackney, S. (1969). Southern violence. *American Historical Review,* 74: 906–925.

Hamnet, C. (1979). Area-based explanations: A critical appraisal. In: Herbert, D.T. and D.M. Smith (eds.) *Social problems and the city: Geographical perspectives.* New York: Oxford University Press, Chapter 13, pp. 244–260.

Hansmann, H.B. and J.M. Quigley (1982). Population heterogeneity and the sociogenesis of homicide. *Social Forces,* 61:206–224.

Harlow, C.W. (1985). *Reporting crimes to the police.* Washington D.C.: U.S. Department of Justice, Bureau of Justice Statistics.

Harries, K.D. (1971). The geography of American crime. 1968. *Journal of Geography,* 70: 204–213.

Harries, K.D. (1974). *The geography of crime and justice.* New York: McGraw-Hill.

Harries, K.D. (1975). Rejoinder to Richard Peet: The geography of crime, a political critique. *Professional Geographer,* 27:280–282.

Harries, K.D. (1976). A crime-based analysis and classification of 729 American cities. *Social Indicators Research,* 2:467–487.

Harries, K.D. (1980). *Crime and the environment.* Springfield, IL: Charles C Thomas.

Harries, K.D. (1985). The historical geography of homicide in the United States. 1935–80. *Geoforum,* 16: 73–83.

Harries, K.D. (1986). Commentary on the geography of social control. *Annals,* Association of American Geographers, 76:577–579.

Harries, K.D. (1986). Serious assault in Dallas, Texas: The roles of spatial and temporal factors. *Journal of Justice Issues,* 1:31–45.

Harries, K.D. (1987). Comparing assaults in Dallas and Baltimore, 1981–85. Paper read to conference entitled "Black homicide and public health," The Johns Hopkins University School of Hygiene and Public Health, Baltimore, MD. March 23.

Harries, K.D. (1987). Homicide and assaultive violence. In: A.Z. Reed (ed.), *Violence in America.* Austin, TX: Lyndon B. Johnson School of Public Affairs, University of Texas at Austin, pp. 97–102.

Harries, K.D. (1989a). They went wilding. *Washington Post,* May 6, p. A20.

Harries, K.D. (1989b). Homicide and assault: A comparative analysis of attributes in Dallas neighborhoods. 1981–1985. *Professional Geographer* 41:29–38.

Harries, K.D. (1990). *Geographic Factors in Policing.* Washington D.C.: Police Executive Research Forum.

Harries, K.D., and S.D. Brunn (1978). *The Geography of Laws and Justice.* New York: Praeger.

Harries, K.D. (1995a). Regional variations in attitudes toward crime issues in the U.S. *Indian Journal of Psychological Issues,* 3:21–27.

Harries, K.D. (1995b). The ecology of homicide and assault: Baltimore City and County, 1989–91. *Studies in Crime and Crime Prevention,* [Stockholm, Sweden]. 4:44–60.

Harries, K.D., and D. Cheatwood (1996). *The Geography of Execution: The Capital Punishment Quagmire in America.* Lanham, MD: Rowman and Littlefield.

Harries, K.D., and A. Powell (1994). Juvenile gun crime and social stress: Baltimore, 1980–1990. *Urban Geography,* 15:45–63.

Harries, K.D., and S.J. Stadler (1983). Determinism revisited: Assault and heat stress in Dallas, 1980. *Environment and Behavior,* 15:235–256.

Harries, K.D., and S.J. Stadler (1986). Aggravated assault and the urban system: Dallas, 1980–81. *Journal of Environmental Systems,* 15:243–253.

Harries, K.D., and S.J. Stadler (1988). Heat and violence: new findings from Dallas field data, 1980–81. *Journal of Applied Social Psychology,* 18:129–138.

Harries, K.D., and S.J. Stadler (1989). Assault and heat stress: Dallas as a case study. In: D.J. Evans and D.T. Herbert (eds.) *The Geography of Crime,* London: Routledge, pp. 38–58.

Harries, K.D., S.J. Stadler, and R.T. Zdorkowski (1984). Seasonality and assault: Explorations in interneighborhood variation, Dallas, 1980. *Annals,* Association of American Geographers, 74:590–604.

Harris, F.R. and R.W. Wilkins (1988). *Quiet riots: Race and poverty in the United States.* New York: Pantheon.

Harriston, K. (1988a). Living with fear, Part 1. Drugs overrun a way of life in Langley Park: Invasion of dealers leaves lasting scars on residents of working-class neighborhood. *Washington Post,* May 19, pp. A1, A19.

Harriston, K. (1988b). Living with fear, Part 2. Drugs erode community's closeness: Cultural, economic differences turn neighbors into strangers. *Washington Post,* May 20, pp. A1, A14.

Harvey, W.B. (1986). Homicide among young black adults: Life in the subculture of exasperation. In: Darnell F. Hawkins (ed.), *Homicide among black Americans.* Lanham, MD: University Press of America, pp. 153–171.

Hawkins, D.F. (1986). Black homicide: The adequacy of existing research for devising prevention strategies. In: D.F. Hawkins (ed.), *Homicide among black Americans.* Lanham, MD: University Press of America, 1986, pp. 211–229.

Hawkins, D.F. (1986). Black and white homicide differentials: Alternatives to an inadequate theory. In: Darnell F. Hawkins (ed.), *Homicide among black Americans.* Lanham, MD: University Press of America, pp. 109–135.

Hawley, A. (1968). Human ecology. In: Sills, D.L. (ed.) *International encyclopedia of the social sciences.* New York: Macmillan and the Free Press, Vol. 4, pp. 328–337.

Hawley, F.F. (1987). The black legend in southern studies: Violence, ideology, and academe. *North American Culture,* 3:29–52.

Herbert, D.T. (1979). Urban crime: A geographical perspective. In: Herbert, D.T. and D.M. Smith, (eds.) *Social problems and the city: Geographical perspectives.* New York: Oxford University Press, Chapter 7, pp. 117–138.

Herbert, D.T. (1982). *The Geography of Urban Crime.* London: Longman.

Herbert, D.T., and K.D. Harries (1986). Area-based policies for crime prevention. *Applied Geography,* 6:281–295.

Hilts, P.J. (1988). Blacks' life expectancy drops: Homicides, accidents called key factors. *Washington Post,* December 15, pp. A1, A22.

Hindelang, M.J. (1974). The uniform crime reports revisited. *Journal of Criminal Justice,* 2: 1–17.

Hindelang, M., Gottfredson, M.R. and J. Garofalo (1978). *Victims of personal crime: An empirical foundation for a theory of personal victimization.* Cambridge, MA: Ballinger.

Hoffman, D. (1989). George Bush: Promises to keep. *Washington Post,* January 20, p. A25.

Holinger, P.C. and E.H. Klemen (1982). Violent deaths in the United States, 1900–1975. *Social Science and Medicine,* 16:1929–1938.

Holt-Jensen, A. (1988). *Geography: History and concepts* (Second Edition). Totowa, N.J.: Barnes and Noble.

Horwitz, S. (1988a). Weapons, drugs, and youths: Formula for the District's bloodiest month. *Washington Post,* February 2, pp. A1, A8.

Horwitz, S. (1988b). A drug-selling machine that was all business. *Washington Post,* April 24, p. A1, A16.

Horwitz, S., and N. Lewis (1988). NE drug gang's war has bloody price tag: 20 deaths since June blamed on rivalry. *Washington Post,* November 20, pp. A1, A22.

Horwitz, S. (1989). D.C. homicide toll reaches 1988 level: Violence highlights scope of drug problem. *Washington Post,* October 30, pages A1, A6.

Horwitz, S., and L. Wheeler (1989). Drug market intensifies violence on Drake Place: SE neighborhood feels crack's impact. *Washington Post,* February 17, pp. D1, D7.

Huff-Corzine, L., J. Corzine, and D.C. Moore (1989). Deadly connections: Culture, poverty, and the direction of lethal violence. Paper read to the Annual Meeting of the American Sociological Association, San Francisco.

Hughes, M.A. (1989). Evermore isolated islands of poverty. *Washington Post,* April 2, p. C8.

Humphrey, J.A. and S. Palmer (1986). Race, sex, and criminal homicide offender-victim relationships. In: D.F. Hawkins (ed.), *Homicide Among Black Americans.* Lanham, MD: University Press of America, pp. 57–67.

Humphries, D., and D. Wallace (1980). Capitalist accumulation and urban crime, 1950–71. *Social Problems,* 28:179–193.

Inciardi, J.A., and D.C. McBride (1990). Legalizing drugs: A gormless, naive idea. *The Criminologist,* 15:1–4.

Inciardi, J.A., and D.C. McBride, C.B. McCoy, H.L. Surratt, and C.A. Saum (1995). Violence, street crime, and the drug legalization debate: A perspective and commentary on the U.S. experience. *Studies in Crime and Crime Prevention,* [Stockholm, Sweden]. 4:105–118.

Innes, C.A. (1988). *Drug Use and Crime.* Washington D.C.: U.S. Bureau of Justice Statistics.

Isikoff, M., and E. Pianin (1989). Bennett gives D.C. top priority in drug war. *Washington Post,* March 14, pp. A1, A6.

Isikoff, M. (1989). Drugs top problem in U.S., poll finds. *Washington Post,* August 15, p. A4.

Isikoff, M. (1989). Drug buy set up for Bush speech: DEA lured seller to Lafayette Park. *Washington Post,* September 22, pp. A1, A22.

Jackson, P., and S. Smith (1984). *Exploring social geography.* London: George Allen and Unwin.

Jacobson, A.L. (1975). Crime trends in southern and non-southern cities: A twenty year perspective. *Social Forces,* 54:226–242.

Jamieson, K.M. and T.J. Flanagan (eds.) (1987). *Sourcebook of Criminal Justice Statistics—1986.* Washington D.C.: U.S. Department of Justice, Bureau of Justice Statistics.

Jargowsky, P.A. (1989). Urban ghettos and changes in the labor market. Paper read to the Association of American geographers Annual Meeting, Baltimore, MD, March.

Jargowsky, P.A., and M.J. Bane (1990). Ghetto poverty: basic questions. In: Lynn, L.E., Jr. and M.G.H. McGeary (eds.) *Inner-city poverty in the United States.* Washington D.C.: National Academy Press, pp. 16–67.

Jason, J., Flock, M., and Tyler, C.W. (1983). Epidemiological characteristics of primary homicides in the United States. *American Journal of Epidemiology,* 117:419–428.

Jason, J. (1984). Centers for Disease Control and the epidemiology of violence. *Child Abuse and Neglect,* 8:279–283.

Jason, J., Strauss, L.T., and Tyler, C.W. (1983). A comparison of primary and secondary homicides in the United States. *American Journal of Epidemiology,* 117:309–319.

Jaynes, G.D., and R.M. Williams (eds.) (1989). *A common destiny: Blacks and American society.* Washington D.C.: National Academy Press.

Jeter, J. (1996). Maryland tops Virginia as D.C. gun supplier. *Washington Post,* January 28, pp. A1, A20.

Jung, R.S., and L.A. Jason (1988). Firearm violence and the effects of gun control legislation. *American Journal of Community Psychology,* 16:515–524.

Kalish, C.B. (1988). *International Crime Rates.* Washington D.C.: U.S. Department of Justice, 1988.

Kalkstein, L.S., and K.M. Valimont (1986). An evaluation of summer discomfort in the United States using a relative climatological index. *Bulletin of the American Meteorological Society,* 67:842–848.

Kalkstein, L.S., and K.M. Valimont (1987). An evaluation of winter weather severity in the United States using the Weather Stress Index. *Bulletin of the American Meteorological Society,* 68:1535–1540.

Kasarda, J. (1989). Race, space, and the urban underclass. Paper read to the Association of American Geographers Annual Meeting, Baltimore, MD. March.

Kenrick, D.T., and S.W. MacFarlane (1986). Ambient temperature and horn honking: A field study of the heat/aggression relationship. *Environment and Behavior,* 18:179–191.

Klaus, P. and M.R. Rand (1984). *Family Violence.* Washington D.C.: U.S. Department of Justice.

Klaus, P. (1988). Bureau of Justice Statistics, U.S. Department of Justice, Washington D.C. Personal communication, February 2.

Klebba, A. (1975). Homicide trends in the United States, 1900–74. *Public Health Reports,* 90:195–204.

Kleck, G. (1991). *Point blank: Guns and violence in America.* New York: Aldine de Gruyter.

Kleck, G. (1995). Using speculation to meet evidence: Reply to Alba and Messner. *Journal of Quantitative Criminology,* 11:411–424.

Klein, L.R., B. Forst, and V. Filatov (1978). The deterrent effect of capital punishment: An assessment of the estimates. In: A. Blumstein, J. Cohen, and D. Nagin (eds.), *Deterrence and Incapacitation: Estimating the Effects of Criminal Sanctions on Crime Rates.* Washington D.C.: National Academy of Sciences, pp. 336–360.

Knight, A., and T. Sherwood (1989). "We've got to find a way to stop all of this": Frustrated city leaders call for help from Bush, the National Guard, in ending violence. *Washington Post,* February 17, p. A16.

Knox, P.L. (1988). Disappearing targets? Poverty areas in central cities. *Journal of the American Planning Association,* 54:501–508.

Kohfield, C.W., and J. Sprague (1988). Urban unemployment drives urban crime. *Urban Affairs Quarterly,* 24:215–241.

Koller, A.J. (1937). *The Abbe' du Bos—his advocacy of the theory of climate.* Champaign, IL: The Garrad Press.

Kozel, N.J., R.L. DuPont, and B.S. Brown (1972). Narcotics and crime: A study of narcotic involvement in an offender population. *The International Journal of the Addictions* 7:443–450.

LaFraniere, S. (1989). Stray bullet from drug fight kills SE woman on her porch. *Washington Post,* July 17, pp. A1, A5.

Lander, B. (1954). *Towards an understanding of juvenile delinquency.* New York: Columbia University Press.

Landsberg, H.E. (1969). *Weather and health: An Introduction to biometeorology.* New York: Doubleday Anchor Books.

Lane, R. (1980). Urban homicide in the nineteenth century: Some lessons for the twentieth.

In: J.A. Inciardi and C.E. Faupel (eds.) *History and Crime: Implications for Criminal Justice Policy.* Beverly Hills, Sage, pp. 91–109.

Langan, P.A., and C.A. Innes (1985). *The Risk of violent crime.* Washington D.C.: U.S. Department of Justice, Bureau of Justice Statistics.

Laub, John H. (1987). Data for positive criminology. In: Gottfredson, M.R. and T. Hirschi (eds.) *Positive Criminology.* Newbury Park, CA: Sage, Chapter 4, pp. 56–70.

Lemann, N. (1986a). The origins of the underclass *The Atlantic Monthly,* 257 (June), pp. 31–55.

Lemann, N. (1986b). The origins of the underclass *The Atlantic Monthly,* 257 (July), pp. 54–68.

Lemann, N. (1988). Battleground: The inside story of the wars behind the war on poverty. *The Atlantic Monthly,* 262 (December), pp. 37–70.

Lemann, N. (1989). The unfinished war. *The Atlantic Monthly,* 263 (January), pp. 52–71.

Lewis, N. (1988). As night falls, guns rule many city streets. *Washington Post,* December 11, pp. B1, B10.

Lewis, L.T., and J.J. Alford (1975). The Influence of season on assault. *The Professional Geographer,* 28:214–217.

Ley, D. (1974). *The Black inner city as frontier outpost.* Washington D.C.: Association of American Geographers Monograph No. 7.

Ley, D. (1975). The street gang in its milieu. In: Gappert, G., and H.M. Rose (eds.) *The Social Economy of Cities.* Beverly Hills: Sage Publications, 247–273.

Linsky, A.S. and M.A. Straus (1986). *Social stress in the United States.* Dover, MA: Auburn House Publishing Company.

Lizotte, A.J. (1986). The costs of using gun control to reduce homicide. In: Homicide: The Public Health Perspective, *Bulletin of the New York Academy of Medicine,* 62:539–549.

Loftin, C., and R.N. Parker (1985). An errors-in-variable model of the effect of poverty on urban homicide rates. *Criminology* 23:269–285.

Loftin, C. (1986). The validity of robbery-murder classifications in Baltimore. *Violence and Victims,* 1:191–204.

Loftin, C., and R.H. Hill (1974). Regional subculture and homicide: An examination of the Gastil-Hackney thesis. *American Sociological Review,* 39:714–724.

Loftin, C., D. McDowell, B. Weirsma, and T.J. Cottey (1991). Effects of restrictive licensing of handguns on homicide and suicide in the District of Columbia. *New England Journal of Medicine.* 325:1615–1620.

Lottier, S. (1938). Distribution of criminal offenses in sectional regions. *Journal of Criminal Law and Criminology,* 29:329–344.

Lowman, J. (1986). Conceptual issues in the geography of crime: Toward a geography of social control. *Annals,* Association of American Geographers, 76:81–94.

Luckenbill, D.F. (1984). Murder and assault. In: Meier, R.F. (ed.) *Major Forms of Crime,* Beverly Hills: Sage Publications. Chapter 2.

Macdonald, J.M. (1971). *Rape offenders and their victims.* Springfield, IL: Charles C Thomas.

Mann, J. (1989). Another feather in Barry's cap. *Washington Post,* January 11, p. B3.

Marsden, G.M. (1987). In: M. Eliade (Ed.) *The encyclopedia of religion,* Vol. 5. New York: Macmillan, pp. 190–197.

Martin, G.J. (1973). *Ellsworth Huntington, his life and thought.* Hamden, CT: Archon.

Martin, M.J., T.K. Hunt, and S.B. Hulley (1988). The cost of hospitalization for firearm injuries. *Journal of the American Medical Association,* 260:3048–3050.

Maxfield, M.G. (1989). Circumstances in supplementary homicide reports: Variety and validity. *Criminology* 27:671–695.

Mayhew, H. (1862). *London, labor and the London poor.* 4 vols. London: Griffin.

McCarthy, C. (1989). Medical price of violence: Guns and drugs are stretching emergency rooms to the limit. *Washington Post,* Health Supplement, February 21, pp. 14–17.

McClain, P.D. (1984). Urban neighborhoods, black residents, and homicide risk. *Urban Geography,* 5:210–222.

McCord, J. (1989). Theory, Pseudotheory, and Metatheory, in: W.S. Laufer and F. Adler (eds.), *Advances in Criminological Theory,* Vol. 1, New Brunswick, NJ: Transaction Publishers, pp. 127–145.

McDowell, D., C. Loftin, and B. Weirsma (1992). A comparative study of the preventive effects of mandatory sentencing laws for gun crimes. *Journal of Criminal Law and Criminology,* 83:378–394.

McGarrell, E.F. and T.J. Flanagan (1985). *Sourcebook of criminal justice statistics, 1984.* Washington D.C.: U.S. Government Printing Office.

McGovern, J.R. (1982). *Anatomy of a lynching.* Baton Rouge, LA: Louisiana University Press.

McKenzie, R.D. (1925). The ecological approach to the study of the human community. In: R.E. Park, E.W. Burgess, and R.D. McKenzie (eds.), *The City* Chicago: University of Chicago Press.

McKinney, J.C., and Bourque, L.B. (1971). The changing South: national incorporation of a region. *American Sociological Review,* 36:399–412.

Mercy, J.A., and P.W. O'Carroll (1988). New directions in violence prediction: The public health arena. *Violence and Victims,* 3:285–301.

Messner, Steven F. (1983a). Regional and racial effects on the urban homicide rate: The subculture of violence revisited. *American Journal of Sociology,* 88:997–1007.

Messner, S.F. (1983b). Regional differences in the economic correlates of the urban homicide rate. *Criminology,* 21:477–488.

Messner, S.F., and K. Tardiff (1985). The social ecology of urban homicide: An application of the "routine activities" approach. *Criminology,* 23:241–267.

Miller, W.B. (1958). Lower class culture as a generating milieu of gang delinquency. *Journal of Social Issues,* 15:5–19.

Milloy, C. (1988). Ending the "Quiet riots" in cities across America. *Washington Post,* November 6, p. B3.

Mills, C.A. (1942). *Climate Makes the Man.* New York: Harper.

Monahan, J., and D. Klassen (1982). Situational approaches to understanding and predicting individual violent behavior. In: M.E. Wolfgang and N.A. Weiner (eds.) *Criminal Violence.* Beverly Hills, CA: Sage. pp. 292–319.

Monkkonen, E. (1981). *Police in urban America.* New York: Cambridge University Press.

Moore, T., et al. (1989). Dead zones. *U.S. News and World Report,* April 10, pp. 20, 22–25, 28–32.

Morganthau, T., et al. (1988). The drug gangs. *Newsweek,* March 28, 20–27.

Morin, R. (1989a). Drugs force many to adjust their lives. *Washington Post,* January 2, pp. A1, A14.

Morin, R. (1989b). Many in poll say Bush plan is not stringent enough. *Washington Post,* September 18, pp. A1, A18.

Morris, T. (1957). *The criminal area.* London: Routledge & Kegan Paul.

Mulroy, E.A., and T.S. Lane (1992). Housing affordability, stress, and single mothers: Pathway to homelessness. *Journal of Sociology and Social Welfare,* 19:51–64.

Mulvihill, D.J., M.M. Tumin, and L.A. Curtis (1969). *Crimes of Violence,* Vol. 11. Washington D.C.: National Commission on the Causes and Prevention of Violence.

Murray, R., and F.W. Boal (1979). The social ecology of urban violence, in: Herbert, D.T.

and D.M. Smith, (eds.) *Social Problems and the City: Geographical Perspectives.* New York: Oxford University Press, Chapter 8, pp. 139–157.

Nadelmann, E.A. (1989). Drugs: The case for legalization. *Washington Post,* October 8, p. C3.

National Commission on the Causes and Prevention of Violence. (1969a). *Violent Crime: Homicide, Assault, Rape, Robbery.* New York: George Braziller.

National Commission on the Causes and Prevention of Violence. (1969b). *Crimes of Violence* Vol. 12. Washington D.C.: U.S. Government Printing Office.

NBC News. (1989). Gangs, Cops, and Drugs. August 15, 16.

Nelson, J. (1989). Fear of violence changes the way Washingtonians live. *Washington Post,* July 24, pp. D1, D7.

New York Academy of Medicine. (1986). *Homicide: The Public Health Perspective.* New York Academy of Medicine.

Newman, O. (1972). *Defensible Space: Crime Prevention through Environmental Design.* New York: Macmillan.

Norris, M.L. (1989a). The Dooney lessons: He's the poster kid, but there are so many others. *Washington Post,* September 10, p. C1.

Norris, M.L. (1989b). Violence scars psyches of area's children. *Washington Post,* February 5.

Nurco, D.N. (1972). An ecological analysis of narcotic addicts in Baltimore. *The International Journal of the Addictions,* 7:341–353.

Nurco, D.N., T.E. Hanlon, T.W. Kinlock, and K.R. Duszynski (1988). Differential criminal patterns of narcotic addicts over an addiction career. *Criminology,* 26:407–424.

Nurco, D.N., and M. Lerner (1972). Characteristics of drug abusers in a correctional system. *Journal of Drug Issues,* 2:49–56.

Nurco, D.N., J.W. Shaffer, and I.H. Cisin (1984). An ecological analysis of the interrelationships among drug abuse and other indices of social pathology. *International Journal of the Addictions,* 19:441–451.

Nurco, D.N., N. Wegner, H. Baum, and A. Makofsky (1979). *A Case Study: Narcotic Addiction Over a Quarter of a Century in a Major American City* Washington D.C.: National Institute on Drug Abuse, Public Health Service, Alcohol, Drug Abuse and Mental Health Administration, U.S. DHEW.

O'Carroll, P.W., and J.A. Mercy (1986). Patterns and recent trends in black homicide. In: D.F. Hawkins (ed.) *Homicide Among Black Americans,* Lanham, MD: University Press of America, pp. 29–42.

O'Carroll, P.W., and J.A. Mercy (1989). Regional variations in homicide rates: Why is the *West* so violent? *Violence and Victims,* 4:17–25.

O'Carroll, P., and J.A. Mercy (1986). Patterns and recent trends in black homicide. In: Darnell F. Hawkins (ed.), *Homicide Among Black Americans,* Lanham, MD: University Press of America, pp. 29–42.

O'Connor, J.F., and A. Lizotte (1979). The "Southern subculture of violence" thesis and patterns of gun ownership. *Social Problems,* 25:420–429.

OCJPA [Office of Criminal Justice Plans and Analysis] (1988). *Homicide in the District of Columbia.* Washington D.C.: Government of the District of Columbia.

Oliver, J.E., and A.K. Siddiqi (1987). Climatic Determinism. In: J.E. Oliver and R. Fairbridge, (Eds.), *The Encyclopedia of Climatology,* Encyclopedia of Earth Sciences Series, Vol. XI, New York: Van Nostrand Reinhold Company.

Oliver, J.E. (1973). *Climate and Man's Environment.* New York: John Wiley & Sons.

Pappas, G., S. Queen, W. Hadden, and G. Fisher (1993). The increasing disparity in mortality between socioeconomic groups in the United States, 1960 and 1986. *The New England Journal of Medicine*, 329:103–109.

Parker, R.N., and M.D. Smith (1980). Type of homicide and variation in regional rates. *Social Forces*, 59:136–147.

Parrot, A., and L. Bechofer (eds.) (1991). *Acquaintance rape: The hidden crime.* New York: Wiley.

Patterson, J.T. (1986). *America's struggle against poverty, 1900–1985.* Cambridge, MA: Harvard University Press.

Pearlin, L.I. (1989). The sociological study of stress. *Journal of Health and Social Behavior,* 30:241–256.

Peet, R. (1975). The geography of crime: A political critique. *Professional Geographer,* 27:277–80.

Perez, J. (1992). *Patterns of robbery and burglary in 9 states, 1984–88.* Washington D.C.: U.S. Department of Justice.

Persinger, M.A. (1980). *The weather matrix and human behavior.* New York: Praeger.

Pervin, L.A. (1978). Definitions, measurements, and classifications of stimuli, situations, and environments. *Human Ecology,* 6:71–105.

Pittman, D.J., and Handy, W. (1964). Patterns in aggravated criminal assault. *Journal of Criminal Law, Crime, and Police Science,* 55:462–470.

Pokorny, A.D. (1965). Human violence: A comparison of homicide, aggravated assault, suicide, and attempted suicide. *Journal of Criminal Law, Crime, and Police Science,* 56:488–497.

President's Commission on Law Enforcement and Administration of Justice (1967). *The Challenge of Crime in a Free Society.* New York: Avon Books.

Prothrow-Stith, D. (1985). Interdisciplinary interventions applicable to prevention of inter-personal violence and homicide in black youth. In: *Report of the Surgeon General's Workshop on Violence and Public Health.* Washington D.C.: U.S. Department of Health and Human Services and the U.S. Department of Justice, pp. 35–43.

Prothrow-Stith, D. (1989). The fight against adolescent violence: A public health approach. *The Criminologist,* 14:1, 15–17.

Pyle, G.F. (1980). Systematic sociospatial variation in perceptions of crime location and severity. In: D.E. Georges-Abeyie and K.D. Harries (eds.), *Crime: a Spatial Perspective.* New York: Columbia University Press, pp. 219–246.

Pyle, G.F., et al. (1974). *The Spatial Dynamics of Crime.* Chicago: University of Chicago Press.

Radelet, M.R., and M. Vandiver (1986). Race and capital punishment: An overview of the issues. In: D.F. Hawkins (Ed.), *Homicide Among Black Americans.* Lanham, MD: University Press of America, pp. 177–195.

Rand, M.R., M. DeBerry, P. Klaus, and B. Taylor (1986). *The use of weapons in committing crimes.* Washington D.C.: U.S. Department of Justice, Bureau of Justice Statistics.

Rand, M.R. (1982). *Violent crime by strangers.* Washington D.C.: U.S. Department of Justice, Bureau of Justice Statistics.

Raper, A.F. (1933). *The Tragedy of lynching.* New York: New American Library.

Raspberry, W. (1989). Maybe Schmoke is right about drugs. *Washington Post,* October 9, p. A21.

Ratner, C. (1992). Concretizing the concept of social stress. *Journal of Social Distress and the Homeless,* 1:7–23.

Ratzel, F. (1882–1891). *Anthropogeographie,* 2 vols., Stuttgart: Englehorn.

Read, K. (1993). *Preliminary Findings of Intentional Injury Study.* Baltimore, MD: University of Maryland at Baltimore, Center for Health Policy Research. Unpublished paper.

Reed, J.S. (1971). To live—and die—in Dixie: A contribution to the study of southern violence. *Political Science Quarterly,* 86:429–443.

Reed, J.S. (1982). *One South.* Baton Rouge: LSU Press.

Reid, T.R. (1989). Patchwork pattern of abortion rules. *Washington Post,* April 17, pp. A1, A8.

Reidel, M., Zahn, M.A. and Mock, L.F. (1985). *The Nature and patterns of American homicide.* Washington D.C.: U.S. Government Printing Office.

Reiss, A.J., and J.A. Roth (eds.) (1993). *Understanding and preventing violence.* Washington D.C.: National Academy Press.

Rengert, G. (1989). Behavioral geography and criminal behavior, in: D.J. Evans and D.T. Herbert (eds.) *The Geography of crime,* London: Routledge, Chapter 8, pp. 161–175.

Rengert, G., and J. Wasilchick (1985). *Suburban burglary.* Springfield, IL: Charles C Thomas.

Reuter, P. (1983). *Disorganized crime: The economics of the visible hand.* Cambridge, MA: The MIT Press.

Rich, S. (1989a). Infant mortality rate drops in South, rises sharply in District [of Columbia]. *Washington Post,* August 10, p. A11.

Rich, S. (1989b). The eternal poverty gap? *Washington Post,* June 30, p. A21.

Robinson, W.S. (1950). Ecological correlations and the behavior of individuals. *American Sociological Review,* 15:351–57.

Rohe, W.M., and R.J. Burby (1988). Fear of crime in public housing. *Environment and Behavior,* 20:700–720.

Rose, H.M. (1977). Urban violence: The case of homicide. In: J. Odland and R.N. Taafe (eds.), *Geographical Horizons,* Dubuque, IA: Kendall/Hunt Publishing Company, pp. 130–146.

Rose, H.M. (1978). The geography of despair. *Annals,* Association of American Geographers 68:453–464.

Rose, H.M., and D.R. Deskins, Jr. (1986). Handguns and homicide in urban black communities: A spatial-temporal assessment of environmental scale differences. In: Darnell F. Hawkins (ed.), *Homicide Among Black Americans.* Lanham, MD: University Press of America, pp. 69–100.

Rosenbaum, D.P. (1986). (Ed.) *Community Crime Prevention: Does it Work?* Beverly Hills, CA: Sage.

Rosenberg, M.L., and J.A. Fenley (eds.) (1991). *Violence in America: A Public Health Approach.* New York: Oxford University Press.

Rosenberg, M.L., J.A. Mercy, and J.C. Smith (1984). Violence as a public health problem: a new role for CDC and a new alliance with educators. *Educational Horizons,* 62:124–127.

Rosenberg, M.L., and J.A. Mercy (1986). Homicide: epidemiologic analysis at the national level. *Bulletin of the New York Academy of Medicine,* 62: 376–399.

Rotton, J. (1986). Determinism redux: Climate and cultural correlates of violence. *Environment and Behavior,* 18:346–368.

Rotton, J., and I.W. Kelly (1985). Much ado about the full moon: A meta-analysis of lunar-lunacy research. *Psychological Bulletin,* 97:286–306.

Rotton, J. (1993). Geophysical variables and behavior: LXXII. Ubiquitous errors: A reanalysis of Anderson's (1987) "Temperature and Aggression." *Psychological Reports.* 73:259–271.

Sampson, R.J. (1985a). Race and criminal violence: A demographically disaggregated analysis of urban homicide. *Crime and Delinquency,* 31:47–82.

Sampson, R.J. (1985b). Structural sources of variation in race-age-specific rates of offending across major U.S. cities. *Criminology,* 23:647–673.

Sampson, R.J. (1987). Communities and crime. In: Gottfredson, M.R. and T. Hirschi (eds.) *Positive Criminology,* Newbury Park, CA: Sage, Chapter 6, pp. 91–114.

Sampson, R.J. (1989). The promises and pitfalls of macro-level research. *The Criminologist,* 14, pp. 1, 5, 8, 10.

Sampson, R.J., and W.B. Groves (1989). Community structure and crime: Testing Social-disorganization theory. *American Journal of Sociology*, 94:774–802.

Sanchez, R. (1988). Drugs as child's play: Experts fear that District youngsters are learning by mimicking adult deals. *Washington Post*, June 5, A1, A19.

Sanchez, R., and L. Wheeler (1989). Shootings, drugs, make street in SE a hostage to violence. *Washington Post*, February 17, pp. A1, A14.

Sawhill, I.V. (1989). The underclass: An overview. *The Public Interest*, 96:3–15.

Sawhill, I.V. (1988). Poverty in the U.S.: Why is it so persistent? *Journal of Economic Literature*, 26:1073–1119.

Schmalz, J. (1989). On battleground of the street, few see a victory over drugs. *New York Times*, September 7, pp. A1, B14.

Schmidt, S., and Goldstein, A. (1988). Maryland assembly enacts strict gun control, *Washington Post*, April 12, pp. A1, A12.

Schmoke, K. (1988). Testimony of the Honorable Kurt L. Schmoke submitted to the U.S. House of Representatives Select Committee on Narcotics Abuse and Control. September 29.

Sellin, T. (Ed.) (1967). *Capital Punishment.* New York: Harper and Row.

Seltzer, R., and J.P. McCormick (1987). The impact of crime victimization and fear of crime on attitudes toward death penalty defendants. *Violence and Victims*, 2:99–114.

Shannon, L.W. (1986). Ecological evidence for the hardening of the inner city. In: R.M. Figlio, et al. (eds.), *Metropolitan Crime Patterns.* Monsey, N.Y.: Criminal Justice Press, pp. 27–54.

Shannon, L.W. (1954). The spatial distribution of criminal offenses by states. *Journal of Criminal Law and Criminology*, 45:264–273.

Shaw, C.R. and McKay, H.D. (1942). *Juvenile delinquency and urban areas.* Chicago: University of Chicago Press.

Sherman, L.W., P.R. Gartin, and M.E. Buerger (1989). Hot spots of predatory crime: Routine activities and the criminology of place. *Criminology*, 27:27–55.

Shishkin, J., Young, A.H., and Musgrave, J.C. (1967). *The X-11 Variant of the Census Method II Seasonal Adjustment Program.* Washington D.C.: U.S. Government Printing Office.

Sinclair, M. (1988). Homes becoming prisons for fearful D.C. elderly: High-crime areas house one third of aged. *Washington Post*, May 31, pp. A1, A4, A5.

Skogan, W.G., and M.G. Maxfield (1981). *Coping with crime: Individual and neighborhood reactions.* Beverly Hills, CA: Sage.

Skogan, W. (1986). Fear of crime and neighborhood change. In: A.J. Reiss, Jr. and M. Tonry (eds.) *Communities and Crime*, Chicago: University of Chicago Press, pp. 203–230.

Sloan, J.H., Kellerman, A.L., Reay, D.T., Ferris, J.A., Koepsell, T., Rivara, F.P., Rice, C., Gray, L. and J. LoGerfo (1988). Handgun regulations, crime, assaults and homicide. *New England Journal of Medicine*, 319:1256–1262.

Smith, C.J., and G.E. Patterson (1980). Cognitive mapping and the subjective geography of crime. In: D. Georges-Abeyie and K.D. Harries (eds.), *Crime: A Spatial Perspective.* New York: Columbia University Press, pp. 205–218.

Smith, D.M. (1973). *The Geography of social well-being.* New York: McGraw-Hill.

Smith, M.D. (1986). The era of increased violence in the United States: Age, period, or cohort effect? *The Sociological Quarterly*, 27:239–251.

Smith, M.D., and R.N. Parker (1979). Deterrence, poverty, and type of homicide. *American Journal of Sociology*, 85:614–24.

Smith, S.J. (1986). *Space, Crime, and Society*, Cambridge: Cambridge University Press.

Smith, S.J. (1987). Fear of crime: beyond a geography of deviance. *Progress in Human Geography*, 11:1–23.

Span, P., and H. Kurtz (1989). Aftermath of assault: New Yorkers shocked by vicious attack. *Washington Post*, April 27, 1989, pp. A1, A34.

Spate, O.H.K. (1952). Toynbee and Huntington: A Study in Determinism. *Geographical Journal*, 118:406–428.

Spilerman, S. (1971). The causes of racial disturbances: Tests of an explanation. *American Sociological Review*, 36:427–442.

Sproule, C.F., and D.J. Kennett (1988). The use of firearms in Canadian homicides 1972–82: The need for gun control. *Canadian Journal of Criminology*, 30:31–37.

Sproule, C.F., and D.J. Kennett (1989). Killing with guns in the U.S.A. and Canada 1977–1983: Further evidence for the effectiveness of gun control. *Canadian Journal of Criminology*, 31:245–251.

Stadler, S.J., and K.D. Harries (1985). Assault and deviations from mean temperatures: An inter-year comparison in Dallas, *Papers and Proceedings of Applied Geography Conferences*, 8:207–215.

Stadler, S.J., K.D. Harries, and L.S. Kalkstein (1989). A climatological interpretation of heat stress and criminal assault. *Preprints, Sixth Conference on Applied Climatology*. Boston, MA: American Meteorological Society, pp. J5–J11.

Staples, R. (1986). The masculine way of violence. In: Darnell F. Hawkins (ed.), *Homicide Among Black Americans*. Lanham, MD: University Press of America, pp. 137–152.

Straus, M. (1986). Domestic violence and homicide antecedents. In: Homicide: The Public Health Perspective. *Bulletin of the New York Academy of Medicine*, 62:446–465.

Straus, M. (1988). Primary group characteristics and intra-family homicide. Paper read to the American Society of Criminology, Chicago, November.

Stringham, P., and Weitzman, M. (1988). Violence counseling in the routine health care of adolescents. *Journal of Adolescent Health Care*, 9:389–393.

Sullivan, M.L. (1989). Absent fathers in the inner city. In: William Julius Wilson (ed.) The Ghetto Underclass: Social Science Perspectives. *The Annals of the American Academy of Political and Social Science*, 501:48–58.

Sutherland, E.H., and D.R. Cressey (1978). *Criminology*, 10th ed, Philadelphia, PA: Lippincott.

Swidler, A. (1986). Culture in action: Symbols and strategies. *American Sociological Review*, 51:273–286.

Taylor, R.B., S.D. Gottfredson, and S. Brower (1980). The defensibility of defensible space: A critical review and a synthetic framework for future research, in: Hirschi, T., and M. Gottfredson (eds.) *Understanding Crime: Current Theory and Research*, Beverly Hills: Sage, Chapter 3, pp. 53–72.

Tennenbaum, A.N., and E.L. Fink (1994). Temporal regularities in homicide: Cycles, seasons, and autoregression. *Journal of Quantitative Criminology*, 10: 317–342.

Thomas, P. (1994). Beyond grief and fear is crime's bottom line: Consequences put financial burden on U.S. *Washington Post*, July 5, pp. A1, A6.

Thomas, P. (1995a). The new face of murder in America. *Washington Post*, October 23, pp. A1, A4.

Thomas, P. (1995b). In a reversal, U.S. homicide numbers fall. *Washington Post*, December 31, pp. A8, A9.

Timrots, A.D., and M.R. Rand (1987). *Violent crime by strangers and nonstrangers*. Washington D.C.: U.S. Department of Justice, Bureau of Justice Statistics, 1987.

Tromp, S.W. (1980). *Biometeorology: The impact of weather and climate on humans and their environment*. London: Heyden & Son Ltd.

Twomey, S. (1989). The puzzle of D.C.'s deadly distinction: Experts offer theories, but no certainties, on why Washington leads nation in killing. *Washington Post*, October 30, pages A8, A9.

U.S. Bureau of the Census (1988). *Statistical Abstract of the United States, 1988* (108th Edition). Washington D.C.: U.S. Government Printing Office.

U.S. Department of Health and Human Services (1980). *Promoting Health/Preventing Disease*, Washington, D.C.

U.S. Department of Justice (1981). *Sourcebook of Criminal Justice Statistics—1980.* Washington, D.C.

U.S. Department of Justice (1983). *Report to the Nation on Crime and Justice.* Washington D.C.: U.S. Government Printing Office.

U.S. Department of Justice (1988a). *Report to the Nation on Crime and Justice,* 2nd Ed. Washington D.C.: U.S. Department of Justice. [1,2]

U.S. Department of Justice (1988b). *Bureau of Justice Statistics Data Report, 1987* Washington, D.C.

U.S. Surgeon General (1985). *Surgeon General's Workshop on Violence and Public Health: Report,* U.S. Public Health Service, Washington, D.C.

Vila, B. (1994). A general paradigm for understanding criminal behavior: Extending evolutionary ecological theory. *Criminology.* 32:311–359.

Wacquant, L.J.D., and W.J. Wilson (1989). The cost of racial and class exclusion in the inner city. In: W.J. Wilson (ed.), The ghetto underclass: Social science perspectives. *The Annals of the American Academy of Political and Social Science,* 501:8–25. Newbury Park, CA: Sage.

Walinsky, A. (1995). The crisis of public order. *The Atlantic Monthly,* July, pp. 1–10.

Waxman, C.I. (1983). *The Stigma of Poverty.* New York: Pergamon.

Welsh, P. (1989). Young, black, male, and trapped. *Washington Post,* September 24, pp. B1, B4.

Welte, J.W., and Abel, E.L. (1986). Homicide and race in Erie County, New York. *American Journal of Epidemiology,* 124:666–70.

Wheeler, L. (1989). "The block was at stake": NE neighbors help get rid of crack house. *Washington Post,* March 17, pp. C1, C3.

Wheeler, L. (1988). NW block goes cold turkey and enjoys it: D.C. police wrested Hanover Place from drug dealers and made it stick. *Washington Post,* April 23, p. G1, G5.

Wheeler, L., and S. Horwitz (1988). Operation clean sweep's uncertain future. D.C. police officials seek to revamp program to cut cost. *Washington Post,* January 26, pp. A1, A14.

Whitman, S. (1988). Ideology and violence prevention. *Journal of the National Medical Association,* 80:737–743.

Whitt, H.P., J. Corzine, and L. Huff-Corzine (1995). Where is the South? A preliminary analysis of the Southern subculture of violence. In: C. Block and R. Block (eds.) *Trends, Risks, and Interventions in Lethal Violence.* Washington D.C.: National Institute of Justice, pp. 127–148.

Wilbanks, W. (1986). *Murder in Miami: An analysis of homicide patterns and trends in Dade County (Miami) Florida.* Lanham, MD: University Press of America.

Williams, K.R. and R.L. Flewelling (1988). The social production of criminal homicide: A comparative study of disaggregated rates in American cities. *American Sociological Review,* 53:421–431.

Wilson, J.Q. and G.L. Kelling (1989). Making neighborhoods safe. *The Atlantic Monthly,* February, pp. 46–52.

Wilson, J.Q. (1983). (Ed.) *Crime and public policy.* San Francisco: ICS Press.

Wilson, W.J., R. Aponte, J. Kirschenman, and L.J.D. Wacquant (1988). The ghetto underclass and the changing structure of urban poverty. In: F.R. Harris and R.W. Wilkins (eds.) *Quiet Riots: Race and Poverty in the United States.* New York: Pantheon.

Wolfgang, M.E. (1975). *Patterns in criminal homicide.* Montclair, NJ: Patterson Smith.

Wolfgang, M.E. (1981). Sociocultural overview of criminal violence. In: J.R. Hays, T.K.

Roberts, and K.S. Solway (eds.) *Violence and the Violent Individual.* New York: SP Medical and Scientific, Chapter 7, pp. 97–115.

Wolfgang, M.E. (1986). Homicide in other industrialized countries. *Bulletin of the New York Academy of Medicine,* 62:400–412.

Wolfgang, M.E. and F. Ferracuti (1967). *The subculture of violence.* New York: Barnes and Noble.

Wolfgang, M.E., R.M. Figlio, P.E. Tracy, and S.I. Singer (1985a). *The National Survey of Crime Severity.* Washington D.C.: U.S. Department of Justice, Bureau of Justice Statistics.

Wolfgang, M.E., R.M. Figlio, P.E. Tracy, and S.I. Singer (1985b). *Sourcebook of crime severity ratios for core-item offenses.* (Microfiche # NCJ-96329). Washington D.C.: U.S. Department of Justice, Bureau of Justice Statistics.

Wolfgang, M.E., and M. Reidel (1975). Rape, racial discrimination, and the death penalty. In: Bedau, H.A., and C.M. Pierce, (eds.) *Capital Punishment in the United States,* New York: AMS Press, pp. 99–124.

Wright, J.D., P.H. Rossi, and K. Daly (1983). *Under the gun: Weapons, crime and violence in America.* New York: Aldine, 1983.

Zahn, M.A. (1980). Homicide in the twentieth century United States. In: J.A. Inciardi and C.E. Faupee (eds.) *History and Crime,* Beverly Hills: Sage.

Zawitz, M.W. (1995). *Guns used in crime.* Washington D.C.: Bureau of Justice Statistics.

Zelinsky, W. (1973). *The cultural geography of the United States.* Englewood Cliffs, N.J.: Prentice-Hall.

Zimring, F.E. (1986). Gun control. In: Homicide: The Public Health Perspective, *Bulletin of the New York Academy of Medicine,* 62:615–621.

Zylke, J.W. (1988). Violence increasingly being viewed as problem of public health; prevention programs attempted. *Journal of the American Medical Association,* 260:18, pp. 2621–2625.

INDEX